MARTIAL JUSTICE

MARTIAL JUSTICE

the last mass execution in the united states

RICHARD WHITTINGHAM

BLUEJACKET BOOKS

NAVAL INSTITUTE PRESS
Annapolis, Maryland

For my wife, Ellen

Originally published by the Henry Regnery Company
First Bluejacket Books printing, 1997

Library of Congress Cataloging-in-Publication Data

Whittingham, Richard.
    Martial justice : the last mass execution in the United States /
Richard Whittingham.
      p.   cm.
    Originally published : Chicago, H. Regnery Co., [1971].
    ISBN 1-55750-945-X (pbk. : alk. paper)
    1. Fischer, Helmut, 1922 or 3–1945—Trials, litigations, etc.
    2. Drechsler, Werner, 1923–1944—Death. 3. Courts-martial and
courts of inquiry—United States. 4. Trials (Murder)—United
States. 5. Prisoners of war—Legal status, laws, etc.—United
States. 6. World War, 1939–1945—Prisoners and prisons, German.
7. Executions and executioners—Kansas—Fort Leavenworth. 8. World
War, 1939–1945—Naval operations—Submarine. I. Title.
KF7642.F55W5   1997
343.73′0143—dc21   97-26227

Printed in the United States of America on acid-free paper ∞
04 03 02 01 00 99 98 97   8 7 6 5 4 3 2 1

Contents

Preface to the Bluejacket Books Edition

One can't tie any bonds with the powers of fate. . . . .
Guenther Kuelsen, from a letter to his
family written shortly before he was
executed in 1945

Several decades have intervened since the summer afternoon I happened on that small graveyard tucked so unobtrusively into a wooded hillside on the grounds of Fort Leavenworth.

There was, and still is, a dualism to this anomaly of a military post: in support of its two major functions it provides a genteel home to the high-ranking officers who attend or teach at the U.S. Army Command and General Staff College on the one hand, and cell-block housing for the large contingent of prisoners incarcerated inside the massive stone walls of the military penitentiary known as the U.S. Disciplinary Barracks (USDB) on the other. The army's best and brightest reside here, as do its most dangerous and darkest.

The post itself is only one of the manifold ironies inexorably woven into the story of the seven young Germans buried in that remote and, in those days, unacknowledged prison cemetery.

With two hundred or so traditional white, tablet-shaped headstones, it appears to be a miniature of the sprawling Fort Leavenworth National Cemetery about a mile away. There are, however, dramatic differences. While the national cemetery stands open and proud, an enduring monument to those who served in the armed forces of the United States during one of the nation's various wars or conflicts, the USDB cemetery—tucked out of the way in a silent clearing in the woods—is for the burial of those who either were executed or died while in custody at the prison. Where the meticulously landscaped national cemetery welcomed visitors, the prison plot (accessible back then only by a winding, unmarked dirt road) was surrounded by a cyclone fence, its only gate chained and padlocked.

Less obvious was the pattern of interment, something I was not to discover until much later. In the national cemetery, the graves have an east-west orientation so that the sun will always rise on the inscribed headstones; in the prison cemetery the graves are arranged on a north-south grid, the sun never to grace the markers of those buried without honor and apparently unforgiven even in death.

Out of curiosity I climbed the fence that afternoon and wandered among the uniform tombstones, the oldest dating back to 1884, wondering who were these forsaken souls relegated to such an intentionally isolated resting place. Even more puzzling, who were these seven men in the last row with the German names—Helmut Fischer, Fritz Franke, Guenther Kuelsen, Heinrich Ludwig, Bernhard Reyak, Otto Stengel, Rolf Wizuy— with inscriptions of their German military ranks beneath, all with the same date of death: August 25, 1945, more than four months after the war with Germany had ended.

It did not take long to find out who they were. There was a small file back in the post's public information office, where I was assigned as a news writer then. It was kept in a locked cabinet along with other files on subjects about which the army was reluctant to provide information. In the file were brief vitas identifying the seven as enlisted men in the German U-boat service, all in their early twenties; a legal summation of their crime—killing a fellow prisoner of war whom they claimed was a traitor to Germany—and a copy of the execution orders; a press release that described in detail how the gallows were specially built to handle a mass execution; and the menu of food served at the prison on the last day of their lives.

It took more than six years, however, to unearth the controversial and sometimes bizarre story behind the crime, the investigation and interrogations, the court-martial and sentencing, the review and appeal, the posttrial maneuverings, and finally the execution of the verdicts. After all, this was before the enactment of the Freedom of Information Act in America and the reunification of Germany. Everything relating to the case (except the court-martial proceedings, which were on the public record) had been marked "classified" by the army and therefore was unavailable, and contact with any German military sources or relatives of the prisoners who happened to be in East Germany was virtually impossible.

Eventually I was able to get much of the information declassified and to talk with members of naval intelligence and army authorities as well as case prosecutor Francis P. Walsh and chaplain George A. Towle, who spent the last seven months with the German U-boatmen before they were executed. However, President Harry S. Truman, who signed the orders of execution, declined to be interviewed and refused to answer any written questions regarding the case; in fact, all documents and records relating to the trial and execution disappeared from the Truman Library after I applied for an appointment to research the case there in the late 1960s.

The story grew increasingly complex as it emerged, yet at the same time it clearly and grimly defined the enormous and unpredictable powers of fate Guenther Kuelsen referred to in his last letter home. Left in its wake was a litany of controversies and unanswered questions as poignant today as they were when the seven were led, one after the other, to the special gallows at Fort Leavenworth that August night in 1945.

In the eyes of some, they had committed a crime worthy of capital punishment; in the eyes of others, their act was a patriotic duty. Would we not expect American prisoners of war in a similar situation to act in the same manner as the seven Germans?

The army sent the traitor into the midst of those who knew of his treacheries—despite explicit directions from the navy, when it turned jurisdiction of him over to the army, not to send him where other German naval prisoners might be incarcerated.

The army used torturous methods of interrogation at a secret camp; these went unchallenged at the court-martial. Also, the opinion of the reviewing authority recommended commuting the sentences to life imprisonment. This was ignored by the Department of War and by President Truman.

The lives of the seven Germans were, for a while anyway, considered valuable enough to be used as pawns in a game of exchange for American prisoners of war. But again fate intervened: the war with Germany ended before negotiations could be completed.

There was no more intimate observer of the star-crossed fates of the seven Germans than Chaplain Towle, who befriended them during the last months of their lives. A gentle yet strong soul, he perhaps summed it up as well as any person could when I asked him what, after witnessing their hangings, his personal feelings were. "The boy in Arizona they killed . . . sad," he said. "The boys we killed for it . . . sad, too." Then he shook his head and invoked the seventeenth-century metaphysical poet John Donne: "'Any man's death diminishes me.' I guess that's the way I feel about it."

Acknowledgments

Many persons have helped in many ways during the course of researching and writing this book and I wish to extend to them my sincere appreciation. Foremost is C. Carter Smith whose collaboration on the research over the last six years essentially laid the foundation for writing this book and whose interest and ideas were a contribution of inestimable proportion.

Those who willingly and helpfully participated in a series of long interviews also deserve a special thanks; especially Msgr. George A. Towle, who better than anyone else in the United States knew and understood the seven central figures in this story, and Mr. Francis P. Walsh, who as prosecutor of the case provided important insights that would otherwise have been unavailable. I would also like to thank Lilo Weyhing, the sister of Guenther Kuelsen, for her gracious cooperation, and Hilke Niemann, the daughter of Otto Stengel, for entrusting me with photographs and documents concerning her father.

In addition, I would like to express my appreciation to the following organizations: the Department of the Army, especially the office of the Deputy Undersecretary of the Army, the office of the Judge Advocate General, the Public Information Office (Washington), the Fort Leavenworth Public Information Office, and the Army Intelligence Command at Fort Holabird, Maryland; the Department of the Navy, especially the Magazine and Book Branch of the Office of Information, and the Office of Naval Intelligence; the National Archives; and the WAST Records Center in Berlin. There were many other persons, offices and record depositories, in various governmental departments and agencies whose cooperation provided a distinct contribution to my efforts and to whom I also express my thanks, although they are too numerous to mention here by name.

A printed acknowledgment is only a token of the appreciation I have for the many people who have helped in all phases of putting this book together.

1

Fort Leavenworth

THE United States Disciplinary Barracks sits high on a bluff overlooking the Missouri River at the north end of Fort Leavenworth, Kansas. The surrounding hills, gently sloping, heavily wooded, and rich in vegetation, contrast sharply with the stark austerity of the prison compound. The prison is not as massive as the neighboring federal penitentiary in the city of Leavenworth, but is big enough to accomodate as many as 2,000 prisoners. It looks much like any other major prison: heavy stone walls with gun towers and a central detention building standing coldly within the walls, its great barred windows unmistakably revealing its function. In only two ways, perhaps, does the disciplinary barracks vary from other prisons: its inmates, except in rare circumstances, come from the ranks of the U.S. army and the U.S. air force and its guards are soldiers, not civilians.

Within the initial-conscious military world, the prison is succinctly referred to as the USDB, a name it has carried since it was formally designated the United States Disciplinary Barracks by act of Congress in 1915. As a prison, however, it dates back to 1874, when it was established as the first strictly military prison in the United States. Until that time, military prisoners were confined either to state penitentiaries or to the stockades on military posts. The USDB was essentially the result of efforts by Major Thomas F. Barr, and its purpose was to alleviate the condition and humanize the treatment of prisoners in those days, doing away with such practices as flogging, branding, tattooing, shackling with ball and chain, and other assorted punishments.

Through the years, jurisdiction over the USDB has passed back and forth several times between the War Department and the Justice Department, which used it as a federal penitentiary. But since November 6, 1940, it has been entirely under the control of the Department of the Army.

World War II brought to the disciplinary barracks the largest aggregate of inmates in its history. By the summer of 1945, with the war in Europe over and the war in the Pacific swiftly drawing to an end, the disciplinary barracks was virtually overflowing its capacity. The large-scale population of the prison, problems created by the war, and the fragmented transition back to a peacetime existence combined to pose a variety of unique, often unprecedented situations for the administrators of the disciplinary barracks. Colonel William S. Eley, who had taken over as the prison commandant in October, 1943, almost daily confronted tasks and decisions that no commandant before him had been forced to face.

Each morning, Colonel Eley arrived at his office in the prison's administration building and, as a matter of course, first went through the mail that had been screened and personally directed to him. On an oppressively hot Kansas morning in early July, 1945, a directive from the office of the Secretary of War made him stop and sit back for a moment, even though Colonel Eley had become accustomed to the unusual. Almost at once, however, he walked into the outer office with the paper still in his hand and told one of the sergeants to send for Lieutenant Colonel Raymond Orr, the USDB quartermaster officer.

A few moments later, the sergeant appeared in the doorway to Colonel Eley's office. "Excuse me, sir. Colonel Orr's signed out for central detention. Do you want me to try and get him over there by phone?"

"Yes, I want to see him this morning," Colonel Eley answered.

The central detention building, paradoxically nicknamed the "castle," is by far the largest structure in the prison compound. Five stories high, it has eight separate wings, each of which empties into a large rotunda. The massive granite building, completed in 1921, was constructed for the most part by prisoners with rock they had quarried themselves. Inside, it is a metallically clean, cold, and hollow dormitory. Each wing is cut off from the rotunda by a heavily barred sliding door that effectively isolates the wing from all other parts of the building. The largest wings each contain five tiers of cells and together house all of the inmates, with the exception of trustee prisoners, who are permitted to live in other, less secure buildings, and those others who are on death row or in solitary and are confined to the basement level of the castle.

When Colonel Orr received the message from the commandant, he concluded his business and walked across the rotunda toward the large door that barred off the main entrance hall. A sergeant at a desk on the outside pushed a button and the huge door slid open, barely paused as the colonel stepped through, and then slid shut again.

The colonel picked up a pencil from the sergeant's desk, signed out on the roster, and then walked briskly into the prison yard—actually a well-gardened mall that stretches the length of a city block, from the entrance of the central detention building all the way up to the rear of the administration building. A few trustee prisoners working on the mall appeared busier than they actually were as the colonel strode past. The lanes on each side of the mall are bordered by other prison buildings, two to three stories high. Behind them stand the huge granite walls, which range in certain places up to a height of 41 feet. The walls enclose a total area of twelve and one-half acres and are also the result of prison labor, a monument perhaps to the confinement at "hard labor" of the past.

Colonel Orr walked the length of the mall and entered the back door of the administration building. The building itself is part of the front wall of the prison; a sally port running through the center of the building is in fact the main entrance to the disciplinary barracks. Large iron gates at each end of the sally port, which are operated independently and are never opened simultaneously, separate the prison from the outside world.

Upstairs, the colonel first went to his office to get a pad of paper and a pencil and then reported to the commandant.

"You were looking for me, sir?" Colonel Orr said as he stepped into the commandant's office.

"Yes, Ray," Colonel Eley said and motioned for Colonel Orr to sit down.

The commandant opened a manila folder, took a thick stack of papers from it, and handed them to Colonel Orr. The top sheet was the directive from the office of the Secretary of War in Washington.

"You don't have to read them now. Generally, you already know what they're about — the Germans we've got in the basement of the castle."

Colonel Orr put the papers in his lap and looked across the desk at Colonel Eley.

"You're going to have to build a special set of gallows," Colonel Eley continued. He paused to see if the statement had carried any impact, but the impassive expression on Colonel Orr's face had not changed. "Word came through today from Washington that we're going to have to hang some of them. The President signed the orders two days ago."

Colonel Orr nodded but remained silent. He was indeed

aware of the fifteen German prisoners of war who sat idly in the dark corridors of the castle's basement. Between the fifteen, they accounted for four separate murders. All fifteen had been tried by courts martial, convicted, and sentenced to death. In two of the cases, the sentence had been confirmed by the President over a year earlier, but the execution of the sentences had been postponed several times by high authorities in Washington for reasons Colonel Orr was not privy to and could only conjecture about. One of the cases involved five prisoners of war—Walter Beyer, Berthold Seidel, Hans Demme, Willi Scholz, and Hans Schomer —all of whom were convicted of the "willful, deliberate, felonious, unlawful and premeditated murder of Johannes Kunze, a fellow prisoner of war, at Camp Gruber, Oklahoma." The other case involved only two prisoners of war—Erich Gauss and Rudolf Straub—who were convicted of the murder by strangulation of German Prisoner of War Horst Guenther at Branch Camp Aiken, South Carolina. The directive from the Secretary of War's office in Washington, which now rested in Colonel Orr's lap, set forth the order to carry out the sentences in these two cases—death by hanging.

The other two cases still floated in the limbolike halls of Washington. One case, however, would be resolved in the next few days when President Harry S Truman would commute the death sentence of Edgar Menschner for beating to death German Prisoner of War Hans Geller in the POW camp at Camp Chaffee, Arkansas. Menschner would be removed from his moribund cell in the castle's basement and, in effect, given back his life to begin serving a twenty-year sentence at Fort Leavenworth. The remaining seven Germans on death row were still waiting to see if the President of the United States would commute their sentence for the murder of POW Werner Drechsler at the Papago Park, Arizona, camp. And they entertained some hope that they would live since, by July, 1945, the war in Europe was over and since, further, no action had yet been taken by the President, even though they had been convicted and sentenced almost a year earlier. In addition, the reviewing authority of their case had recommended commutation to life imprisonment.

For the moment, however, Colonel Eley and Colonel Orr were concerned only with expediting the orders at hand—not with the actual prisoners—and that required the immediate construction of a set of gallows that could effectively accommodate at least five and perhaps later seven consecutive hangings in one evening.

Colonel Eley foresaw certain problems in the situation that confronted them. First, now that the orders were signed, the executions would have to be carried out as quickly as possible. All courses of appeal had been exhausted, and it was necessary to play out the final scene with as little delay as was humanly possible. However, Colonel Eley could not set the date until the gallows were erected and tested, a point that was made very clear to Colonel Orr.

Second, Colonel Eley was convinced that it would not be wise or convenient to use the central detention building as the gallows site. The German prisoners of war housed there were already very anxious, and he did not want to agitate the situation. In all, there were 120 German and 18 Italian POWs incarcerated at the disciplinary barracks, and Colonel Eley knew the tensions that ran through his overcrowded prison.

Third, while there would be no way to hide the executions, at the same time there was no need to make a spectacle of them. Therefore, another requirement was that the gallows be portable, so that they could be constructed shortly before the execution and then torn down immediately afterward.

Colonel Orr duly noted all of the stipulations, and then assured Colonel Eley that he would handle the mission as immediately and efficiently as possible. He left the commandant, went back to his own office, and called in the three civilian engineers who worked for the disciplinary barracks. Together they quickly worked out a plan that they felt was feasible. Blueprints were drawn up and the proposal typed for Colonel Eley's approval.

Meanwhile, the public information office at Fort Leavenworth was advised of the pending executions, and it was to notify the press and handle any publicity in regard to this grim bit of newsmaking. It was hardly the type of thing that the USDB would want to solicit much publicity for.

The site that had been selected was an old salvage warehouse, inconspicuously located about 150 yards from the central detention building. A few things would have to be requisitioned, but Colonel Orr's engineering task was actually more a matter of conversion than construction.

Within two days the gallows were operable. Colonel Eley walked across the prison yard to inspect the finished product with Colonel Orr and the three civilian engineers. Colonel Orr had arranged a test to expose dramatically its potential, using a stuffed and weighted dummy, so that Colonel Eley could in good faith get on with his orders from Washington. The demonstration was brief, but it was enough to reassure the commandant that Colonel Orr and his engineers had successfully carried out their mission. The gallows were icily efficient.

The best description of Colonel Orr's creation was set forth in a news release put out by the Fort Leavenworth Public Information Office. Why the release was written has been lost somewhere in the intervening years, but the release itself has been preserved in its entirety. Its militarily precise wording relates in transparent detail the construction of the gallows and how they would be operated.

INFORMATION ON THE CONSTRUCTION
AND OPERATION OF THE GALLOWS

The United States Disciplinary Barracks at Ft. Leavenworth was confronted with the problem of devising a set of gallows on which to execute a number of inmates of the institution who were condemned to die. Many problems confronted the officials of the USDB when they were first notified that they must hang some of their inmates.

First, the gallows could not be constructed outdoors, due to the inclement weather—rain, snow, etc. Second, they must be constructed in some place where they would not attract too much attention of the inmates, thereby causing nervousness and talk in the institution. Third, the gallows should be prefabricated so that they could be assembled and taken down again rapidly.

Lt. Colonel Raymond Orr, Quartermaster officer of the USDB, was given the mission of surveying the situation and devising the gallows to be constructed. With the assistance of some civilian engineer employees, the solution was found to be to use an old elevator shaft in the Salvage Warehouse within the walls of the institution.

Two floors and a basement are necessary for the functioning of the gallows. On the first floor level, a portable floor is the trapdoor, trimmed in black, with a black circle in the center indicating the position where the condemned man is to stand. On the second floor of the shaft is a cross-beam where the rope is made secure.

The trapdoor is operated by manipulating a large brake-like handle. Pushing the handle releases the belt that lets the trap fall. The condemned man falls from the first floor level into the basement below, slightly more than his own height. Medical officers in the basement then examine the body at frequent intervals to determine when death is absolute.

During each execution, Lt. Colonel Orr, with three enlisted men as assistants, are continually on hand to supervise the operation of the trapdoor and to re-tie a new noose in the rope at the end of each execution.

After the executions have been completed, the false floor that is placed on the first floor level is removed in three sections, the beam on the second floor is removed, and then the elevator shaft so uniquely used reverts to its original role as a cargo elevator in the Salvage Warehouse. No one would suspect that it could be converted so quickly and so effectively into an execution chamber.

At midnight, July 10, the gallows received their first real test. One by one, Walter Beyer, Berthold Seidel, Hans Demme, Willi Scholz, and Hans Schomer were led from their cells and across the prison yard to the salvage warehouse, where within the prescribed formality of such an occasion, even to the legendary black hood for the victim, each man was hanged. A team of doctors waited in the basement for the five Germans, who, each in his turn, came plummeting down and at the appropriate moment was pronounced dead. As each execution was successfully completed, the body was wrapped in an army blanket and carefully placed off to the side. The whole operation took almost four hours, a good deal longer than had been expected, but then everybody involved was new at this sort of thing.

At midnight, July 14, Erich Gauss made the identical trip, followed approximately 45 minutes later by his accomplice Rudolf Straub. The procedure was basically a reenactment of the scene that had transpired a few nights earlier, only this time it was carried out more smoothly and was proportionately more expeditious.

Still in death row were seven young German submariners: Helmut Fischer, 22; Fritz Franke, 21; Guenther Kuelsen, 22; Heinrich Ludwig, 25; Bernhard Reyak, 21; Otto Stengel, 26; and Rolf Wizuy, 23. When July 15 dawned, the German prisoner-of-war population at the disciplinary barracks had slipped from 120 to 113; the sentences of the last seven still remained unconfirmed. The old adage, "no news is good news," made its way among the seven, but the enthusiasm with which it was said had flagged considerably in the last few days as they had watched their comrades depart. The hope that had replaced their initial bitterness at the sentence was not extinguished, but it gave way steadily to frustration and vituperation rising out of their helpless situation and their overwhelming desire to live.

Somewhere in Washington the papers that described their

crime, court martial, sentencing, and review were waiting for the action of the President who was their last source of appeal. Among the papers was a 22-page document entitled simply "Opinion of the Board of Review"; its first page effectively synopsized their crime and the action of the military court and the last sentence contained the substance of the one fragile shred of hope that all seven still clung to even though they had no way to gauge its strength.

Accused were tried upon the following Charge and Specification:
CHARGE: Violation of the 92nd Article of War.
SPECIFICATION: In that Prisoner of War Helmut Fischer, Prisoner of War Fritz Franke, Prisoner of War Guenther Kuelsen, Prisoner of War Heinrich Ludwig, Prisoner of War Bernhard Reyak, Prisoner of War Otto Stengel, and Prisoner of War Rolf Wizuy, all of Prisoner of War Processing Station, Angel Island, California, acting jointly and in pursuance of a common intent, did, at Prisoner of War Camp, Papago Park, Phoenix, Arizona, on or about March 12, 1944, with malice aforethought, willfully, deliberately, feloniously, unlawfully, and with premeditation kill one Prisoner of War Werner Drechsler, a human being, by strangulation.

Each pleaded not guilty to and was found guilty of the Charge and its Specification. Each was sentenced to be hanged by the neck until dead. The reviewing authority approved the sentence as to each and forwarded the record of trial for action under Article of War 48 with a recommendation that the sentence of each accused be commuted to life imprisonment.

The root of the frustration of the seven men, however, went even deeper. It was incomprehensible to them that they were tried *at all* by court martial. In their minds they had not committed a crime. Rather, they had done their patriotic duty to Germany. Their fellow prisoner of war, Werner Drechsler, they alleged, was a traitor to Germany; he had betrayed his country and had suffered the just consequences of his treachery. Germany had still been at war at the time of the crime, they claimed, and

it was their duty to destroy this man before he could do any further damage to their fatherland.

The U.S. army obviously did not view the matter with the
same eyes. Under the authority of the Articles of War and within the rules laid down by the Geneva Convention, they saw it
only as a crime of murder that clearly warranted a just resolution within the laws of the land.

In any case, these questions had already been resolved, at
least in the minds of the prosecuting authorities, as the present
state of the seven men amply illustrated. What was of supreme
importance now was the final decision to confirm or commute
their sentence, the ultimate answer as to whether they would live
or die. And that was still in abeyance.

2

Seven Men

THE journey to death row at Fort Leavenworth, Kansas, had not been simple for the seven young Germans, who had come from different towns by different paths but shared one distinction — in their brief adulthood they had seen an enormous slice of life. They had observed as well as played intimate and active roles in the most grotesque aspect of human existence, the death and destruction of war; they had experienced deep emotions of friendship, loyalty, and dedication to a cause; and they themselves had killed another human being with their own hands.

Yet, despite the depth and raw exposure of their experiences within the framework of human emotion, all seven had actually emerged from a narrow, rigid corridor of life fashioned by forces beyond their control, which had made them, at least subjectively, frighteningly alike.

They had all been born in the desolate years immediately following World War I, into a society that was thoroughly depressed and struggling desperately to put some order back into a way of life that had been shattered. They entered the world under less than ideal circumstances and grew up within it but without the knowledge that it was destined to get much worse. As very young boys, Helmut Fischer, Fritz Franke, Guenther Kuelsen, Heinrich Ludwig, Bernhard Reyak, Otto Stengel, and Rolf Wizuy were no different from most children growing up in Germany. In Berlin, young Rolf Wizuy, with ears that seemed far too big for his head, was often seen kicking a soccer ball in the street, scooping it up under one arm and running to his home in an apartment building on Magazinstrasse. Another little boy with dark hair and nervous eyes could be seen running freely through a field on the outskirts of Munich; he was Otto Stengel. In Dusseldorf, a little blond-haired, blue-eyed boy with porcelain skin, Guenther Kuelsen, was a perfect prototype for the Hitler posters of ideal German youth only a few short years in the future.

When the seven first went to school, the German public school system was still intact, dedicated only to the purposes of good education. But before they graduated, an intense program of Nazification had replaced all other forms of education. The Hitler youth was formed and became a turgid reality, and all seven young men drifted into it—and that was really the beginning of the long corridor that would finally empty out at Fort Leavenworth, Kansas.

As young men, Helmut Fischer, Fritz Franke, Guenther Kuelsen, Heinrich Ludwig, Bernhard Reyak, Otto Stengel, and Rolf Wizuy comprised a remarkable cross-section of urban German youth, representing metropolises of all sizes from Berlin to Neuss And in their backgrounds was the striking similarity of education and their indoctrination into Nazi Germany. Finally, as a unit of seven prisoners of war, they also had a number of other things in common. They were members of the German navy, had received much the same training, and had served in the elite U-boat command of Admiral Karl Doenitz. They had suffered through the sinking of their submarines, seen many of their shipmates die hideously in the frantic moments of attack, and together adapted wearily and begrudgingly to the dismal life of a prisoner of war. All seven shared a certain spirit and pride in the U-boat command they represented, which even several years of imprisonment could not diminish, and, if they had it to do all over again, not one of them, they admitted freely, would have chosen another branch of the German armed forces.

Otto Stengel was the oldest but not the ranking man nor the leader of the seven prisoners. He had rather joyously acknowledged his twenty-sixth birthday on February 9, 1945, with a fanfare that was strangely out of place in his basement cell at Fort Leavenworth.

Born in the small town of Aunkofen, he had moved with his family to Munich while he was still a baby. After 8 years in a public school and 3½ years in a trade school, he had gone to work as a locksmith in Munich, a trade he worked at until he enlisted in the German navy in 1939. He had grown up under Hitler and was fiercely loyal to both Germany and the Fuehrer. In fact, of the seven, Stengel was one of the strongest followers of Hitler.

Stengel was a strikingly handsome young man. His dark brown hair, which he did not part, was swept straight back; and his eyes, when they lingered on anyone for more than a few fleeting seconds, which was seldom, were deeply penetrating. After joining the U-boat force, he grew a beard and mustache that gave him the appearance of a kind of second-rate matinee idol, but it was a respected symbol of the service command he belonged to and was sincerely proud of.

Stengel was the only member of the seven who was married. His wife, Anna, had given him two children — a daughter, Hilke, and a son born after he left for sea duty whom he consequently had never seen.

In the summer of 1941, Stengel joined the crew of the U-352, a submarine still in the last stages of construction, and began his training as a machinist in the port town of Flensburg on the northernmost peninsula of Germany, only a mile or two from the Danish border, while the boat was still being completed. The U-352, a 500-ton boat that bore on its conning tower the emblem of the coat of arms of the town of Flensburg, was commissioned in October, 1941, and placed under the command of Kapitanleutnant Hellmut Rathke. Rathke conducted the new boat's trial runs throughout the remainder of the autumn of 1941, and in December the crew was given leave. Otto Stengel went home to his wife, Anna, and their daughter, to spend their last Christmas together as a family. On December 29, he returned to Flensburg, and shortly afterward the U-352 set out on its first war cruise.

The base of operations of the U-352 was designated as St. Nazaire, the beautiful French coastal city at the mouth of the Loire River. On the open sea, the order of the day was almost constant drills and exercises, with a sharp eye kept for any Allied ships that might be sailing the North Atlantic. If any were sighted, however, it mattered very little because the U-352 reached St. Nazaire on March 5, 1942, without incident. The submarine docked for adjustments and supplies, and Otto Stengel and the other members of the crew were given their last shore leave.

While they were at St. Nazaire, a crack British commando force staged a daring raid on the port. Stengel, along with most of the crew of the U-352, were in town, staying at a special "U-boatmen's home," and only heard the sounds of the assault coming from the bay several miles away. The U-352 was not damaged, but other U-boats were, and Stengel and the crew were required to take a special oath of secrecy that, if they were later captured, they would never divulge any information in regard to the damage done there. One of Stengel's shipmates later said: "I would undoubtedly be stood against a wall and shot on returning to Germany if it ever became known that I had given away any information [about the raid]."

Toward the middle of April, the U-352 left St. Nazaire and headed across the Atlantic. Most of the time, it cruised on the surface, but no Allied ships were encountered. During the voyage, the crew went about their normal duties and participated in a few simulated emergency-situation exercises as well as a few real ones. Aircraft were frequently observed, and when they were, the U-352, amid the sounds of its alarms, would quickly submerge. Other than that, however, it was a leisurely cruise. The food was good—fresh meat, vegetables, and canned fruit, a limited amount of alcohol was permitted, the crew were allowed to sunbathe in small groups on the deck of the submarine, and when the boat neared the United States coast, music from radio stations in the United States was picked up and broadcast over the boat's loudspeaker system.

After about three weeks, on May 7, 1942, an aircraft suddenly appeared and was sighted by the deck officer, but not until it was too late. The submarine was spotted, and as the U-352 crash-dived, the plane swooped down to attack. As the boat surged deeply into the water, seeking the relative protection of the ocean's depths, two bombs hit the water above it, much too close for comfort. The boat balked, and its sides writhed under the impact of the explosion above. The men were knocked about the cabin like fragile twigs, but the boat held together and remained submerged, silently and steadily making its way out of danger.

Two days later, the U-352, at periscope depth, cautiously ventured quite near the North Carolina coast off Cape Lookout, in search of Allied ships that might be plying their way close-in along the coast.

Almost immediately, the U.S. coast guard cutter *Icarus* detected the submarine's presence on its sonar equipment. At approximately the same time, Kapitanleutnant Rathke spotted the *Icarus* through the U-boat's periscope and saw it bearing down fast. "Action stations" was sounded, and the submarine's crew madly scrambled to their posts. Rathke maneuvered the submarine into position and let go with a bow torpedo, which set out on target but then suddenly dipped and went straight to the bottom, where it exploded harmlessly. The *Icarus* was now almost on top of tthe submarine, and there was no time to fire another torpedo. Rathke was calm and at the same time dreadfully aware of his boat's precarious situation. They were trapped in shallow water with the U.S. coast on one side of them and an enemy ship moving in for the attack from the other side, one of the worst predicaments that could haunt a U-boat commander. The U-352 began to take evasive action, but it could not go deep. Finally, Rathke grounded it in the shallow waters to begin the tense and fearful wait for the cutter to pass and, all on board hoped, lose them. As the marauding ship steamed toward their position, Otto Stengel and his crewmates in the submarine froze in silence at their station.

Suddenly the depth charges began to hit, seemingly on all sides. Dishes smashed to the floor of the galley; loose equipment flew wildly about the boat; lockers burst open as if an explosion had detonated inside each one; the men pitched against the walls of the submarine and crumpled to the floor in heaps as the entire boat twisted and groaned in agony. The damage was extensive; the electric motors finally failed; the boat was enshrouded in total darkness.

In the pitch black tube, Rathke reluctantly ordered the men to don their life jackets and then blew the tanks, sending the submarine quickly to the surface. The men rushed through the hatch of the conning tower, racing for the two antiaircraft guns on deck, but the guns of the *Icarus* were too close and too sure. No one was able to reach the submarine's guns to use them. Over the chaos, Rathke shouted to abandon ship, and the men began plunging into the water. As the men were swimming away from the submarine, two muffled explosions from the scuttling charges split the U-boat apart, and it quickly sank to the bottom, the second U-boat in World War II to be sunk by an American warship and the fourth to be sunk by the U.S. armed forces.

Otto Stengel had been one of the first to hit the cold water off Cape Lookout. He swam strongly away from the sinking boat and was picked up by coast guardsmen of the *Icarus*. When the other survivors were brought aboard, the count revealed that of the four officers and 42 enlisted men of the U-352, two officers and 12 men had either been killed in the attack or drowned in the aftermath.

Stengel's head felt as if it were about to burst as he stood dripping wet on the deck of the *Icarus*, he complained to one of the surviving officers of the U-352, who told him that it was probably a result of the speed at which the submarine surfaced and mentioned that he, too, was suffering from the same intense pain. But other than that, and a few rather painful bruises, Otto Stengel was in pretty good shape.

The *Icarus* quickly sent word of its success back to the United States and then set out with its catch of German U-boatmen for the port at Charleston, South Carolina.

Two days later, Otto Stengel and his fellow prisoners were led off the ship and placed under the jurisdiction of U.S. army authorities for interrogation and imprisonment. They were taken first to Camp Moultrie, South Carolina, and then to Fort Bragg, North Carolina. At both places, Stengel was interrogated, but he refused to give any information other than that required by the Geneva Convention. Under threats and other psychological pressures, Stengel remained steadfast, although he was now fearful and extremely nervous. He knew for him the war was over, but he had no idea what the future held in store. Stengel then began a tour of prisoner-of-war camps from Massachusetts to New Mexico until he finally found himself in late 1943, at the POW camp at Stringtown, Oklahoma, where he joined a large contingent of other captured U-boatmen. On January 3, 1944, he was transferred to the permanent POW camp at Papago Park, Arizona.

Heinrich Ludwig, the second oldest of the condemned seven, had spent the second longest time as a prisoner of war. On September 14, 1945, he, too, would reach the age of 26—if he lived that long. However, he looked much younger than Otto Stengel. In fact, with his short blond hair and very light complexion, almost beardless, he appeared a good deal younger than he actually was.

Ludwig was born in Essen and grew up there under the shadows of the huge Krupp steel works. Like most young men raised in that part of the industrial Ruhr valley during the 1930s, Ludwig was eventually drawn into the vast Krupp network. He had had only eight years of public school in Essen and did not qualify for any particular trade, so he finally went to work in the mines of an affiliated company of Krupp. When Germany went to war in 1939, Ludwig was deferred from the draft because of his job as a miner in an industry highly essential to the German war effort; he did not formally enter the German navy until early 1942.

During that year, the U-199 was under construction and being prepared for its launch from the naval shipyards at Kiel, a large port city on the Baltic Sea about 50 miles north of Hamburg. Heinrich Ludwig, with the rank of an ordinary seaman, a gefreiter, joined the crew at Kiel, where he received additional training for his first war cruise in the bowels of a submarine. The command of the U-199 had been given to Kapitanleutnant Hans Werner Kraus, who, despite the fact that he was only 28 years old, was already a seasoned submarine commander. Kraus had served as executive officer on the U-47 and was then promoted and given command of the U-83, which he led through eight war cruises in the North Atlantic and the Mediterranean before being reassigned to supervise the construction of the new U-199 and the training of its crew. Ludwig looked upon his new commander as a very likable leader who was at the same time a strict disciplinarian and extremely security conscious.

The U-199 cast off from Kiel on its first and last war cruise at eight in the morning on May 13, 1943. Life on the submarine for Heinrich Ludwig was a great deal cleaner than in the mines. Everything, in fact, was much better than the existence he had been used to, and this prompted him to begin thinking about making the navy his career.

Accompanied by a mine sweeper which steamed ahead, the U-199 sailed out of the Bay of Kiel and made its way up through the Kattegat between Denmark and Sweden. As it entered the North Sea, the mine sweeper departed, and the U-199 headed on to its first port of call, Kristiansand, on the southern tip of Norway, arriving on May 15. The submarine fueled up and took on supplies of fresh food and water, but no shore leave was granted, even though this was to be the last port until the war cruise was over. Then early on the morning of May 16, the U-199 cast off from Kristiansand.

The U-199 headed not for the North Atlantic, as Ludwig presumed, but for the South Atlantic, just below the equator and in the vicinity of the coast of Brazil, an area that Admiral Doenitz had selected for a massive U-boat assault on convoys moving in and out of what had recently become the very active port of Rio de Janeiro. Thus, in the early summer of 1943, the U-199 joined a number of other submarines to begin a series of devastating attacks on the freighter and tanker traffic in that area. The U-199 operated independently and not as a part of a "wolf pack," the tactic developed by Admiral Doenitz that had been used with frightening effect in many other parts of the Atlantic.

On June 25, the U-199 was spotted on the surface by a Brazilian plane off Cape Frio, about 100 miles north of Rio de Janeiro; Kapitanleutnant Kraus gave the order to crash-dive and safely eluded the plane. The area was abundant with prey, and Captain Kraus informed the crew that it was going to be both a very active and a very dangerous voyage.

About a month later, the U-199's troubles began; by this time, Heinrich Ludwig had become a hardened veteran of submarine warfare. He knew his duties well, and he had carried them out in a number of different emergency situations. Everything started off well on July 25: the U-199 was at periscope depth and Kraus had sighted a lone ship, a 4,000-ton British vessel, the *Henzada*, headed west toward the port of Santos, Brazil. Kraus moved into position and called out: "Depth setting, three meters, set speed for 30 knots," and unleashed three torpedoes from the bow. All three were wide. Kraus brought his boat to the surface, proceeded full speed ahead to a position well in front of the oncoming British ship, and then lay in wait. When the ship approached, the U-199 adjusted its position and fired two torpedos from the stern, one of which hit the *Henzada* directly amidships, and Kraus watched through the periscope as the ship broke in two and sank. Kraus and the crew celebrated their clean kill that night.

The next day, the U-199 was cruising on the surface when it was surprised by an aircraft that Captain Kraus could not immediately identify. He screamed for an emergency turn and for the engines to be thrust full speed ahead. Crew members ran to the guns on deck, but before they could align the sights, the plane suddenly exploded and plunged into the sea nearby. Heinrich Ludwig was standing on the deck, and he watched, astonished, at the strange scene, unable to understand what had caused the aircraft suddenly to burst into flames and crash. It was, he thought, one of those strange, unfathomable quirks of war. Perhaps fate really was on his side.

Four days later, the U-199 made its next encounter, this time not far from Rio de Janeiro, when it happened to meet a single ship on its way out of port. The U-199 was not within torpedo range, and Kapitanleutant Kraus decided to wait until dark before surfacing, which, as it turned out, was too late because the ship had disappeared into the darkness. Kraus remained on the surface to recharge the U-199's batteries until the next morning when, as a consequence, the boat was discovered by a Brazilian plane. Kraus, who was below when he heard the emergency orders given by the officer on deck, rushed topside. The guns on deck were manned, but they could not stop the plane, which bore down on them, its guns blasting several large holes in the conning tower. The plane also dropped six bombs as it passed, close enough to cause damage below deck. A large oil slick began to trail off behind the submarine, and billows of black smoke issued from the conning tower. The Germans' only relief was that the plane, out of ammunition, disappeared back into the sky.

Ludwig was not injured in the attack, although the crew itself had suffered a number of casualties. Even more serious, the boat could not submerge; in fact, it could move on the surface only at a very slow speed. But Kraus determined that it was repairable, despite the heavy damage it had sustained, and so he set out for water shallow enough for him to put the submarine on the bottom and repair it there, out of sight of the enemy. He did not make it, however. A Brazilian aircraft located the limping submarine and moved in for the kill, finally wiping out the gun crews by blasting them right off the decks of the boat. Several depth charges were dropped, and the U-boat absorbed a tremendous amount of punishment. Then another Brazilian plane appeared, joined the attack, and on its first pass laid two depth charges close enough to destroy the boat.

Kraus was on deck and immediately ordered the few men left to abandon ship. He, too, dived into the water only moments before the submarine's bow raised up out of the water and the boat slid to the bottom stern first.

Heinrich Ludwig was one of the fortunate ones; he was on deck and into the water at the first cry to abandon ship. Only 11 other men of the ship's original crew of 61 survived along with him. As they floundered in the water, Kraus shouted for all the men to swim to him, and when they did, he reminded them of their oaths of secrecy and the allegiance they had sworn to Germany.

Ludwig and the other survivors were hauled from the water

later that day by the crew of the U.S.S. *Barnegat,* a small sea-plane tender. They were issued dry clothes and then taken to the Brazilian port of Recife, where they were interrogated briefly. From Recife, Ludwig was flown to the 4th Service Command, Miami, Florida, and again was questioned by naval intelligence personnel. He adamantly refused to divulge any information and showed a surprising degree of fearlessness to his captors, who had for some reason not expected quite that reaction from a sailor who looked so young. The other survivors were obviously just as constant, as evidenced by the report of the naval interrogators who were so impressed that they noted that the survivors of U-199 were "the most security-conscious group ever interrogated in this country."

The United States was not about to give up, however, and Ludwig was transferred to a secret interrogation center at Fort Meade, Maryland, just outside Baltimore. Ludwig and other prisoners of war who were sent there were under the impression that they were in Washington, D.C., and later always referred to Fort Meade as "the interrogation camp in Washington." The operation at Fort Meade was supervised by the Army Provost Marshal General's office, and it involved a well-planned and detailed scheme of interrogation. Intelligence officers from all branches of the service participated in their respective interrogations. A great deal of pressure was thrust upon the new arrivals and the tenuous nature of the thread by which their lives hung was made abundantly, even if not truthfully, clear to them.

Heinrich Ludwig arrived at Fort Meade on August 18, 1943, exactly eighteen days after his boat was sunk. He had no idea what might happen to him but, despite the fear for his life by this time engendered in him, he had made up his mind that he would not reveal a single thing to the enemy. After he was processed in, he was led to his quarters, which were a cross between a jail cell and an ordinary room, having elements of both but not definable as either. Ludwig was told that he was going to share a room with another prisoner, an obermaat, a rank equivalent to a U.S. army sergeant or a navy mate. The man was not there when Ludwig arrived, but Ludwig was told the obermaat would be brought back later. When he was, Ludwig met for the first time Werner Drechsler, although he did not know it then. The young NCO introduced himself as "Obermaat Limmer," and Ludwig's first thought was that the man was quite friendly and with no affectations despite his higher rank. That was on August 18; when Ludwig left Fort Meade a few weeks later, on September 14, his feelings about the man were radically different, but he tried to put them out of his mind because he felt certain that he would never see Limmer again.

The other five condemned prisoners had been shipmates aboard the U-615, which was sunk only one week after Ludwig's submarine. By July, 1945, at Fort Leavenworth, Helmut Fischer, Fritz Franke, Guenther Kuelsen, Bernhard Reyak, and Rolf Wizuy had been comrades for more than three years. They had shared the same cramped quarters for months on the U-615; they had been together at the same POW camps, usually housed in the same barracks with one notable exception: they were segregated at the interrogation center at Fort Meade. From these experiences, they had developed a closely knit comradeship and loyalty and a certain dependence on each other that went beyond what is required in an ordinarily friendly human relationship.

Helmut Fischer was not only the ranking member of the group at Fort Leavenworth; he was also a natural leader, and no one, with the exception perhaps of Otto Stengel, was even to conceive of contesting this. At the same time, Fischer was one of the youngest of the seven; he was only 22 in 1945. He was a very good-looking young man with brown wavy hair and a certain sincerity and honesty about him that came across to almost everyone who came in contact with him.

Fischer had been born and raised in the town of Ravensburg,

set in one of the most beautiful areas of southern Germany, only a few miles from Lake Constance. As a boy, with blond hair that slowly turned brown, he went to a German public school in Ravensburg and was one of the better students in his class. For the first five years, his schooling was relatively normal, but during the last three he was inculcated with a new form of education that centered all academic disciplines around the core of Naziism. He attended trade school after graduation and also joined the Hitler youth, in which he was moderately active but not a leader. Upon graduation from trade school, he went to work in Ravensburg as a tool and die maker.

Because of his trade, Fischer avoided conscription for about two years, although this was by no means his choice. In fact, Fischer was discontent serving the war effort from a factory in Ravensburg, so just before his twentieth birthday he enlisted in the German navy. He easily qualified for the U-boat service and willingly volunteered after basic training. Finally, he was brought to train with the other crew members of the U-615 in the historic city of Breda, The Netherlands.

At Breda, he met the youngest of the seven, Fritz Franke, who in 1942 was only 18 years old and looked more as though he should still be toting school books down a high school corridor. Franke was tall and very slender, carrying only about 155 pounds on his six-foot frame. He was coldly quiet to everyone except his closest comrades in the crew, and despite, or perhaps because of, his age he was the most resolute Nazi and least cooperative prisoner of the seven men.

Franke grew up in Frankfurt an der Oder, the smaller of the two cities named Frankfurt in Germany, about fifty miles southeast of Berlin and exactly on the border of Poland. It was an industrial town, and most of the boys growing up there were trained in skills that would insure them of work in the town itself. Franke studied to be a mechanic, but after three and a half years in trade school he decided not to stay around

Frankfurt. He had taken his participation in the Hitler youth very seriously, and at the first opportunity he joined the navy, not only as a deeply felt duty but also with a definite feeling of excitement. He adapted easily to the rigid discipline and the hard training, and he was extremely proud when he was accepted into the U-boat service.

Guenther Kuelsen was only about five months older than Franke, but he did not look nearly so young. Kuelsen came from Dusseldorf, where he had gone to school and where he had risen in the ranks of the Hitler youth to a position of leadership. In trade school, he studied to become a machinist and later worked at that trade for three and a half years in Dusseldorf.

Guenther Kuelsen was the exact image of what Hitler dreamed the German youth to be: blond, blue-eyed, strong, proud, fervently dedicated to the Germany Hitler was building, and enthusiastically aggressive. By the time he was 16, Kuelsen had stood up and fervently repeated the oath of the Hitler youth: "In the presence of this blood banner, which represents the Fuehrer, I swear to devote all my energies and strength to the savior of our country, Adolph Hitler. I am willing and ready to give up my life for him, so help me God." And he actively participated in the organized training that bred a Hitler youth for survival in war. On February 7, 1942, he volunteered for the navy and was sent to Breda for training as a U-boatman, an assignment he was quite pleased with. At Breda, he immediately struck up a friendship with Helmut Fischer, and the two became the closest friends among the group.

As time passed and the terrible realities of war were exposed to him, Guenther Kuelsen's admiration for Hitler as a man and a leader began to pall but his devotion to Germany and its success in the war was never touched. Through the wordless days of waiting at Fort Leavenworth with his six comrades, he managed to hold out the single strongest hope that something or someone would reverse the flow of fate and they would all survive. As he wrote to his parents in February, 1945, from his cell in death row: "But I really believe that it won't take too long . . . and that we will see each other in Dusseldorf."

As a boy, Bernhard Reyak was a plump, cherubic type whose soft features and corpulent face carried over into adulthood. He had been born and raised in the small town of Neuss on the banks of the Rhine River. Although he was only 21 at Fort Leavenworth, his bushy eyebrows and dark brown hair made him look older than most of the others. Reyak had worked as a metalsmith in Neuss for two years before joining the navy in 1941. While he was a member of the Hitler youth program, he was not too active and probably carried quietly more doubts about Hitler than any of his fellows.

Reyak met Fischer, Franke, Kuelsen, and Wizuy at Breda and began the concentrated training of a submariner along with them. He had a certain warmth and friendliness that was contagious, and he was liked by the others. They all felt Reyak was an extremely hard worker who more than held up his end of the load. And of the seven men at Fort Leavenworth, Bernhard Reyak was the least inhibited about expressing his great desire to live; he definitely did *not* want to die. He would not relinquish the righteousness he felt about the deed they had committed, but at the same time he made it crystal clear that he did not think he should be executed for his role in it.

Rolf Wizuy was the most unpredictable of the seven, moody and nervous to the extent that when he was placed under a certain amount of pressure he visibly showed it, yet at the same time he was militant and stubborn in his beliefs. A chaplain at Fort Leavenworth would often refer to Wizuy as "that strange little duck" because Wizuy was so erratic in his behavior and because underneath his physical appearance and bearing he was a considerably different person from what one might expect.

At 5 feet 11 inches and 138 pounds, Wizuy was downright skinny, but he had been this way all his life, even as a wispy little boy playing in the streets of Berlin. Because he had lived all his life in Berlin, he had seen much more of the politics and actions of the Nazi party than his comrades, though he had actually ingested no more knowledge about the party and its leader than any of the others. He had watched in awe the massive parades and attended the huge rallies that were so much a part of life in Berlin during the late 1930s and the first few years of the 1940s. He worked during the day as an electrician and at night he studied the writings of Hitler, Goebbels, and Baldur von Schirach, the virulent leader of the Hitler youth.

Rolf Wizuy was only 23 in 1945, but having enlisted during the autumn of 1940, he had been in the navy longer than any of the others with the exception of Otto Stengel. He had drifted about the navy for almost two years before his deepest ambition reached fruition—he was accepted into the U-boat service. The U-615 was his first assignment, and he enthusiastically boarded the train for Breda and the new training that lay ahead of him. When he arrived, he quickly made friends with Helmut Fischer and Guenther Kuelsen, both of whom he not only liked but also respected. In 1945, despite the urbanity of his background, he was in many ways still a little boy with winglike ears and an ever-present pout.

Fischer, Franke, Kuelsen, Reyak, and Wizuy worked hard along with the other crew members training at Breda, and by the time their training was completed they were confident they could cope with any contingency, even though they had never been to combat in a submarine. They were anxious to be off on an actual mission despite the rumors that had been drifting back about the hazardous change that had come about in the submarine situation in the Atlantic. Of late, the U-boats had been suffering horrendous losses, and though the losses were cloaked in closely-guarded security, word could not be kept from other members of the brotherhood of the U-boat service. Yet it still did not sway the ebullience of the new crew of the

U-615. As Helmut Fischer remarked to several of his crew-mates:"Because some people are getting killed doesn't mean we will. In fact, we're going to be a lot safer than the poor bastards on the ships we're going to sink." They all agreed with him.

The U-615 could not leave port until the end of the winter of 1943. The crew was given shore leave; then, when spring finally arrived, they moved out to join the war in the Atlantic.

Helmut Fischer, a radioman first class, had as his primary duties the manning of the boat's radio communications system. Kuelsen, Franke, and Wizuy were mechanics in the engine room, and Bernhard Reyak was a fireman first class. All, with the exception of Fischer, were obergefreiters, the equivalent rank of a U.S. army private first class or a navy seaman first class. Fischer outranked them slightly; he was a funkoberge-freiter, a rank equal to an army corporal, but he was not con-sidered a noncommissioned officer.

The U-615 was placed under the command of Kapitanleut-nant Ralph Kapitzky, an experienced and able captain who demanded and received unswerving loyalty from his junior officers and crew. Kapitzky did not announce the destination of the U-615 to the crew, but he did tell them they were headed to an area where the hunting would be spectacular and that they would no doubt see a great deal of action. As the U-boat made its way across the Atlantic, Kapitzky continually drilled his inexperienced crew in a variety of situations so that they would be able to react quickly and effectively to any emergency that arose. In the back of Kapitzky's mind, he knew that all of these situations would probably arise before this war cruise was over. His orders were to take his boat to the Caribbean and disrupt the heavy sea traffic that was flowing unhindered between Venezuela and some of the southern Caribbean islands, such as Trinidad and Curaçao. They were indeed hostile and dangerous waters, but the potential prizes far out-weighed the risk, Kapitzky believed.

The Atlantic crossing was uneventful, however, and the U-boat usually traveled on the surface with four crew members on watch duty at all times, carefully scanning the sea and the skies around them. As they approached the Virgin Islands, Kapitanleutnant Kapitzky revealed to the crew the actual area in which they would be operating. He told them how vital it was for them to be acutely alert at every moment, that the safety of the entire submarine depended on the actions of each man. But this was only a restatement of their long months of training, and Fischer, Franke, Kuelsen, Reyak, and Wizuy already felt that they were distinct but integral parts of a single unit.

The U-615 submerged as it neared enemy waters, traveling underwater during the day and surfacing at night to recharge its batteries. The submarine silently moved into the Caribbean through the Anegada Passage, about 100 miles east of Puerto Rico, passing close to the islands of St. Thomas and St. Croix and then heading south to begin its mission. A feeling of excitement among the crew was definitely noticeable to Kapitzky, who tried to keep it within certain bounds so that it did not adversely affect their functioning.

Rolf Wizuy was physically nervous, but he was no more afraid than anyone else on the boat. One morning as he was having breakfast in the galley, he turned to Guenther Kuelsen and said, with a kind of brooding seriousness: "You know what I'd really like. I'd like to see the fruits of our work. Watch a ship go down. But I guess we'll never get to see that, will we?"

Kuelsen nodded his head in agreement and then shrugged his shoulders slightly; his mouth was too full to answer.

"What do you think our chances are? I mean of really getting a lot of them?" Wizuy went on.

"I'd say damn good," Kuelsen answered, wiping some crumbs from the corner of his mouth. "Otherwise we wouldn't be here, right?"

"It also betters their chances of getting us," Wizuy said dejectedly.

Kuelsen smiled. "I don't think about that. I don't think they're that lucky. The odds are on our side anyway."

The U-615 patroled the waters of the southern Caribbean for two weeks, its periscope in constant motion scanning the sea and straining to catch sight of some unsuspecting vessel. But as the days wore on, Kapitzky became more and more restless. He began to wonder if his information about the fecundity of the hunting grounds had been wrong. His feelings reached the crew as well, and they were noticeably on edge as the stalking of seas that remained empty dragged on from days to weeks.

Finally, on July 27, their patience was rewarded. Kapitzky sighted a small tanker riding quite low in the water; he knew immediately that it was loaded to capacity. He ordered the crew to their battle stations, and he brought the U-615 into position for attack. After carefully charting the positions and distances, he fired two bow torpedos at the slowly moving tanker. Kapitzky watched through the periscope as the torpedoes surged through the water toward their victim. Inside the submarine, the almost total silence of the men was suddenly interrupted by the jubilant shouts of their captain: "Hit! Hit!" One of the torpedoes, directly on target, had torn into the side of the tanker. An explosion sheared the ship almost in two. Flames immediately poured over the ship, leaping hundreds of feet into the air. Huge columns of dense black smoke also rose into the sky, and there was not the slightest question in Kapitanleutnant Kapitzky's mind that his victim was on its way to the bottom of the Caribbean. The crew, as happy as Kapitzky, shouted excitedly, slapping each other on the back and participating in a weirdly chaotic dance about the cabin. Kapitzky let two of the officers view the gothic spectacle through the periscope and then extended it to several of the crew members who were nearby, including Bernhard Reyak but not Rolf Wizuy, who was still in the back of the engine room. Then, Kapitzky turned his boat around and hightailed it out of the area.

Kapitzky promised his men a special meal in celebration of their first hit; the first of many, he told them. He then walked over to Helmut Fischer and ordered him to radio their success back to the war office in Berlin. With a smile of satisfaction, Fischer said, "Yes, sir," and dutifully went about transmitting the captain's message.

Unfortunately for the U-615 the transmission was picked up by observers at a tracking station in Puerto Rico, who accurately calculated the location from which the U-615 was broadcasting. Immediately, even though Kapitzky and his crew were not aware of it, the hunter had suddenly become the hunted. Planes took to the air to scour the area that the U-615 was now known to be operating in, and a methodical and meticulous search got under way.

It was not until two nights later, however, on July 29, that an American bomber finally located the U-615, which was idly cruising on the surface to regenerate its batteries. The plane attacked once and its bombs caused some damage to the submarine, but the U-boat was able to crash-dive and escape temporarily from the attacker. Kapitzky turned the submarine eastward, heading in the direction of the Atlantic. But for the next few days, it became a desperate game of run and hide in an attempt to elude the attackers from the sky. Two planes successfully managed a bombing and depth charge attack that stunned the U-615 and caused a considerable amount of damage, enough to cripple the submarine seriously, before somehow losing the boat in the night.

The crew of the U-615 worked feverishly to repair the damaged submarine. Franke, Kuelsen, Wizuy, and Reyak spent all of their time working on the repairs—salvaging parts and redesigning and making new parts for those that had been completely destroyed. They used anything makeshift that, through their strained ingenuity, might possibly become an operable part and put their boat back into full function. Fischer, too, spent much of his time working with them in what was beginning to look like an endless and impossible job. In the meantime, the submarine was making very little progress.

By August 6, the U-615 had traveled only about 200 miles east from Curaçao, and it was still a long way from the Atlantic. Kapitzky had the boat on the surface that afternoon in a crash attempt to complete some badly needed repair work. Under the brutal sun and drenched with perspiration and seawater, the crew labored frantically on the decks of the boat. Everyone was aware of their awful vulnerability. Then, despite four men on bridge watch scanning the skies with binoculars, the U-615 was caught off guard by an American bomber, which roared down on them and laid a well-placed spread of bombs about the stern of the submarine. The submarine lurched and then reared up as water rushed into the stern section. The bow of the boat rose completely out of the water.

Guenther Kuelsen was below when the bombs first hit, and he and the other crew members there were thrown violently against the walls of the cabin. There was immediate chaos and panic below, but in the terrible urgency of the moment the men managed to seal off the hatches to the stern and save the entire boat from flooding. Kuelsen and Fritz Franke had helped to close off the stern, and as they rushed for the hatch to the conning tower, both knew there was at least one and possibly more men trapped in the water-filled tomb they had just sealed.

On deck, some members of the crew reached the two heavy antiaircraft guns, and as the American plane moved in for its second attack, they blasted it out of the air. There was no celebrating about this hit, however, as there had been when they had sunk the tanker. Kuelsen and Helmut Fischer, dazed, stood on the deck and watched as several crewmates lifted a bloody and limp body that was lying in a gnarled heap near one of the guns and unceremoniously dropped what had been one of their comrades into the sea. Kapitzky ordered the men back to their emergency stations, and the frenzied efforts to keep the boat afloat and moving began again. The submarine was now so badly damaged that it would be impossible for it to submerge, but it still limped slowly and miserably eastward. The U-615 did not get much farther. Another wave of attackers soon appeared in the sky, as Kapitzky had known was inevitable, and the men rushed to the guns again. They threw up a barrage of flak that damaged two planes, but the U-615 also absorbed a great deal of punishment. Kapitzky was on deck one moment and below the next, shouting orders and trying desperately to keep the crew functioning and fighting. Fischer, Kuelsen, and Wizuy were below at their emergency stations. Reyak and Franke were on deck helping with the gunnery, replacing two men who lay dead next to them. A deadly accurate strafing attack almost completely wiped off the deck, and Franke fell beside the gun clutching a searingly painful wound in his shoulder. With blood rolling down his arm, he made it back to the conning tower hatch and down into the submarine. Others were not so lucky; an on-target bombing run hit on both sides of the submarine and the boat suddenly began to submerge of its own accord. It was under only momentarily, but long enough to wash the dead and wounded from the decks. Then somehow the boat popped back to the surface, and Kapitzky ordered the men back to the antiaircraft guns. Kuelsen and Fischer joined Reyak on deck to help man the guns against the brutal strafing of the attacking planes. As night began to fall, the aircraft, out of ammunition and running low on fuel, began to peel off one by one and return to their bases. Finally in the darkness it was quiet again.

The dead from the U-615 were placed in the sea before the glazed eyes of those who had survived. Below, the wounded were treated in what now looked like an infirmary instead of the cabin of a submarine. Franke's injury proved to be more painful than serious, and Helmut Fischer helped dress the wound after a steel fragment had been removed from the young sailor's shoulder. The men were grimly quiet, overcome by the death and destruction of the afternoon, and aware that they themselves could meet the same fate. But somehow the U-615 managed to keep moving through the night.

The next morning, shortly after the sun pushed over the horizon in front of them, Kapitzky heard his officer of the deck sound "battle stations" again and quickly went topside. The lieutenant handed him the binoculars and Kapitzky focused on an American destroyer steaming directly toward them from the south. He put the binoculars down and gazed out across the sea in the direction of the destroyer; he knew that it was now utterly hopeless. Kapitzky told the lieutenant to pass the word to the rest of the crew to abandon ship. It was all over; there was no other recourse. Kapitzky watched what was left of his crew leave the boat, and then he lowered himself back through the hatch into the submarine and personally guided it to the bottom of the Caribbean Sea.

The destroyer was the U.S.S. *Walker,* and it did not have to fire a shot. It moved in on the survivors and brought 43 German submariners aboard. Then it turned around and headed back for Port of Spain, Trinidad.

Among the survivors were Helmut Fischer, Guenther Kuelsen, Bernhard Reyak, and Rolf Wizuy, all of whom miraculously escaped uninjured except for a few cuts and bruises, and Fritz Franke, who was given immediate treatment aboard the U.S.S. *Walker* before being allowed to rejoin his fellow prisoners. At Port of Spain the prisoners of war were given a temporary issue of clothing and then put on a ship bound for Norfolk, Virginia. Briefly at Port of Spain and periodically on the voyage to Norfolk, the men were interrogated by naval officers, but they were steadfast in revealing nothing other than what was permitted under the terms of the Geneva Convention. After docking at Norfolk, the prisoners stepped onto American soil for the first time, and the frustration of being in the land of the enemy was almost overwhelming. At Norfolk they were transferred to the command of the Army Provost Marshal General's office and it was there that, for the first time in many months, they were separated. Guenther Kuelsen and Fritz Franke were taken across Chesapeake Bay to Newport News, Virginia, for interrogation by naval intelligence authorities, and Helmut Fischer, Bernhard Reyak, and Rolf Wizuy were transported by truck to Fort Meade, Maryland, for more intensive questioning. The five men were not to meet again until several weeks later, when they would finally come together at the POW camp at Stringtown, Oklahoma.

All five were fearful about what was in store for them as they were shipped out for the interrogation centers; they had heard many rumors about the inhuman treatment and even outright murder of prisoners of war who were not cooperative—that had been part of their training before they ever went to sea—and in the short time since their capture they had already heard threats on their lives from some of their interrogators.

For the moment, anyway, they were alive; not well, they would be the first to admit, but at least still in existence, something many of their comrades could not claim. Their fears made them wonder just how long that situation would last, but deep behind the fearful faces was the iron conviction that if they died, they would die as good German fighting men.

3

Werner Drechsler

THE city of Chemnitz is in the hill country of East Germany, not far from Dresden and less than thirty miles from the Czechoslovakian border. After World War II, its name was changed to Karl-Marx-Stadt but it remained an odd mixture of picturesque old castles and bustling modern industry, with a population of more than 250,000. In the days before the war, Chemnitz was a good place to live; jobs were relatively plentiful and the standard of living was more than adequate. It was in this atmosphere that Werner Drechsler grew up, a good-looking little boy with a long rectangular face whose most salient feature was a large pair of soft, almost sad, blue eyes. He lived in a modest but pleasant home at Number 1 Sebastian Bach Strasse and could walk to the nearby public school, which he first started attending in the autumn of 1928.

In school, he was a better than average student, a likeable boy with a quick smile and a somewhat devilish disposition.

37

He stayed in the public school system for ten years, graduating in 1937 after experiencing the radical changes that were brought about in his training as Hitler began to intrude in the education of German youth. In effect, his early interest in history and the arts changed to interest in the more practical subjects of an industrial state. In the public school, he had picked up a smattering of both French and English, more French than English, and probably would not have been diverted into a technical school if the times had been different. But Germany was mobilizing and the emphasis was strictly on the useful and critical trades, so Werner Drechsler went to trade school to become a mechanic. He attended the school for one year and then, in the summer of 1938, as a 16-year-old boy, began his apprenticeship. He worked for about two and one-half years in Chemnitz before joining the navy in 1941.

Drechsler volunteered for U-boat service and was sent to Kiel for advanced submarine training. His first assignment was to the crew of the U-118, which, even though it was a U-boat, was not a fighting sub but rather a submarine supply boat and minelayer, sometimes referred to as a "milch cow." The U-118 was still under construction when Drechsler arrived at Kiel. It was a large boat, 1,600 tons, assigned to join the 12th Flotilla, which was headquartered at the German naval base at Bordeaux, France. Drechsler became intimately acquainted with the boat while it was undergoing its last stages of construction and he was moving through the final days of his training. He was present at the dock as the last touch was added before launching, the painting of the boat's emblem on the conning tower: the coat of arms of the city of Bad Gastein, Austria. And on December 8, 1941, the day after Pearl Harbor and three days before the United States officially declared war on Germany, the U-118 was commissioned.

The U-118 had been placed under the command of Korvet-

tenkapitan Werner Czygan, who was relatively old at 38 for a
U-boat command. Although this was Czygan's first U-boat
command, he was truly an old salt who had seen quite a bit
of the German navy from many different bridges, including the
old battleship *Schleswig-Holstein*. Czygan was from the North
Sea port city of Wilhelmshafen, but because of the heavy bombings of that city, he had moved his wife and daughter the
length of the country to the mountain resort town of Berch-
tesgaden on the Austrian border. He was a strict commander,
but his men were very fond of him, probably because he
made it exceptionally clear at the outset that their welfare was
his prime concern. Werner Drechsler especially liked Czygan
and had nothing but good things to say about him. The one
officer Drechsler did not like, and in this opinion he was in tune
with most of the other crew members, was Kapitanleutnant
Felix Müller, the boat's first engineering officer. Drechsler
came to refer to him disdainfully as "Felix the Strong" because of his harsh, bullying tactics.

Czygan took the U-118 out of Kiel for its U-boat acceptance
commission trial runs between December 10 and 20, and
then granted the crew leave for the Christmas holidays. Werner Drechsler went home to Chemnitz, enthusiastic and proud
of his assignment; he was 19 and this was to be the last
Christmas he would spend with his family before going to
war. Drechsler reported back to Kiel shortly after New Year's
Day and the U-118 finally put out to sea on January 6.
The boat traveled on the surface eastward, heading for
Danzig, Poland, and it was a treacherous and tricky cruise
through the bitter cold and rapidly forming ice in the Baltic
Sea. Czygan, however, brought the U-118 safely into the
Gulf of Danzig the next day and tied up next to a German
cruiser, on which Drechsler and the other members of the
crew were berthed in roomy and relative comfort. Diving
trials were held the following day, but the ice had gotten so
thick that the U-118 had to be led back to port by an ice-

breaker. After docking his ship, Czygan knew that they would not be going anywhere in the near future, at least until the ice began to break up.

Drechsler lived aboard the cruiser for the next two and one-half months but worked and trained daily on the U-118. Life was pleasant, food was good, and the war was a long way away. But finally on March 29, the U-118 slowly steered a course out of the harbor behind an icebreaker and made its way to the Hela peninsula. For most of the next two months, the U-118 stayed in the Baltic Sea, conducting various tactical exercises and drills. One of the exercises Werner Drechsler was most excited about was the test firing of the torpedoes. Even though it was not a fighting U-boat as such, the U-118 carried a load of torpedoes and would be constantly on the alert to use them if the opportunity ever presented itself, and among Drechsler's duties was that of a torpedo man.

Eventually the U-118 sailed out of the Baltic Sea, following the now well-worn submarine lane up through the Kattegat, down to the North Sea, and out into the North Atlantic. The first two war cruises of the U-118 were principally to supply other submarines operating in the mid-Atlantic. During the cruises, Drechsler worked hard and maintained a good rapport with the rest of the crew. He held up his end of the work and was accepted even by the more experienced U-boatmen as a good submariner.

One member of the crew, Herman Polowzyk, was from occupied Poland. He had, surprisingly, been *drafted* into the U-boat service, a fact that was later interpreted by United States naval intelligence authorities as a strong indication that Admiral Karl Doenitz was having difficulty finding volunteers for his elite but now highly hazardous underwater service. Because Polowzyk was not a German, he was not fully accepted into the innermost confidences and camaraderie of the crew. Not that he was isolated; that just could not be on a submarine where each man was important as an individual for his own duties, and all the men were forced together into an uncommonly close environment. But Polowzyk was ignored as much as possible and he was indeed aware that his crewmates looked on him as a Pole, not a German.

Two men on the submarine, however, went out of their way to be friendly with Polowzyk. One was Korvettenkapitan Czygan, who on occasion would personally invite the young seaman to his quarters for a game of chess, an effort to keep Polowzyk's morale up and to make him feel that he was accepted as part of the crew, and probably as an example to the other men of the boat. The other person to befriend Polowzyk, even though it was in a somewhat guarded way, was Werner Drechsler, perhaps because Drechsler did not share the Third Reich's racial and nationalistic attitudes and hence did not feel any strong alienation for people other than those born and raised in Germany. In another way Drechsler felt sorry for Polowzyk, whose vanquished country was now in ruins and who had made the large decision to allow himself to be conscripted into the navy of the conqueror. But whatever the extent of Drechsler's reasons, they were, at least at that time, appreciated by Herman Polowzyk.

At the end of the second war cruise of the U-118 Werner Drechsler had his first terrifyingly close encounter with death. The last U-boat had been supplied and Czygan was preparing to take his submarine back to port. He took the boat under but as they were submerging, the U-118 began to tilt, stern first, and descend, almost sliding, backward, deeper and deeper. The consistently increasing angle of inclination reached a full 55 degrees. Czygan ordered the entire crew to move to the bow of the boat in a desperate attempt to alter the angle of descent, but by this time the angle was too steep for any of the men to move forward. Everything that was not battened down came crashing to the floor and then clattered toward the boat's stern. Drechsler and Polowzyk, who were in the stern section, looked at each other with horror. The depth gauge registered 190 meters. For a chilling moment every man on the submarine, with the possible exception of Czygan, thought that there was no way that they could be saved and that any moment the pressure would crush their boat like a paper cup and they would be spilled out to a watery grave.

The engineering officer, Felix Müller, "Felix the Strong," gave way to panic and screamed wildly at Czygan, "What shall I do?"

"Blow the tanks," Czygan screamed back at him.

Müller momentarily regained some of his composure and managed to blow the tanks, but in his frenetic state neglected to close one of the diving tanks at the bow of the boat. Czygan again shouted at the engineering officer who reacted automatically and was able to rectify his almost fatal mistake. The submarine then began to surge rapidly upward at the same steep angle that it had been descending. When it broke the surface, its bow leaped right out of the water and then slapped down violently on the water's surface. Drechsler's eyes were laden with fright, and there was an awkward silence for a few seconds before he and the rest of the shaken crew realized that they were now safe. They found the cause of their near-fatal accident—during their last supply transfer one of the negative buoyancy tank valves had become clogged with debris that prevented it from being closed while they were submerging. It was quickly remedied and the U-118 was safely back on its way to port.

On the following day, December 8, 1942, the crew held a dual celebration—it was the first anniversary of the ship's commissioning and they had all survived the previous day's dilemma. Czygan ordered a special meal to be served, replete with beer to drink and cake for dessert. Drechsler even proposed a toast at his table; he was very happy to be alive and on his way back to safer waters.

Their destination was Lorient, France, an Atlantic coastal town where German subs put in for repairs. When they arrived, however, they found that the concrete shelters built to protect U-boats while they were docked were not large enough for the U-118, and so Czygan was forced to tie up next to them, vulnerably exposed to any air attack. The U-118 stayed there for three weeks until the routine overhaul was completed and Czygan's constant apprehensiveness about the nakedness of his boat was finally relieved.

The U-118 embarked on its third war cruise on January 26, leaving Lorient for the dangerous waters around the Straits of Gibralter. As soon as they were under way, Czygan informed the crew that they would be traveling submerged most of the time and that their mission was to be the very dangerous one of laying mines in the strait itself. On February 5, Czygan brought the U-118 to rest on the bottom of the sea between Casablanca and Tangiers to wait for weather suitable for the intricate job of minelaying in obviously hostile waters. The boat remained submerged for two days and the crew's mild excitement about their mission began to give way to a distinct fear for their lives. Drechsler was already having deeply disturbing thoughts, not only about his decision to volunteer for the U-boat service but also about the war in general and Hitler in particular. He did not, however, let his feelings be known to his fellow crew members. In any case, as they began their mission, Drechsler and the rest of the crew were too busy to think about anything other than successfully carrying it out. Eventually, their mission accomplished, the crew and the U-118 returned to port.

The fourth and final war cruise of the U-118 was also a minelaying mission, this time in the vicinity of the Azores. Part of the morning of June 12, a beautifully clear day with the sun bright in the sky and angled off the sub's bow, Werner Drechsler was on deck with several other crew members, sunbathing. Shortly before noon they went below for lunch, leaving on deck the four men on bridge watch. No more than two minutes after Drechsler had closed the conning tower hatch, however, one of the bridge watch suddenly screamed, "Planes, planes," and sounded the alarm.

Seemingly from out of the core of the sun two airplanes were streaking directly for them. The four men ran to the U-boat's gun but the planes' machine guns were already zeroed in and strafing the deck. Three of the men fell seriously wounded as Czygan threw open the hatch and rushed on deck. The planes were already circling for another attack. He immediately gave the order to submerge and held the hatch open as the one un-injured man on deck, Werner Reinl, dragged the other three men to relative if only temporary safety. Reinl pushed the last man into the submarine and then jumped in himself, closing the hatch only seconds before the water rushed over the diving U-boat. Below, it was absolute chaos.

When the boat had reached a depth of about 35 meters, the first depth charges hit and exploded near the stern. The damage was considerable and the submarine began to angle downward, stern first. More depth charges hit and the U-boat's motors went dead, the electrical steering failed and the hydroplanes and rudder were wrenched loose. Czygan gave the order to surface and fight it out with the planes. But as they flung open the hatch and started for the guns, the men were astounded to see not *two* but *nine* planes circling overhead. The planes dove to the attack and the gunnery submariners never made it to the guns; they were cut down in their tracks by machine gun fire. Others tried to reach the guns but with no better luck. Czygan was on deck and wounded, blood streaming from a vicious gash in his leg. Werner Drechsler was still below, but then one of the motors suddenly exploded and burst into flames. Drechsler watched helplessly and in horror as the young seaman tending it turned into a screaming sheet of flame and crumpled to the floor. And then Drechsler clambered out onto the deck.

A depth charge exploded just forward of the conning tower

and the submarine began to break in two. A fragment from the explosion tore into the side of Drechsler's neck; at almost the same moment a bullet ripped into his right knee. He collapsed on the deck. Czygan gave the order to abandon ship and Drechsler half-dragged himself and half-crawled to the edge and plunged into the water. He was able to swim with difficulty and did not look back at the sinking submarine. If he had, he would have seen his captain, Werner Czygan, kneeling on the forward deck, covered now with blood from several wounds, as the boat went under in a dazzling fountain of spray and debris.

Drechsler managed to stay afloat and watched in fear as one of the attacking planes swooped down at the men struggling in the water, but instead of opening fire, it dropped a life raft and then streaked off into the sky. Two of the survivors helped Drechsler into the raft, and then he helped pull in two other seamen who were also seriously wounded, one of whom was obviously dying. About an hour later, the survivors were picked up by the destroyer U.S.S. *Osmond Ingram*. Of the 58 men that had been aboard the U-118, only 17 were alive when the *Ingram* arrived on the scene, and the most seriously wounded sailor died shortly after being lifted onto the destroyer.

Werner Drechsler was taken directly to the ship's sick bay. His right knee was operated on at sea by the ship's doctor and he remained in bed for most of the eight-day voyage to Norfolk, Virginia. The day of their arrival in the United States he rejoined the other prisoners, but he could only walk with great difficulty and a good amount of pain. At Norfolk, he was helped off the ship by his friend from Poland, Herman Polowzyk, and led to a waiting ambulance. Drechsler and the other wounded prisoner were taken to the naval base hospital; the other fourteen prisoners were shipped directly to Fort Meade, Maryland for interrogation. It was the last time Werner Drechsler would see his crewmates until he finally caught up with them nine months later. Drechsler was hospitalized for the next nine days and so it was not until June 30 that he was finally transferred to Fort Meade and the interrogation center. When he arrived there, the other survivors of his crew had already gone on to other POW camps.

The usual stay at Fort Meade for new prisoners varied from a single day to several weeks, depending on the intelligence authorities' opinion as to the amount and type of information the prisoner might have and the possibility of his revealing it. Werner Drechsler, however, was a different case altogether. Reports preceded him to the interrogation center; the U.S. Navy informed the army that Werner Drechsler was not only an anti-Nazi but also a most cooperative prisoner—so cooperative, in fact, that the navy later stipulated emphatically that *he should never be sent to a prisoner of war camp where other German naval prisoners of war were held.* Besides that, he was also a valuable commodity—a German prisoner of war who might be able to win the confidence of subsequent prisoners who would pass through the interrogation center at Fort Meade. Therefore, Werner Drechsler took up his quasi-permanent residence at the fort.

It was at Fort Meade during the next few months that Werner Drechsler was able to refresh his language skill in English, and by the end of that period he could speak it fluently. He enjoyed a relatively comfortable existence and the war seemed very distant, even though many new prisoners passed through the interrogation center while Drechsler was at Fort Meade. He met and lived with quite a few of them. During these encounters, he still had an eager smile and a warm and friendly attitude that he tried sincerely to convey to all of the new men he met. Drechsler talked enthusiastically and freely with them about Germany, the war, and especially the submarines they were from. But most of his transient roommates were skeptical of him; the one feeling he apparently could not convey was trust.

Finally, on February 3, 1944, seven months after his arrival, the army for reasons nobody seems able or willing to explain to this day decided to transfer him temporarily to Fort Leonard Wood, Missouri. He arrived there the following day.

The other prisoners from the U-118 had been assigned to the POW camp at Stringtown, Oklahoma, the same camp that almost all U-boat prisoners were being sent to in 1943. It was army policy in those days to keep prisoners from particular branches of the service together. Therefore, almost all naval prisoners were kept together at specified camps. At Stringtown, one of the compounds was composed almost completely of captured U-boatmen, which was obviously much to their liking because of their proud confraternity. The U-boatmen often talked together, comparing their experiences in the war as well as their lives as prisoners of war. Among the most emotional subjects that continually came up in conversation were those Germans they had known who had either sold out to the Americans as traitors or those who had denounced Hitler and Naziism and had been sent to special prisoner of war camps—in most instances, they concluded, the two types were one and the same.

At Stringtown, Rolf Wizuy met Heinrich Ludwig for the first time. They talked about the interrogation center at Fort Meade, and both told how a "so-called U-boatman" had tried to ask them about military information, and as Wizuy and Ludwig talked they realized they had both encountered the same man.

"His name was Leimi," Wizuy said. "He claimed to be an obermaat."

Ludwig shook his head. "He used the name 'Limmer' with me. He said he was from the U-118."

"That's right, that's what he told me. It has to be the same person. Have you talked to anyone from the U-118?"

"Nobody knows a Limmer from the U-118. The only two from the U-118 who aren't accounted for are Drechsler and another one, and they think it must be Drechsler. The description fits him, they said."

Wizuy moved about nervously as they talked. "Are they sure?"

"I guess so. A lot of others were with him there and they all describe the same person."

The others included several non-commissioned officers, the highest ranking of which was Funkobermaat Friedrich Murza. There were also Obermaats Siegfried Elser, Lothar Mandelkow, and a few others, who altogether made up a rather substantial and responsible group of witnesses as far as Wizuy and Ludwig were concerned. In addition, at least fifteen other ordinary seamen claimed to have been interrogated by the same man, and their descriptions were all strikingly similar.

As the days passed at Stringtown, a prime subject for conversation was the situation involving "Leimi," "Limmer," "Nimmer," or whatever name the man used in a given instance. All of the men involved discussed the situation among themselves and with the crew of the U-118. Funkobermaat Murza also pointed out: "The rooms were bugged. That's why he wanted to get us to talk about those things. They put him there to get us to talk to him." The whole story hung together just too well — the descriptions were the same, they all fit Werner Drechsler who was still unaccounted for as a prisoner of war, the man in question knew too much about the U-118 to be anyone other than a member of that boat's crew. It was unanimously concluded at Stringtown that the man was a traitor and that the man was Werner Drechsler. But there was nothing they could do about it.

The submariners assumed that Stringtown would be their permanent camp and that they would stay there until the war was over. By the end of 1943, most of them had been at the camp for several months and had adjusted to the camp life and their jobs, which consisted of farming in the fields or the numerous jobs within the camp that were necessary to make the prison self-supporting and self-functioning. But Stringtown was not to remain their home, and in January, 1944, all of the prisoners from the U-boats were loaded a-board a train and transported to Papago Park, Arizona, a POW camp within the city limits of Phoenix. Among the list of prisoners going to Papago Park were Herman Polowzyk and Werner Drechsler's other crewmates; Helmut Fischer, Fritz Franke, Gunther Kuelsen, Bernhard Reyak, and Rolf Wizuy from the U-615; Heinrich Ludwig from the U-199; Friedrich Murza, Siegfried Elser, and all of the others who knew Drechsler personally or from the stories they heard about him.

The trip by train was not unpleasant and the prisoners soon learned that the move was nothing other than routine; that they would simply have to adjust to the new surroundings, new guards, and the new *modus operandi* of the camp. When they arrived, they quickly learned that, from the German 'point of view at least, everything and everyone in the camp at Papago Park was under the command of Fregattenkapitan Jurgen Wattenburg, who ruled with an iron discipline and a philosophy that was deeply embedded in the tenets of Naziism.

Papago Park was by no means an improvement over String-town, yet it was no worse, either. Arizona was warmer and drier than Oklahoma but the living facilities, the issues of clothing and equipment, and the assigned duties of the men differed little from those at Stringtown.

True to the policy of keeping units together, the crew of Drechsler's boat were all billeted in the same barracks and Fischer, Franke, Kuelsen, Reyak, and Wizuy were similarly kept together. Murza and Elser joined the other noncommissioned officers in a special barracks, but they were not isolated from the enlisted men, and hence they could keep good control of the chain of command that was still very much in effect at all POW camps.

In January, 1944, at Papago Park, the food was equivalent
to that served to U.S. military personnel. It was destined to
get much worse, however, as the war dragged on and food became more scarce. The typical day began with reveille at
5:30 A.M., breakfast at 6:00, and work at 7:30. If the men
were working in the fields, lunch was provided there; if not,
they were marched to the mess halls in the camp. All the
prisoners were back within their compound by 5:00 P.M.
for formation and then dinner. The evenings were their
own, and each compound had its own canteen where the
prisoners could buy various items like toiletry articles,
tobacco, and even beer—out of their "salaries" of 80 cents a
day if they worked in the American interest and 10 cents
a day if they didn't. They could write and receive well-
censored letters and packages, but the mail service left a
great deal to be desired.

They were forbidden to use the Nazi salute or to wear anything other than the army issue of POW clothing. If they refused
to work, they would not be fed—a simple but effective maxim
that usually kept the prisoner labor force full and active. They
were prisoners in the truest sense; the barbed wire, gun towers,
rigid discipline, fears, threats, and unveiled distaste of their
captors all bore witness to that fact.

Fischer, Franke, Kuelsen, Reyak, and Wizuy remained close,
and Heinrich Ludwig remained an occasional friend. They
did not know Otto Stengel, and their associations with Funk-
obermaats Murza and Elser were all strictly within the accepted protocol of the chain of command. During the evenings,
the five men from the U-615 often just sat in their barracks
talking. They would talk of escape and its possibilities, but
they were not planning anything; they would talk about home,
but Germany was an enormous distance and time away; they
spoke of the war, but that was very disheartening; and they
talked about their experiences as prisoners of war, but that was
bitter and extraordinarily depressing. Life at Papago Park
soon drifted from the initial excitement of a new camp to the
dismal routine of just another ordinary POW camp.

4

Sunday at Papago Park

$\mathbf{M}$ARCH 12, 1944, a Sunday, is not a particularly historic date. The events that would occur that day would do little to stir a world that in the last five years had become almost casually accustomed to news reports of immediate and often far-reaching significance. Not that little was happening; on the contrary, the war on all fronts was moving along at a brisk pace. The fighting was bitter and costly, but neither side had yet let go of the ubiquitous dream of victory; even Germany accepted its setbacks in North Africa, Italy, and Russia and the incredible pounding they were taking in their own cities from the savage force of allied air power, not as a prognosis of eventual disaster, but simply as unfortunate developments in a hellish war. Behind the war fronts, the political, economic, and industrial forces on all sides were involved in an exhaustive campaign to keep their respective war machinery running smoothly.

Much of what was going on that day would make outstanding news later but it was still in the planning stage and
shaded with secrecy. In London General Eisenhower and his
top echelon staff at Supreme Headquarters Allied Expeditionary
Force (SHAEF) were clandestinely putting together the last
details of *Overlord,* an operation that would erupt on the
shores of Normany in less than three months. *Overlord* was
being drawn up under a tight veil of security and although
the German high command knew that an Allied assault and
landing on the continent was inevitable, they could only spec-
ulate as to where, when, or even how large the invasion
would be. But on March 12 *Overlord* was still a vague plan;
an astronomical number of details had to be sorted out and
coordinated.

Less than 600 miles away in Berlin, another highly secret
operation, code name *Valkyrie,* was being planned by a high-
ranking, select group of German army officers. It was a well-
organized and calculated conspiracy to remove Hitler from
power. How this was to be done had not yet been decided.
Much of the conspiracy, however, was keyed to Count Klaus
von Stauffenburg, a young, good-looking lieutenant colonel
who had lost an eye, an arm, and two fingers from his remaining hand in defending the Reich. He had direct access
to Hitler and was prepared for the sake of Germany to carry
a bomb to the Fuehrer's bunker and destroy the leader for
the ultimate well-being of the country. Not everyone involved
in the intrigue agreed with Stauffenburg's method, but they
were gradually being drawn to his side. The plot was being formulated in Berlin, but the list of conspirators em-
braced all elements of the German high command and
reached out to the war fronts themselves. Unlike *Overlord,*
however, *Valkyrie* would fail. Not only would Stauffenburg die, but the vengeance of Hitler would leave a death
toll in the thousands from a brutal purge designed to rid
Germany of all traitors to the Reich; among the eventual

victims would even be Germany's most famous field marshal, Erwin Rommel.

No one besides those directly involved, of course, were aware of the surreptitious plans that were being formulated in Europe on March 12, least of all the prisoners of war at Papago Park. In their enforced state of isolation, they were not even aware of the general course of the war, attributing the various dribbles of news they did hear to the workings of American propaganda. Above all, as the morning of March 12 dawned at Papago Park, the prisoners had no idea whatsoever that they, too, would be involved in a desperate plot before the day was over. It would prove to be a day unlike any other day they had experienced at the prisoner of war camp. For Helmut Fischer, Fritz Franke, Guenther Kuelsen, Heinrich Ludwig, Bernhard Reyak, and Rolf Wizuy, and for Otto Stengel, who at this point did not even know the other six men, it would be the most decisive day of their lives. They were about to enter into their own personal conspiracy, one that would have a greater effect on their lives than any of the operations and schemes that were being hatched in London, Berlin—or anywhere else in the world.

As they slept through the last few morning hours before reveille, Werner Drechsler was already aboard a train on his way to join them. His days at Fort Meade were over. The Department of the Army had, despite the previous explicit warning from U.S. naval intelligence authorities, decided to transfer him from the temporary camp at Fort Leonard Wood to the Prisoner of War Camp, Papago Park, Arizona. Whether it was through the sheer stupidity of some army officers or the bungling of red tape or whether it was a preconceived and sadistic attempt to send him to his death now that he was no longer needed has obviously never been documented, but whatever the reason, the result was still the same—Werner Drechsler was reassigned to the one camp that housed practically all of the German U-boat prisoners in the United States.

March 12 began much like any other day at the POW camp. At 5:30 the sharp blast of a whistle in each barracks building cut through the silence of the early morning. The sun had not yet edged over the eastern horizon. The men moved slowly at first, trying to shake off the lethargy of the early hour. It was a ritual they had grown used to; it had its own rhythm and almost in synchronization the pace quickened as the prisoners prepared to fall out for the morning formation. Once outside, the men moved to their assigned positions in front of each barracks, perhaps more enthusiastically today because it was Sunday and for most of them Sunday was a day off. They stood rigidly at attention as the roll calls began, the sounding-off from each group mingling together and becoming indistinguishable in the otherwise quiet, dry Arizona air.

Sundays at Papago Park were leisurely, or at least as leisurely as a person could expect at a POW camp. There were only two formations, one in the morning and the other at five o'clock that afternoon. Some of the prisoners would be on duty in the mess halls and at other odd jobs, but most would be on their own for the day. They could attend religious services in the morning if they desired, but this had not proved to be one of the more popular Sunday diversions at the camp. The movie theater, on the other hand, which opened in the afternoon, drew the largest crowds even though the bill was usually nothing more than a super-saccharine, well-censored American movie. This particular Sunday looked as if it would be more pleasant than average. It was a clear day, the sun was out, and it was comfortably warm for a March morning.

At camp headquarters, the staff of U. S. army personnel were operating on a skeleton force. Captain Leland Hebblewaithe, the camp's classification and identification officer, was one of the officers on duty that day. He was at his desk promptly at eight o'clock in the morning, organized for the day's work, when orders came through directing him to assemble a unit of troops and proceed to the train station at Tempe, Arizona, to pick up a large group of new prisoners. Captain Hebblewaithe was a

28-year army veteran and his precise neatness and order were the result of almost three decades of military discipline and procedure. Most of the 28 years he had spent in the ranks of enlisted men, but the war had brought about his promotion to captain and finally the assignment and responsibility for classifying, identifying, and maintaining the records of all prisoners of war at Papago Park.

A total of 350 prisoners of war were being shipped by train to Papago Park for permanent incarceration. They were scheduled to arrive at the depot in Tempe at noon that day, where the authority for their custody would be turned over to the command at Papago Park. Captain Hebblewaithe was to classify and identify the new prisoners at the train station and then take charge of them, assign them to available barracks, and see that they got there that afternoon.

It was a routine assignment. Hebblewaithe had spent eight years in classification work, trained by both the army and the Federal Bureau of Investigation, and he knew pretty much all there was to know about fingerprint and photographic identification. He could process all 350 prisoners in less than two hours. The logistics of getting the prisoners from Tempe to the POW compounds at Papago Park was basically a standard procedure by that time.

The details of the logistics were left to the motor pool; all they needed to know was the number of men to be transported, the distance, and any special requisition of the officer in charge. All Captain Hebblewaithe had to do was set the operation in motion and to telephone the camp's medical detachment to order an ambulance in the event that some of the prisoners might be sick or injured.

The distance to the train station at Tempe was less than ten miles, and the trip by army convoy took about half an hour. By eleven o'clock, the convoy was formed and Captain Hebblewaithe took his seat in the staff car at the front. Behind the staff car was the army ambulance and a long row of heavy, dark troop transport trucks with their canvas-covered tops and the familiar white star painted on each door. The rumbling procession moved down the camp's main road and out through the front gates; the appearance of such a cold and harsh caravan had become a rather common sight in Phoenix.

Meanwhile, in Compound 4, most of the prisoners had decided to go to the movie. Fischer and Kuelsen talked about going together. Franke and Reyak planned to go with some other friends and were trying to talk Heinrich Ludwig into joining them. Ludwig had KP duty for the evening meal and had to report to the prisoners' mess hall at four o'clock. He wasn't sure whether he would make it back in time, but he finally agreed to accompany Franke, Reyak, and the others and asked them to remind him when it was 3:30 if the movie was not over by that time. Rolf Wizuy would have to miss this week's movie. He was on KP duty for the day at the officer's mess on the other side of the camp, which would keep him unhappily occupied until 6:30 that evening.

Captain Hebblewaithe and his convoy arrived at the train station well ahead of the train. The train finally pulled in a little after one o'clock, and the new prisoners were herded off and lined up in a clearing near the trucks. They stood at ease in silence, their small duffle bags containing all their worldly possessions beside them. The train commander and several aides approached Captain Hebblewaithe. They exchanged salutes and then got down to the business of transferring command of the prisoners to Captain Hebblewaithe. The train commander turned over the records of all the prisoners and then Captain Hebblewaithe began the tedious procedure of checking each man against his records and photograph. By three o'clock that afternoon, however, the classification of all 350 prisoners was completed.

Three of the prisoners were singled out of the formation and led over to the ambulance. Sergeant Fred R. Bornstein, the medic noncom in charge of the ambulance detail, leaned against the vehicle and watched the prisoners as they walked toward him, an armed guard on either side of them. One of the prisoners limped slightly, the sergeant noticed as they approached, but other than that they appeared to be in pretty good shape.

One of the guards handed Sergeant Bornstein the prisoners' records and the orders that told where to take them. Before the sergeant let them get into the ambulance, however, he asked the prisoners what was the matter with them. The prisoner who had been limping answered for all three of them in English. None of them had anything seriously wrong, it turned out, and the man with the limp simply stated that he had hurt his leg but that he could walk without any real problem.

"You can ride sitting up, if you want," Sergeant Bornstein told them. "It makes no difference to me. It's a short ride."

The three men did not answer. The sergeant turned to the ambulance driver and handed him the prisoners' records. "All three go to Compound 4."

The sergeant looked back at the prisoners. "Okay, which is it—sitting up or on the stretchers?"

The men looked at each other and then their spokesman said, "We'll ride sitting."

The three men climbed into the ambulance and sat hunched over on the bottom stretcher. The three tiers of stretchers prevented them from sitting straight, and the guard who followed them in took the single small seat at the back. Sergeant Bornstein closed the back doors and took his seat in the front beside the driver. The ambulance waited until the rest of the convoy was loaded and then joined in the long column that started back toward Papago Park.

Sergeant Bornstein turned in his seat to look at the prisoners. The man closest to him was the prisoner who had spoken for the others. "You the only one who speaks English?" he asked.

"Yes. They speak only German," the prisoner said nodding toward the other two.

"Your name's Drechsler, isn't it?"

"Yes, Werner Drechsler."

"You been a prisoner very long?"

Drechsler did not answer immediately and appeared to be lost in thought. "Almost a year," he said finally. "Pretty long, I guess."

"Where did you learn how to speak English?"

"I went to school in England. Before the war."

"You speak it pretty well."

"Thank you."

Werner Drechsler still had a boyish face that could break into a soft grin or a cold uncomprehending stare with very little provocation. This, combined with his squared-off crewcut, almost shaven at the sides, made him look even younger than his actual age. He had celebrated his 21st birthday without ceremony at Fort Meade less than two months earlier, but this fact and his youthful appearance are somewhat meaningless in attempting to describe a young man whose experiences over the preceding two years were more than most men would be exposed to in a lifetime. For a while, Drechsler had grown a beard, a short goatee that barely formed a "U" around his chin, and a thin mustache, which succeeded in making him look older but at the same time slightly Faustian. He had shaved them off, however, before leaving Maryland.

Drechsler's days as a prisoner of war had apparently had little effect on him physically; stocky, he could be best described as athletically muscular, and he gave every appearance of being capable of handling any form of rugged manual labor.

Sergeant Bornstein had turned back to the front and the group rode on in silence until the prison camp came into view and the convoy slowed as it neared the front gates.

"Are we going to the hospital?" Drechsler finally asked.

"No, you're all going to Compound 4. The barracks."

"I thought we were supposed to go to the hospital. On the train they said we would go to the hospital."

"Well, they were wrong. The orders say Compound 4." Sergeant Bornstein paused for a moment, and then added, "Maybe they'll send you over in the morning."

"What time do they have sick call here?"

"In the morning, right after reveille formation. You go to your company orderly room. What's the matter with your leg anyway?"

"I was wounded. Shot in the leg." Drechsler rolled his pants leg up to reveal a circular scar about an inch in diameter and marked by small perforations. "It's been bothering me a lot lately. Also I fell on the train coming here, which didn't help it at all. I think a doctor should look at it."

The convoy moved through the front gates of the camp and came to a halt. A corporal directed three trucks to pull out of the column and proceed down the main road; then he motioned for the ambulance to follow them.

Compound 4, at the far south end of the camp, was completely enclosed by a chain-link fence, topped by three rows of heavy-duty barbed wire. To the east of it was a large recreation area for the prisoners of all four compounds, to the west was the hospital complex. North of the compound, a heavy barbed wire fence and a patrol road separated it from Compound 3. It was the most isolated of the four enlisted men's compounds, only slightly less insular than the small compound that housed the German officers.

The ambulance followed the three trucks to the far end of Compound 4 and finally came to a halt just south of the complex of barracks. Werner Drechsler looked over the shoulder of the ambulance driver to catch a glimpse of what was to be his new home and absently reached down and rubbed his right knee. Spirals of thick black smoke curled upwards from the chimneys of the dreary one-story barracks buildings. Through the open window of the ambulance drifted the flat, acrid odor of burning coal. The stale smell was quite familiar to Drechsler, as it was to practically everyone in the United States army;

it hung in the air even when the barracks stoves were not in use and was as representative of all old army barracks as a butt can nailed to a beam support.

A few prisoners had gathered near the barracks to watch the new arrivals as they clambered out of the backs of the three trucks. Word of the arrival of new prisoners always spread quickly through the camp. The prisoners were anxious to learn who the new men were and what news they had of Germany and the war. From the ambulance Drechsler watched, too, as the men were disgorged from the trucks, and then he slowly followed the other two prisoners out of the ambulance. He was not too enthusiastic, however, about meeting other prisoners, and he no longer needed or wanted to hear what information they had about Germany.

Drechsler and the other two prisoners from the ambulance walked over to the group and stood with them in silence. Of the 350 new prisoners, 58 had been assigned to Compound 4. A sergeant assembled them into a formation and took roll call. The men were assigned bunks and told that their bedding, what there was of it, was ready and would be issued at the supply room next door to their barracks. The sergeant ended the formation abruptly. "The mess hall's open until 16:30. You will fall out for formation at 17:00 in front of your barracks. Dismissed."

The welcoming of new prisoners had become almost a ritual at Papago Park. It began with an immediate but friendly quiz of the new prisoner to establish some kind of association—a hometown, a unit, a battle, or even a campaign, the place captured, another interrogation camp or POW camp in the United States, a mutual friend—anything they might even remotely have in common that would serve to cement a relationship in their collectively helpless situation.

It was now nearly four o'clock and the prisoners who had not gone to the movie began to filter in among the new arrivals and set the ritual in motion. Drechsler went directly to his

bunk and tried to keep himself occupied. Besides his POW issue of clothes and toiletries, he carefully laid out his three personal effects—a pipe, a tobacco pouch, and a pair of bathing
trunks, though what he was going to do with the trunks must
have been a mystery, even to him. He worked quietly, trying
to avoid the others by ignoring what was going on around
him. Anonymity, however, in a crowded POW barracks was
virtually impossible. He had to talk to the prisoners who approached him and he could not help overhearing the conversations that were going on around him. And it soon became
apparent to Werner Drechsler that he had arrived in a prisoner of war compound inhabited primarily by members of the
German navy, many of whom had served in the Reich's U-
boat command, some who had been aboard his own submarine,
the U-118, and others who had passed through the same
interrogation center in Washington.

Werner Drechsler reluctantly talked to the stream of prisoners
that wandered through his barracks, answered their questions,
and tried to act as complacently as possible. Shortly, however,
he began to have the uneasy feeling that some of the veteran
prisoners had established an association with him that he
desperately wished would not materialize. It was not a certain
feeling, rather an intuitive notion, that he felt, perhaps, might
be founded more in his own fear and guilt than on actuality.
And, with these ambivalent feelings, he had the overwhelming
desire for the night to end and morning sick call to present
itself.

5

Discovery

A few minutes before four o'clock, the movie let out and the prisoners filed out into the street. It had not been a particularly memorable movie but it did occupy the afternoon and the men had, perfunctorily if not enthusiastically, enjoyed it. Heinrich Ludwig had left early and was already back at the mess hall by the time the movie ended. He was among the first of the moviegoers to learn of the arrival of new prisoners, hearing the news as he walked back to the mess hall. He couldn't go to see the new prisoners at once, he thought, when he heard the news, but he would definitely go over after he came off duty to see if he knew any of them.

As he entered the mess hall, he announced excitedly to the other KP's, "New prisoners have arrived. Over fifty of them, I hear." But the other prisoners on duty were already aware of the fact and they went sullenly about their duties, ignoring Ludwig's statement.

As the main group of prisoners made their way back to the

barracks after the movie, word passed quickly among them about the new prisoners. By the time they reached their barracks, there was scarcely a prisoner in Compound 4 who did not know about the new arrivals, with one notable exception, Rolf Wizuy, who was still toiling in the officer's mess in another area of the camp.

Guenther Kuelsen had walked back from the movie with his friend Helmut Fischer, and when they reached their barracks he turned to him and asked: "What do you say we walk over and meet the new prisoners?"

"I think I'll wait till after supper," Fischer replied.

"Why? We've got plenty of time. It's only four o'clock."

"I know. But I think I'll wait. It won't be so crowded over there later." Fischer took off his shoes and stretched out on the canvas bunk.

"All right. But I think I'll wander over there now." Kuelsen turned and started toward the door.

"Guenther," Fischer yelled after him. "Are you going to the soccer game later?"

"I think so."

"Good, I'll see you there."

Kuelsen nodded and then left the barracks. When he reached the new men's barracks, he saw a few of the new prisoners standing out in front talking to other prisoners he knew. Kuelsen looked at the new men but did not recognize any of them. He went into the barracks and walked down the aisle, but none of the new prisoners looked the least bit familiar. It was crowded inside the barracks so he let himself out the rear door and walked back around the building. The same men were still in front and he joined one of the small groups. The new man was from Essen, a gefreiter who had been snatched from the north Atlantic after his submarine had been sunk about three months earlier. The new man had been at a POW camp in Maine and was transferred to Papago Park for reasons he could not explain but was not particularly happy about, it appeared, when he talked about the treatment and privileges at his former camp and was quickly informed that the same niceties did not exist at Papago Park. Kuelsen talked briefly to the man and then left for the mess hall. He was hungry and even the daily four-ounce ration of meat suddenly seemed very appealing.

After supper and precisely at five o'clock the men assembled in front of their barracks for the last formation of the day. The new prisoners were slightly disorganized, but in a few minutes they were lined up correctly and counted off.

The soccer game began shortly after the formation and many prisoners began to drift over toward the large recreation area to watch it. The game was between the two best teams in the compound and it attracted a large crowd. Guenther Kuelsen stopped back at his barracks to look for Fischer, but his friend had apparently either left for the game or had gone to talk with the new prisoners.

When Kuelsen reached the soccer field the game was underway and a crowd of over two hundred had already gathered to watch. Two prisoners he knew waved to him as he approached.

"Kuelsen, did you hear about the traitor?" one of them asked.

"Traitor?" Kuelsen looked somewhat puzzled. "No! A traitor here?"

"There's a traitor with the new prisoners. Haven't you heard? It's all over the camp."

"No. Are you sure? I mean how do you know he is?"

"He was recognized. A couple of the men knew him from the interrogation camp in Washington." The prisoner paused and looked at Kuelsen for his reaction but found nothing in the flaccid, immobile face of his listener. "You went through the camp in Washington, didn't you Kuelsen? Maybe you know him, too?"

"What's his name?"

"Drechsler. I think his first name is Werner. He's a gefreiter, but I don't know what ship he's from."

The name took Kuelsen by surprise, and for a split second his mind was groping. Then suddenly it hit him.

"He went under a different name in Washington," the prisoner continued. "A different rank too. They said he was called Leimi, Obermaat Leimi, or something like that."

Kuelsen's astounded face now visibly came alive. The second name seemed to slam into him like a sharp, solid blow to the chest and everything suddenly fell into place. "Leimi! My God! That's who Wizuy always talks about."

The two prisoners looked at each other and then back at Kuelsen. "That's what they said, 'Leimi.'"

"Leimi was Drechsler. Christ, yes!" Kuelsen said. "Wizuy was kept in the same room with him in Washington. He swears the bastard was a traitor. He said he tried to get all kinds of information from him." Kuelsen paused to catch his breath. "I was there at the same time. But not with Rolf. We were all kept separate. I never saw Leimi, but Rolf would know him. Has Wizuy seen him yet?" Kuelsen stopped again, suddenly remembering that his comrade was on duty at the officers' mess and wouldn't be back for another hour. "If it's Leimi, Rolf will know. My God."

The two prisoners were startled by Kuelsen's excited recognition and stood staring blankly at him.

"You did say his name was Drechsler," Kuelsen continued, "the one he's using here?" They told him again. "Drechsler," he repeated to himself and started to walk away from them. "I've got to find Fischer."

Werner Drechsler had been in camp less than an hour and a half. Although he didn't know it, in that short period of time he had become the axis of conversation throughout Compound 4. Kuelsen looked briefly through the spectators at the game, but he could not see Helmut Fischer among the faces. He must be over with the new prisoners, Kuelsen thought, and began walking in the direction of their barracks. His mind was in a strange state of agitation; his thoughts recklessly spiraled around the single word "Leimi." Should he even speak to the bastard? he asked himself. Confront him. What if it isn't Leimi? If this is another Drechsler . . . it might not be. It would be better to wait for Rolf. But he also thought that maybe he should question him, so he could tell Rolf. What is there to learn anyway? he tentatively decided. Drechsler was not about to come out with, "Yes, I'm Obermaat Leimi. You probably remember me from Washington. I was a traitor there." Where the hell is Fischer? he thought. I need to talk to Fischer.

A number of men were still milling around the new prisoners' barracks when Kuelsen arrived. He went inside but Fischer was not there. Kuelsen talked to several of the new prisoners, but his heart really wasn't in it, and he could not strike up any kind of association. Finally, he asked one of them, "Is there a Drechsler here? I heard there was, and I think I might know him."

"Drechsler, yes. I think he's out in front," one of the new prisoners answered.

Kuelsen made his way back to the front door of the barracks and looked outside. A few small groups of men stood about talking and he wondered which one included Drechsler. Then as he stepped out the front door, he noticed one man standing alone. The man was leaning up against one corner of the barracks building and smoking a pipe. Kuelsen approached him.

"You just arrived today?" he asked rhetorically. "My name's Kuelsen, Guenther Kuelsen."

"Mine's Werner Drechsler." His words were slow, saddled with a tone of detachment. As he spoke he looked up at Kuelsen briefly and then gazed off toward the football field.

Kuelsen was surprised. He had not expected the man to be Drechsler; somehow he thought Drechsler would be much older. The suddenness of the confrontation was something Kuelsen felt terribly unprepared for, but its mildness left him with a strange feeling—a thickness in his throat and a tingling brilliance spreading somewhere deep within his body, almost sexual in nature, as if he had hinted to a girl that he would like to go to bed with her and she had just looked straight into his eyes and without hesitation told him she would. For a moment he couldn't say anything, and just looked at the man, who was slowly dragging on his pipe, ignoring him. After what seemed to him like an enormous silence, yet in reality was only a few seconds, Kuelsen spoke again.

"Where are you from?"

"You mean my home, or where I was before here?"

"Your home. Where you lived," Kuelsen said.

"In Chemnitz."

"Chemnitz. There are others here from Chemnitz. Have you met any of them?"

Kuelsen paused for a moment, and then said excitedly, "Haase, he's from Chemnitz. He was just here. I saw him over there in front." Kuelsen turned quickly to the groups of men standing near the front door of the barracks. "He's right over there. Have you talked with him?"

Drechsler shook his head negatively.

"Haase," Kuelsen shouted. A man looked over at them from one of the groups. "Haase, come over here. This man's from Chemnitz."

The man strode over to them and shook Drechsler's hand. Drechsler and Haase talked about their home town, but they had not known each other there. Kuelsen listened and felt a strong wave of relief that he was no longer alone with Drechsler. The two men continued to talk for several minutes but they could not find a person in Chemnitz they both knew and their conversation drifted off onto other topics related to Chemnitz—areas of the city, streets, stores, and other things that they both knew.

Drechsler appeared to become more friendly as they talked. He was more animated and began asking questions about the camp, POW life in general, and finally certain things that Kuelsen nervously felt the man had no right to ask. The in-

quiries were fragmented and seemed to have no particular
order or logic, but even fragmentary answers would give information that this man should not have, Kuelsen thought.
Then Kuelsen felt it might all be just his imagination. Perhaps the questions were not out of line at all. At any rate,
he would file them away in his memory and talk to Fischer
and Wizuy about them.

"I'm not even supposed to be here," Drechsler said, as their
conversation appeared to be reaching an end. "I was supposed
to go to the hospital. They brought me from the train station
in an ambulance, but I don't get to go to the hospital until tomorrow."

Drechsler told them briefly, but with a sense of pride, about
his wound and how he was injured in action. The two men listened and then departed when he was through with the story.
Haase went back to the other new prisoners and Guenther Kuelsen set out again to find Helmut Fischer.

Heinrich Ludwig learned that Drechsler was one of the new
prisoners from the others who came to eat in the mess hall
where he was working. At first, he did not believe it. "They
couldn't possibly send him here," he told one of the other
KPs. "Not Drechsler, too many people know about him
here." But as more and more prisoners filed through the
mess hall, talking about Drechsler by name and the fact that
he was the traitor from Washington, Ludwig became very
anxious to go over to the new prisoners' barracks and see
for himself if the Drechsler they were talking about was really
his old room-mate at Fort Meade. If it was, he could easily
identify him and would happily do so, Ludwig said to himself. But it would have to wait because there was no way he
could leave the mess hall until he was released from his duty
there.

Otto Stengel did not live in the same barracks as Fischer,
Franke, Kuelsen, Reyak, Wizuy, or Ludwig. He was quartered
in another barracks about six buildings away, and typical of

the general practice of the camp had his closest friends among those confined within the same four bare-wood walls. Stengel knew the other six men by sight but only one of them, Rolf Wizuy, by name. He had seen the others briefly on work details or at the canteen but never had had any real opportunity to become better acquainted with them. He would have liked to have known them better; his inquisitive nature made him want to know everyone in the camp, but this was, of course, impossible. So he looked on them as simply more of the nameless faces that even in their anonymity were still close comrades, bound together in a common plight.

Every barracks, probably every group of men that lives together for a period of time, has one man among them who is the accepted source of news—a mixture of probing journalist and town crier who is self-appointed to keep all of the rest informed. A woman in this capacity is often unflatteringly pegged the local gossip; a man, especially in circumstances like Papago Park, was a welcome necessity and his activity carried no label, complimentary or uncomplimentary. In his barracks, Otto Stengel was that man. He was a faithful reporter and the men had come to rely on him, even though they knew he tended to embellish most stories. The facts were always there, however, and the men did not mind sifting through the rhetoric to find them. The collection and dissemination of information had achieved the status of a personal quest for Stengel; the embellishments were basically the result of his impetuous sense of the dramatic. Otto Stengel, it could be said, enjoyed his role very much.

Like the others, Stengel had gone to the movie that afternoon and learned of the arrival of the new prisoners as he was returning from it. For some reason, unexplained as well as being ostensibly out of character, Stengel did not immediately go over to meet them. Instead, he ate and then went directly back to his barracks. A while later, he walked alone to the soccer game where, like Kuelsen, he heard there was a traitor among the new prisoners. This was obviously too much for a self-styled correspondent like Stengel to pass up, so he set out hastily for the new prisoners' barracks. He wanted to talk with Drechsler himself and bring back a firsthand interview to his bunkmates, who he knew would want an accurate and comprehensive report on the man whom everybody in the compound now seemed to be talking about.

When he arrived at the barracks, Stengel sought out Drechsler immediately and found him in the same location that Guenther Kuelsen had left him about five minutes earlier. Drechsler was talking to another prisoner, a man named Bruno Faust who coincidentally was a friend of Stengel. Otto joined the two and began an interrogatory conversation that sounded almost like an exact repetition of Drechsler's earlier questioning by Kuelsen. The one exception was that Stengel knew another prisoner from Chemnitz whose name struck a chord of recognition in Drechsler.

"His name is Heinz Richter," Stengel said. "He was on the same submarine with me."

"I know Richter very well." A boyish smile spread across Drechsler's face and for a brief moment he was happily excited.

"He and I used to go to the same dances in Chemnitz. That was before the navy; I haven't seen him since. Where is he now?"

"Probably at the soccer game. Come on, I'll take you to him."

The smile faded, and Drechsler ended the conversation politely but with indifference. "I'll go over later and find him. I've got some things to do around here first."

Stengel took the hint, said good-bye, and walked back to the soccer game. He found Heinz Richter at the far goal. "Heinz, I just talked with a good friend of yours," Stengel said with a tone that bordered on coyness. "He's one of the new prisoners."

"Really, what's his name?"

"Drechsler."

Before Richter could reply, another prisoner standing near-by shouted, "You've got a fine friend there, Richter. He's a traitor." Richter and Stengel looked at the man understand-ingly but said nothing. The prisoner added, "He's going to get the 'holy ghost' tonight, I'd bet on that."

Richter turned to Stengel and said quietly, "I don't want to see him. In fact, I won't see him."

Guenther Kuelsen finally tracked down his friend Fischer in the crowd at the soccer game, where Fischer was standing with Fritz Franke, Bernhard Reyak and several other prison-ers. Kuelsen hurriedly told them about Drechsler and the con-versation he had just had with him. The others had heard the rumor that there was a traitor in the camp, but they had not yet heard his name. Kuelsen's news was an electrifying surprise. The men talked excitedly for a few minutes and then split up—Kuelsen and Fischer went back to talk with Drechs-ler; Franke and Reyak returned to their barracks to wait for Rolf Wizuy. None of the men had seen Drechsler in Washing-ton, with the exception of Reyak, who had met him briefly there but felt he could not positively identify him. Wizuy was the only man who would know beyond a reasonable doubt whether this man was one and the same with the "Leimi" who had gouged his way into their memories by his exploits in Washington.

One other man could identify Drechsler—Heinrich Ludwig, still on duty at the sinks in the mess hall. But somehow his name had not come up in the excited discussions the other four men were having about Drechsler.

Helmut Fischer was the ranking man in the group and the closest they had to an actual leader. He was a quiet, thought-ful young man, and despite the fact that he was only 21 years old, the other men from his submarine relied on him and res-pected him. Fischer did not really know why he wanted to talk with Drechsler, but he was apparently afflicted with the same urge that had earlier driven Guenther Kuelsen to seek out the man. He led the way to the new men's barracks even though it was actually Kuelsen who was taking him to meet Drechsler. They found Drechsler and talked to him for a short time but learned nothing of any consequence. It appeared that Drechsler was getting used to visitors because he talked candidly and without hesitation to the two men. He was obviously unaware of the story spreading through the compound. Either that or he had the facility for masking what had to be a torturous inner panic with an outward composure that was as calm as that of any ordinary sailor relaxing on a Sunday afternoon.

Kuelsen left the group and went back to the soccer game. Guenther Bleise met Helmut Fischer back at the barracks and Bleise reminded him that he had been with Drechsler, too, at Fort Meade, but they decided to wait for the return of their companion Rolf Wizuy.

Werner Drechsler went back into his barracks. It was far too early to go to bed, not even six o'clock, and there was enough noise and activity in the building to make sleep an utter impossibility. But Drechsler was as tired as he was anxious for sleep to come. He lay back on his bunk and stared up at the ceiling.

Shortly after six o'clock, Obermaat Werner Reinl of Drechsler's boat, the U-118, entered the mess hall of Compound 4. Heinrich Ludwig, who was stacking freshly washed trays, looked over his shoulder as he heard the door slam. Obermaat Reinl walked over to him. "You've heard about Drechsler, I take it?" he asked.

Ludwig said that he had, and then slid the trays into the cupboard in front of him.

"Who else besides you were with him in Washington?"

"Wizuy spent the most time with him there," Ludwig answered. Reinl began to write the name down on a piece of paper. "It's Gefreiter Rolf Wizuy. He roomed with Drechsler until he was taken out for an operation."

"Who had an operation?" Reinl asked.

"Wizuy. He had to have his appendix out." Ludwig paused for a moment. "I also roomed with Drechsler, you know."

Obermaat Reinl nodded his head. "Give me the names of anyone else who was in Washington about that time, who might have known or heard about Drechsler."

Ludwig began to dictate a list of names of men from his barracks and a few others he had heard talk of Drechsler at one time or another. Reinl wrote all of the names down and looked up when he heard Ludwig stop.

"Is that all?"

"All that I can think of right now. Are you planning to do anything with him?"

"Not yet. We'll have a meeting when we get more information. We're not certain yet that it's the same man. We want to get all the facts before we bring the thing up to the compound spokesman."

"I could identify him, you know," Ludwig said.

"I know. But we don't want you or any of the other men taking any action, no matter what, until after we have a meeting with the compound spokesman. Do you understand that?"

Obermaat Reinl then left the mess hall and walked over to Wizuy's barracks. The gathering in the barracks had increased; it included Fischer, Franke, Reyak, other prisoners who shared the barracks, a few curiosity seekers, and now Obermaat Reinl. Helmut Fischer talked with Reinl but there was little information he could give him that the obermaat was not already aware of. Fischer asked Reinl if they had decided yet on any course of action in the event Drechsler proved to be the traitor Leimi, and he received the same cursory answer that Ludwig had. Reinl added, however, that the compound spokesman, Franz Hox, was already aware of the situation and would, no doubt, summon all the men later to hear their stories himself. In the meantime, Reinl and several other NCOs would continue to investigate the matter. It was implicit in his words that for the time being the case of Werner Drechsler was out of the hands of the enlisted men; it was not, however, implied that it would *remain* out of their hands.

Rolf Wizuy walked into the barracks about ten minutes earlier than he was expected. It was approximately 6:20, and from the expression on his face it was evident that he had already heard about the arrival of Werner Drechsler. He headed immediately toward Helmut Fischer's bunk at the far end of the barracks, where Fischer sat talking with Reyak and Guenther Bleise. Wizuy's long coltish legs carried him quickly and rather awkwardly as he hurried down the aisle. Despite the loose-fitting, coarse fatigues, Wizuy had a reedy, fragile appearance that now seemed visibly shaken; his face reflected the strange admixture of excitement, anger, confusion, vengeance, and the weight of sudden and unexpected responsibility that now ran through his mind. He began to speak even before he stopped walking.

"Is it true about Drechsler? Is he here?"

"He's here. At least there's a Drechsler here," Fischer said with a surprising degree of calmness. "No one's sure yet if he's the same one. We were waiting for you."

"Where is he now?" Wizuy appeared to be regaining control as he stared down at the three men sitting on Fischer's bunk.

"Probably still at his barracks," Fischer answered.

"Well, let's go. I'll know in a minute if it's Leimi."

As the three men stood up, Fritz Franke appeared, seemingly out of nowhere, and clapped his hand on Wizuy's shoulder. "Are you going over to see Drechsler?" He asked. Wizuy said that they were and Franke told the four that he would like to go along. Guenther Bleise, however, decided to stay in the barracks in the event any of the noncommissioned officers came looking for them. Wizuy, Fischer, Reyak and Franke started down the aisle toward the door. Bleise watched them go and then slowly walked over to his own bunk and lay down.

As they left the building, Fischer turned to Wizuy and said: "I talked with Drechsler. So did Kuelsen. But we couldn't tell anything. Neither of us knew him in Washington. Which reminds me, we should stop by the soccer game and get Kuelsen. He didn't think you'd be back until after 6:30."

"Did Drechsler say anything?"

"No, not really. He talked very freely with me. He didn't seem nervous at all. But Kuelsen said he was asking some strange questions when he talked to him."

As the four approached the soccer field, Kuelsen saw them coming and trotted over to them. The five men continued toward Drechsler's barracks, hardly breaking stride as Kuelsen joined them.

"What kind of questions was Drechsler asking you?" Wizuy asked Kuelsen. "Helmut says they were strange."

"He asked me if we get German news through a short-wave radio. He wanted to know if we had one in camp so we could get the true news about the war. He said they had one in their last camp and all the men were able to get the German news. But I didn't answer him. He also asked me if we had a list of names of the men who were missing from different crews, the ones the Americans said were deserters. I didn't answer that, either."

The five men were now nearing the front entrance to Drechsler's barracks.

"He also said he knew of some officers who deserted," Fischer added. "I don't know how he would know that."

Franke opened the door to Drechsler's barracks and the five men stepped inside. A number of the new prisoners turned to look at the small group when the door slammed shut behind them. Fischer's eyes scanned the room quickly, but it was actually not necessary for him to look very far. Drechsler was stretched out on the second bunk from the door to their right. Fischer looked at Wizuy and nodded toward the bunk. Drechsler had his eyes closed but with his hands clasped behind his head did not appear to be asleep. He was wearing only a tee-shirt and a pair of fatigue pants.

As the five stepped over to the end of his bunk, Drechsler opened his eyes and a fleeting, slightly astonished expression flashed across his face. His hands released his head, but before he could speak, Rolf Wizuy addressed him.

"Obermaat Leimi, what are you doing here, in an enlisted man's barracks?"

"I'm not an obermaat," Drechsler answered. His look of bafflement gave way to a somewhat strained smile. "I'm a gefreiter. And my name is Drechsler."

Wizuy ignored the answer and continued, "I'm sure you won't object if I call you 'you' even though you're an obermaat and I'm only a gefreiter."

Drechsler sat up on the cot. "I told you I'm not an obermaat. I'm a gefreiter, the same as you. You must be mistaken; maybe you have me confused with somebody else."

"Don't you remember me?"

"No. I don't even know you." Drechsler looked beyond Wizuy at the four men standing behind him. "What is this, anyway?"

"Where are you from?" Wizuy asked suddenly.

"Chemnitz."

Before Drechsler could continue, Wizuy broke in. "That's what I thought. And you don't remember me from Washington? You don't remember sharing a room with me there at the interrogation center?"

"You are mistaken. I've never even seen you before."

"You must remember, we were together there for quite a-while. You even got an icebag for me just before they took me away for my operation. You must remember that. I was in great pain and you went and got the icebag."

Drechsler shook his head negatively and mumbled something, mostly incoherent, but to the effect that he was never in Washington.

"And how are your wounds? You were wounded, weren't you?"

"Yes, in the neck and in the leg." Drechsler unconsciously rested his hand on his right knee. Then he looked straight at Wizuy. "I was wounded in action."

"I know. You showed me the wounds in Washington," Wizuy said staring back at him.

Drechsler looked away and said nothing for a moment. Then he looked up, his gaze encompassing all five of the men who were staring back down at him. "Look, I don't know what you're after, but you've made a mistake. I don't know any of you. And I was never in Washington. Now please leave me alone. I'm very tired and I have not been well. We can straighten all this out in the morning, if you want. But now I want to go to sleep."

The five men stood there awkwardly for a few seconds and no one said a word in response to Drechsler. Then Fischer said quietly to Wizuy, "Come on, let's go." Wizuy and the others turned and started toward the door. Drechsler watched them go. As Fischer held the door open, Wizuy, the last man out, looked back over his shoulder at Drechsler, who was still staring after them emptily, as if he saw no one there.

A rush of cold air was sucked into the room through the open door, and the sharp chill made Drechsler suddenly realize that he was sweating profusely. After the door slammed shut, he reached for his fatigue shirt and began wiping the perspiration from his face and neck. He looked down at his bare arms and watched the beads of sweat swelling and then quickly rubbed them dry with the shirt. The beads reappeared almost immediately. He swung his legs over the side of the bunk and looked at the other new prisoners, but none of them looked back. They all appeared busy and it was apparent that they were not going to say anything to him about the incident that had just taken place. It was a very disquieting silence, and Drechsler was acutely aware of it.

Outside, the five men walked about twenty yards before anyone said a word. Then Fischer turned to Wizuy and asked, "Are you sure it's him?"

"I'm positive," Wizuy answered. "He had a beard in Washington, but it's the same person. I'm sure of it."

6

Death in the Shower Room

NIGHTS were the loneliest and saddest times for the prisoners at Papago Park. The few hours between the onset of darkness and the extinguishing of lights at ten o'clock seemed to concentrate their feelings of isolation and focus with terrible poignancy on the vapid existence they had been cast into. During the day, the prisoners could lose themselves, at least temporarily, in work, but the night intensified the realization of the shabbiness of their condition with a copious supply of reminders—the bare light bulbs dangling from the ceiling; the coarse raw-wood walls and unfinished floors and the cold draft that seeped in from every crack and joint; the thick odor of fifty men confined too closely together; the searchlights from the gun towers that methodically patroled the grounds; the brightly-lit chain-link and barbed-wire fences that seemed to glisten in the night; and the city lights of Phoenix, flickering only a short distance to the west, constantly bringing to mind other days in better places. Sleep was the great release, and

the few minutes before it came were the cherished and scrupulously guarded moments when each man could be alone
with himself.

When the night of March 12 finally came and the darkness
had completely settled on the camp at Papago Park, it was
an altogether different kind of night for most of the prisoners
in Compound 4. They were too occupied to think of their
own personal squalor; the fate of Werner Drechsler super-
seded all other thoughts, not only of those men who wanted
to be involved in its outcome, but of those as well who
merely wanted to talk about it or ponder it alone themselves. And for Werner Drechsler, it was an all-consuming
thought after his confrontation with Rolf Wizuy.

On the way back to their own barracks and for a while
once they arrived, Rolf Wizuy and his friends discussed what
should be done with Drechsler. Of the five men, several felt
that all they could safely do was administer the "holy ghost,"
the POW's term for a severe beating. This, followed by a
complete ostracism of Drechsler by all the prisoners, would
suffice, they said. Others, however, felt the only suitable and
just punishment for the crime of treason was death. The discussion itself had a strangely unreal quality because at this
point the five men did not know who would carry out the
verdict, whatever it was, nor even if they would take part in
it once it was determined. They felt the decision would ultimately be made and the sentence directed by the camp's
noncommissioned officers, either on their own volition or as
a result of orders from the German officers who were not too
effectively isolated in their own sector of the camp.

The NCOs had been able to maintain surreptitious communications with their officers despite the determined efforts of the
U. S. army to enforce a strict and complete segregation between the two military classes. A well-planned and constantly
changing system was employed by the Germans to keep each
other informed and to maintain the proper chain of command

even under these difficult circumstances. Accomplishing this and keeping it going was a tax on the ingenuity of everyone concerned. One of the most effective methods was the exchange of written messages between officers and enlisted men who were assigned to work details within the officers' garrison; the messages were left under preselected rocks to be picked up later, the recipients alerted to their existence by a discrete set of signals passed mutely in an environment where conversation between two groups was strictly forbidden.

The highest ranking German officer held at Papago Park was Fregattenkapitan Jurgen Wattenburg, commander of the submarine U-162 that had been sunk by three British destroyers September 3, 1942, who had also been an officer aboard the famous German battleship, the *Graf Spee*. Wattenburg, often referred to in 1944 as a "super-Nazi," exercised rigid command over all German POWs at Papago Park, directly and indirectly, and he was ultimately informed of everything going on within the camp's walls. The problem was not getting messages to him, but rather how long it would take to do so, especially when certain decisions, like the one involving Werner Drechsler, demanded immediate action.

The five men from the U-615 finally decided to send a messenger to the compound spokesman and inform him of Wizuy's positive identification of Drechsler, in the hope that it would hasten a decision as to what should be done. Bernhard Reyak volunteered to take the message and subsequently left the barracks to find Chief Quartermaster Franz Hox. Wizuy and Guenther Kuelsen decided to walk over to the nearby barracks that housed the crew of the U-118 to see if they had any plans for their former shipmate. Fischer and Fritz Franke remained in the barracks to be on hand in the event any of the NCOs were to come looking for them. Heinrich Ludwig had returned from duty at the mess hall and was alone in his barracks; he had not sought out any of the others who knew Drechsler. Instead he had decided to wait for further directions from Obermaat Reinl or one of the other noncommissioned officers.

By 7:30 Reyak had contacted the camp spokesman and was back in his barracks. Hox had accepted the news indifferently and offered no suggestions or ideas to Reyak, except to say that he might want to see all of them later. Wizuy and Kuelsen had likewise returned, bearing the news that Drechsler's crewmates had no plans and were not making any. Their feeling on the subject, Wizuy reported, was that they had not personally known Drechsler to be a traitor and that any action to be taken should be carried out either by those who were directly involved with his alleged treason or by those who were selected by the noncommissioned officers. Wizuy told his friends that he strongly agreed with the former approach.

Shortly before eight o'clock, Guenther Bleise arrived at the barracks and ordered Wizuy, Fischer, Kuelsen, Franke, and Reyak to report immediately to the compound spokesman. The messenger then left to convey the same orders to Heinrich Ludwig.

The compound spokesman's office, actually nothing more than a table and a single chair, was in the orderly room of Compound 4's first company. It was at the opposite end of the compound, and the five men walked quickly through the darkness toward it. When they arrived, about ten other enlisted men were already gathered in front of Chief Quartermaster Hox's desk. Funkobermaat Murza, Obermaat Elser, and several other noncommissioned officers were also present. The other men had apparently already been questioned and had given their stories because as soon as the five new men arrived Hox told the others to step out of the way so he could talk with Wizuy, Fischer, Franke, Kuelsen, and Reyak.

Otto Stengel sat on a bunk in his barracks, smoking a cigarette and thinking about the events that had transpired that day. He had brought his comrades up to date on the situation and related in precise detail his conversation with Drechsler. As the climax to his narrative, he dramatically inquired if they knew what was going to happen that night. They didn't so he told them: "He'll get the 'holy ghost' and possibly will not survive the night." Stengel's friends did not exactly react with uncomprehending disbelief, and several mentioned that they thought something like that might occur but they had not known it as a fact, which was not surprising because in reality neither had Otto Stengel.

Stengel doused his cigarette in a butt can and started out of the barracks. He decided to revisit the new prisoners. Like a good reporter, he wanted to be on the scene in case anything newsworthy happened.

At the new prisoners' barracks, Stengel talked casually with a few of the new men, but, under the circumstances, what they had to say was essentially unimportant to him. He tactfully disengaged himself from them and wandered toward the end of the barracks, where Drechsler was standing alone by his bunk. As he struck up a conversation with Drechsler, he immediately became aware that Drechsler was uneasy and seemed to be scrutinizing him carefully. After a minute or two, however, Drechsler realized that Stengel simply wanted to talk, and he relaxed.

It was then that Stengel began his gentle probing. "How long have you been a prisoner?" he asked.

"About a year and a half."

"That can't be completely accurate," Stengel said with a trace of distrust. "I've been a prisoner not quite two years and you were from the U-118. It was sunk long after I ever became a prisoner. How can it be a year and a half?"

Drechsler ignored the question.

When it became clear that Drechsler was not going to answer, Stengel began anew. "What camp were you at before you came here?"

"A better one than this one," Drechsler said sharply. "These cots aren't worth a damn. We had regular bunks there. Almost everyone had his own radio. In fact, it was so good that I signed a release from the hospital so I could get out and back to the barracks."

Drechsler then told him about his battle wounds and showed him the scars. "Everything was much better there. We even had a newspaper printed in German. Here, it seems to me, we don't have anything."

"That newspaper is an American paper," Stengel corrected him. "It is put out by a German immigrant. But he's an American; he's not on our side."

"How can you prove that?"

"I know. I saw the paper at another camp. I even distributed it to other prisoners until I found out it was filled with lies. It insulted our government. It even insulted Dr. Goebbels and Hermann Goering. And the Fuehrer." Stengel's ruddy face began to redden. "It attacked all our leaders."

Drechsler looked up, a wry, almost mischievous grin on his face. "That paper's right. What it says is true." The grin faded. "What did Hitler tell us? 'We don't want a war.' And then what have we had? Nothing but war. War with everybody."

Stengel's face was now a deep red, and he searched frantically for something to say in answer to Drechsler's sudden and unexpected heresy. He finally blurted out, "You better watch what you say. Otherwise, something is going to happen right here. I'm a good German and I won't let you talk like that."

"What would you like to do about it?" Drechsler said quickly but without any real malice, and then he laughed at Stengel.

"It's better that I leave. I don't want to continue this now. But we'll talk again, I guarantee you that." Stengel turned and stalked out of the barracks. A combination of the knowledge of who Drechsler was and the consummate effrontery of the man – speaking out against Germany and the Fuehrer—so enraged Stengel he did not stop trembling until he reached his own barracks.

Heinrich Ludwig was in the latrine washing his hands when

Bleise entered his barracks. Bleise looked for him at his bunk and asked if anyone knew of his whereabouts, but none of the other prisoners did. Bleise left word to have Ludwig report to the orderly room of the first company as soon as he returned.

Ludwig was taking his time washing; the combination of odors from his work in the mess hall—the grease, garbage, raw detergents, even the metallic smell from the stainless steel trays—reeked, and he slowly and carefully tried to wash them away. About five minutes had elapsed since Bleise had disappeared back into the night when Ludwig, drying his hands as he walked, returned to his bunk. When he received the message, he quickly put on his fatigue shirt and darted out the door. Ludwig knew immediately what Chief Quartermaster Hox wanted to see him about, and he double-timed it across the compound, unaware either of the darkness or of the cool wind from the north into which he was moving. He was thinking only that the time had finally come to identify Drechsler.

Ludwig arrived at the orderly room slightly out of breath. When he entered, he did not see Hox, only the backs of five men he knew—Fischer, Kuelsen, Franke, Reyak, and Wizuy. As he moved up behind them unnoticed, he caught a glimpse of Chief Quartermaster Hox sitting behind the table. The compound spokesman was talking to the five men, and as Ludwig came into range, he heard him say, "Well, it all appears very clear now. It's the same Drechsler."

One of the five men asked what the compound spokesman was going to do about Drechsler, but Ludwig only vaguely heard the question. He was more concerned with the sudden realization that it really was the Drechsler he knew and that there would be no more speculating on his part, no more mind-straining conjurations of Drechsler's face so that he would be absolutely sure when he identified the man. It had already been determined: Werner Drechsler was Obermaat Leimi.

Chief Quartermaster Hox looked at the five men standing before him and for the first time noticed Ludwig behind them. He said nothing to Ludwig but nodded to him in recognition and then spoke to the men in general. "There's nothing I can do personally, you know that. There's no official thing I can tell you to do or have done."

"Are you going to inform Captain Wattenburg?" Wizuy asked.

"When we can. But there is nothing he can do, either." Chief Quartermaster Hox paused and looked up at the ceiling. "Drechsler could be gone from here by the time we got a message to the captain."

"What do you suggest we do, then?"

"I can't really advise you on that, either. You have to determine that for yourselves. I leave it up to you."

From the inflection in the camp spokesman's voice, it was clear the meeting had come to an end. It was also clear that Hox had no intention whatsoever of committing himself to any form of involvement in the eventual disposition of Werner Drechsler. He had done his duty as trial, judge; the evidence had been presented in his crude and spurious courtroom and the compound spokesman was now convinced that Drechsler was indeed the man who wore the gross scar of treason. The verdict of guilty had come from Hox, not so much passed as it was simple concurrence with the opinions of the witnesses and other members of the kangaroo court. The compound spokesman apparently deemed the evidence so overwhelming that it precluded the need for the defendant to appear and testify in his own behalf. Drechsler stood convicted in absentia.

Beyond the finding of the court, Chief Quartermaster Hox implied, it was not within his jurisdiction to pass sentence on this man. So he was returning the case to the people against whom the crime had been committed. It would be they who would have to render the inexorable judgment of the man's fate.

The orderly room emptied quickly, but the kangaroo court reconvened in the darkness outside with only Chief Quartermaster Hox not in attendance. The resolution of the case was now entirely in their hands.

The noncommissioned officers who stayed with the group included Funkobermaat Friedrich Murza and Funkmaat Siegfried Elser. With them was Drechsler's one-time friend, the young Polish draftee, Herman Polowzyk. At first, it was Rolf Wizuy who did most of the talking. With a renewed bitterness, he revealed his feeling with the terse statement, "The traitor should be hanged. It's the only way." He began to reiterate the treachery to which he was exposed in Washington, but he was cut short by Murza and Elser, the two ranking men in the group, who reminded Wizuy that they had already been through that aspect of the case in Hox's office. Now they had to decide what to do with Drechsler. Murza and Elser suggested that the "holy ghost" might be sufficient under the circumstances. They argued that they had no idea what reprisals the Americans might take if they killed Drechsler. They did not know why the Americans had sent Drechsler to the camp or even whether he was still considered important to the U.S. government. To kill him could endanger the entire camp, they said.

Wizuy did not agree. He claimed that Drechsler must have been sent because the Americans wanted him taken care of. "Why else would they have sent him among those who knew he was a traitor?" He had served his usefulness to the enemy, Wizuy continued, and now they didn't need him anymore. Perhaps the United States looked upon traitors with as much disgust as Germans did; perhaps they actually *expected* Drechsler to receive punishment for his crime at the hands of those he betrayed.

Murza and Elser were still not convinced. A sound beating would be punishment, they said. Perhaps a beating would not be enough for the gravity of his crime, but true punishment would be meted out in Germany after the war. In the meantime, they could uphold their duty to Germany as well as satisfy their desire for vengeance without jeopardizing their own lives in the process. They agreed that Drechsler deserved to be hanged, but that did not resolve the question of what might happen to those who carried it out—no matter how right it was in their own minds. Their rights as well as their lives were firmly in the hands of their captors. They were not in a position to bargain for anything.

Wizuy was not to be put off easily, however. He postulated that Drechsler may even have been sent to the camp to continue his espionage activities. He reminded Murza and Elser of the questions Drechsler had put to Guenther Kuelsen, and of some other highly suspicious inquiries brought up at the hearing in Chief Quartermaster Hox's office that Drechsler was alleged to have made since arriving in camp. Wizuy held to his original position—that it was their duty as German fighting men to destroy the traitor. Wizuy's shipmates and their friend Heinrich Ludwig expressed agreement with him, whether out of loyalty, which Wizuy was later to claim, or out of their own deeply rooted feelings cannot be determined. In any case, at this point, in the dark, chilled desert night, they stood with him to the man. Others in the group were not so steadfast; some, in fact, began to drift away into the darkness and by their departure to remove themselves from involvement in the sentencing and from the case as well.

The gathering was reduced to about fifteen men when one of them revived the specter of the special camps into which, it was said, certain prisoners for unexplained reasons would disappear, never to be heard from again. The camps actually existed only in the minds of the prisoners, but to them the camps were real. There was a very real possibility, the prisoners thought, that they all might be sent to these special camps before the war ended, and then there would be no one left to identify Drechsler in Germany. And, of course, no one knew for sure that he would ever get back to Germany. In addition, the group agreed, Drechsler knew that he had been identified. All he would have to do would be to pass on to the American authorities the names of those who could identify him and they themselves might be destroyed while Drechsler was allowed to live and return to Germany.

Justice must be accomplished now, Wizuy repeated; it could not wait until the war was over—and *now* meant *that night,* because Drechsler would no doubt be gone by the morning and their opportunity lost, perhaps forever.

The reasoning of Rolf Wizuy and his five friends was fragmented, almost contradictory, and emotional. It was based on certain premises, such as the special camps (which simply did not exist), and it was riddled with pure conjecture as to, for example, the reason Drechsler had been sent to the camp and whether he would depart the following morning. Yet for all its weaknesses, the argument was convincing, primarily because it called upon all of their deepest feelings of patriotism, something that was inbred with them and had roots that went back many years before they ever entered the German armed forces.

The seriousness of murder was never a part of the discussion, because the thought of execution as murder never entered their minds. Duty, honor, country did, overwhelmingly enough not merely to defer but also totally to preclude the weaknesses of their reasoning and the inequity of taking the law into their own hands. It was from the honorbound appeal to patriotism that Werner Drechsler's sentence was passed, at approximately 8:30 P.M., March 12, 1944, by the small group of men standing in the night shadows of the 1st Company orderly room of Compound 4. The sentence was confirmed when one of the noncommissioned officers, never identified by name even in subsequent interrogations and testimony, asked, "All right, who would like to carry it out?" Rolf Wizuy and his four comrades from the U-615—Helmut Fischer, Guenther Kuelsen, Fritz Franke, and Bernhard Reyak—and their friend Heinrich Ludwig volun-

teered without hesitation. The matter settled, the group dis-
solved into the night to set about the preparations for the execution.

The men met again in an open area in front of the 3rd Company, approximately midway between the 1st Company orderly
room and the barracks in which Werner Drechsler had already
bedded down for the night. There, they made the final plans and
then parted to carry out their individual assignments. They
agreed to meet at 9:00 P.M. in the yard in front of the 4th
Company, which was about fifty yards from Drechsler's barracks.

Helmut Fischer volunteered to obtain the rope and went off
in the direction of the 2nd Company. The men had discussed
several ways they might entice Drechsler out of his barracks.
Kuelsen, for example, offered to go into the barracks and invite Drechsler out under the pretext of showing him some in-
teresting things in the camp, but the others did not feel that
this would work, not only because it was now rather late,
but also because Kuelsen had been present at the confrontation with Wizuy only a short time earlier. Wizuy suggested
they try to persuade an obermaat whom he knew to participate, at least to the extent of luring Drechsler out of his barracks, and he left for the noncommissioned officers' barracks
to see if he could find the man. The other four set out to procure gloves so that they would not leave any fingerprints and
incriminate themselves.

Shortly before nine o'clock the men arrived at their prede-
termined meeting place. Fischer had secured a tent rope and
had already looped and tied a rather crude noose. The
gloves had been obtained and distributed. But there was still
one problem. Wizuy had been unsuccessful in enlisting the
aid of the obermaat.

He now suggested that he go back and talk directly with the
noncommissioned officers from the U-118. They would be the
most likely to help, he said. Wizuy asked Kuelsen and Franke

to go with him because he thought that the three of them might have better luck than if he went alone. Fischer, Reyak, and Ludwig would go to the shower room and prepare the rope so that everything would be in order and they would not have to waste any time or create any additional disturbance at the moment of the execution. Before they separated, however, Wizuy wanted to tie a new noose because he said the one Fischer had tied was not strong enough. As Wizuy knelt in the dirt to tie it, the lights in Drechsler's barracks suddenly went out. The men stared blankly at the darkened building. It had a strange effect on them and for some reason it made them feel they had to act quickly. Wizuy finished the noose and the men hastily departed to carry out their assignments once more.

By 9:15 they had regrouped in the yard in front of the 3rd Company barracks. Wizuy and his two comrades returned with two other men. The two others entered Drechsler's barracks but came out almost immediately and reported simply that Drechsler was asleep and that they were not going in again. All that was left now, the group agreed, was to go in themselves and take Drechsler out by force. Three men would go in the rear door and three would enter the front to prevent any possible escape. They put on their gloves in silence, with the knowledge that the moment had finally arrived.

Near Drechsler's barracks, the area was not empty. On the contrary, a number of small groups of prisoners stood in the shadows of the buildings, talking, and occasionally a dark figure could be seen moving across the prison yard. The night had clouded over, but the moon was still visible through the clouds. The lights in most of the barracks were still on and would remain that way until ten o'clock when, as if a master switch were thrown somewhere, they would be extinguished almost as a single light. The lights from the guard towers burned steadily, illuminating the barbed wire fences, but not reaching into the compound itself. With no particular regularity, a searchlight would beam on and make its painstaking way across the open areas and over the faces of the barracks within its range. The entire effect was that of a shadowy tableau. And through the stillness of the scene, or perhaps more accurately on the periphery of it, Otto Stengel wandered from group to group seeking the latest news of Werner Drechsler.

All of the groups of men were talking about what was in store for Werner Drechsler. News had traveled quickly of the verdict reached in Chief Quartermaster Hox's orderly room, and by this hour it was common knowledge throughout Compound 4. The men outside could hardly have failed to notice the six men walking rapidly across the yard toward Drechsler's darkened barracks, and consequently, like all of the other prisoners in the compound who were aware of the situation, were involved to the extent of being, through passive acceptance of what was to happen, witnesses in substance and accomplices in spirit.

As the six men neared Drechsler's barracks, they slowed their pace and finally came to a halt altogether about ten feet from the front door. A figure emerged from somewhere out of the shadows but in the excitement and intensity of the moment no one really knew from where he had come; all they were aware of was that he was suddenly there in their midst. It was the ever-probing Otto Stengel.

"What are you going to do with Drechsler?" Stengel asked. The purpose of the six men was apparently so evident that Stengel felt he could go directly to the heart of the matter.

The six men looked at each other briefly, and then one of them said icily, "Kill him. Why?"

Without pausing for Stengel to answer, another man added, "He's a traitor. Did you know that?"

"I heard that he was. How are you going to do it?"

"Hang him. It's all been taken care of."

"Good. It's the only way. It's what he deserves." Stengel could physically feel the hatred he had acquired for Drechsler move within his body. "How are you going to get him out of the barracks?"

"Drag him out."

"Do you need another man?"

"Yes, we could use one."

"I'll help you, then."

Otto Stengel had changed roles; he was no longer simply the reporter. Instead he had joined in the drama he had set out to report. His decision for complicity was abrupt and was made with feeling. It would prove to be the worst decision he ever made.

The seven men now separated into two groups. Fischer, Kuelsen, Wizuy, and Ludwig were to enter the front door; Reyak, Franke, and Stengel were to come in through the rear door and meet the other four at Drechsler's bunk. The two doors opened almost simultaneously and the sound of the three men coming in from the rear and hurrying down the aisle caused a stirring among the other prisoners in the barracks. Several of them sat up in bed, but none got out of his bunk. Drechsler, however, did not stir. He was sound asleep. The men moved into position on each side and at the foot of the bunk, but Drechsler still did not budge. For a few seemingly interminable seconds, the seven men stood in silence. It was one of those awkward, gaping intervals that, when viewed out of context, borders on the absurd —Drechsler asleep and surrounded by seven deadly serious young men who suddenly realized their mission was at hand and for the moment did not really know what to do. Then, as a slice of time, the interval ended when one of the men at the head of the bunk finally reached down and shook Drechsler by the shoulder.

Drechsler jumped; his eyes opened on seven black silhouettes; and, despite his surprise, he immediately understood the terrible implications. His voice was thick from sleep and impeded by a mounting panic, but he managed somehow to get out: "What's the matter? What's going on here?"

"What the hell do you think?" a voice from the darkness shot back. "What did you do to us in Washington?"

"Wait a minute." Drechsler, halfway sitting up in bed, looked toward the slender, gaunt figure at the end of the bunk who had just spoken. The man's face was slowly coming into focus, and Drechsler recognized it as belonging to the same man who had confronted him earlier in the evening about his activities in Washington. And Rolf Wizuy, staring back at him, was as tense as a frightened animal. Drechsler spoke directly to him: "Let me explain."

"That's what we want," one of the others said. "Admit you're a traitor."

"No. That's not true." Drechsler looked quickly to the side to find the voice that had just spoken. "You don't understand; I can explain everything. Just give me until tomorrow morning. Then you'll see you're making a mistake. Please..."

"Tomorrow you'll be gone. You'll be back with your fucking friends, the Americans. Tell us now."

"You bastard, you betrayed us in Washington. You betrayed Germany. We know what you did. You don't have to tell us."

"You're a traitor."

"No, it's not so." Drechsler's voice tapered off into a thick moan, and he no longer looked up at the men who surrounded him. "I couldn't help it. In Washington they made a pig out of me." His doleful admission was heard by all seven of the men standing above him, but they answered him only with silence. Then suddenly he looked up, his voice regaining clarity. "But I can explain, comrades. Give me until tomorrow. Please, comrades, then I'll tell you everything."

It was the German word *kameraden*, spilling freely from Drechsler's lips, that proved to be the hair-trigger to act. The word, so meaningful and so universally respected by the prisoners of war as a symbol of their unity, slashed through the seven men. Someone shouted: "You have no comrades anymore, you bastard." But it was lost in the noise as the men pounced on Drechsler.

Wizuy and Stengel grabbed at his legs, which were still covered by the GI blanket, and hands reached out for his arms and neck. But Drechsler reacted quickly and fiercely, terrify-

ingly aware that he was now fighting for his life. He kicked
out at the two men who had his legs, sending Wizuy skid-
ding onto the floor. At the same time he rolled out of the
bunk and grabbed for one of the men on his right. Stengel
lost his grip on the other leg, and Drechsler scrambled to
his feet, still clinging to the man he had grabbed. Drechsler's
momentum sent both of them crashing into the next bunk,
which teetered for a moment and then slid out from under
them, spilling them onto the floor. The prisoner in the bunk,
who had half leaped and was half slammed out of it, stood
back, and clad only in a pair of boxer shorts stared dumbly
at the desperate struggle taking place at his feet. Drechsler
was on top and for the moment he was clearly getting the
best of the other man. Other hands, however, grabbed at
Drechsler and tore him off the man. Drechsler fought wildly,
his strong arms flailing out with such force that he managed
to break free of his attackers and send one of them sprawling
across the overturned bunk.

Drechsler had made his way to the center of the aisle before
three of the men had him again. His arms were still free, but
he felt sharp, disabling kicks to his legs and someone had him
by the neck, wrenching his head backward. He struggled desperately to stay on his feet, to break loose and get to the door
only ten feet away, so close but at the same time so far away.
The men grabbed for his flailing arms, but he fought them off;
he absorbed the punches and kicks, but he could not free his
neck. He grabbed at the man's arm to pry it loose, but as he
did, the others grabbed his arms. Suddenly Drechsler felt the
electrifying pain of a kick that had squarely caught him in the
shin. His legs buckled and he felt himself going over backward.
They all dropped in a heap to the floor. A punch glanced off
Drechsler's forehead, but he continued to struggle ferociously,
trying to shake free of the mass of savage arms, hands, legs,
and feet that were beating and tearing at him. A knee to the
groin, not exactly on target, was close enough momentarily

to stun him into immobility with a shock of excruciating pain. An incredulous expression lingered on his face and then a fist came smashing into it and the bone in his nose utterly collapsed. Blood gushed from both nostrils, and even though his eyes were still open, he was stunned into unconsciousness.

The seven men dragged Drechsler toward the door. Bernhard Reyak let go and opened the door to see, staring back at him, a large group of prisoners who had gathered close to the barracks to watch, at least, a hundred, he thought. At first he was startled by their presence, but then something of more pressing importance diverted his attention and he turned quickly to his co-conspirators. "The patrol jeep's coming. Wait." But the men had already lifted Drechsler and were halfway through the door.

Someone said, "Just hurry, they won't see us," and they carried Drechsler down the three steps and into the yard.

They had gotten no more than ten feet into the yard, however, when Drechsler regained consciousness. Urged by the desperateness of his situation and despite his condition, he kicked out violently and began to scream. The men struggled with him, but from some hidden recess in his body Drechsler summoned up an enormous amount of strength, and the seven men had great difficulty holding him. His screaming attracted the attention of the American guards in the patrol jeep, which came to a sudden stop. The beam from its large spotlight scanned the grounds. At the same time the searchlight from the guard tower bore down on them, and the seven men, suddenly aware of their own vulnerability, released Drechsler and scattered into the darkness. Drechsler got to his feet, still screaming at the top of his voice, but no one could understand what it was he was shouting. The searchlight passed across him but did not pause. Drechsler made it back up the steps of his barracks and stood there, shouting at the men who had attacked him and who were now out of sight, but the real audience he sought were the American guards in the patrol jeep and the guard tower. He presented a grotesque sight as he stood there in his shorts and tee-shirt, blood streaming from his nose and already matted on the front of his shirt, weaving slightly from side to side and all the while screaming for someone to pay attention. The searchlight, however, had passed on and Drechsler's desperate cries failed to summon it back. The beam of light from the jeep went out and the vehicle began to move slowly down the patrol road. Drechsler opened the door and went back into the barracks, still dark and still silent despite everything that had happened in the preceding few minutes. He sat on the edge of his bunk and wiped the blood from his face, then threw his head back in an effort to staunch the flow of blood.

Outside, the prison yard appeared deserted. The spectators had disappeared quickly into the night when the searchlight played across the yard. But in the shadows of the last barracks of the 4th Company, the building directly opposite Werner Drechsler's barracks, the seven men were gathering again to discuss the sudden and unnerving turn of events that had disrupted their plan. And in other corners, groups of men were beginning to reappear.

Some of the men expressed serious reservations about continuing; the propriety of pursuing their goal was highly questionable if only from the standpoint of their own safety. In addition, there were now doubts about the possibility of actually achieving success. The first man to express his doubts was, surprisingly enough, Rolf Wizuy. "It's no use now," he said to the others. "The beating will have to be enough. It's too dangerous." The other men seemed to agree. An unidentified voice said softly, "We can hang him later, but we should probably get back to our barracks now in case the Americans come back to see what was going on."

Bernhard Reyak agreed strongly, "I think he's right, the punishment was enough. Let's leave it at that."

"We can't," Stengel said, moving into the center of the

group. "We must go on and finish it once and for all. Otherwise he'll be out of the camp, maybe even by tonight. Especially after what's happened. And, besides, he can identify all of us. What happens when he tells the American authorities about tonight?"

The men listened to Stengel, and despite the ambivalence of their feelings, most of them had to agree that what Stengel was saying made sense. After all, it was the same reasoning that had launched them into the operation in the first place; the basic thesis had not changed.

It was very quiet in Compound 4, and it did not appear as if the American guards were planning to return. So the men a- greed to go back with Stengel and finish the job. All of them, that is, except Bernhard Reyak.

"I don't think I want any more of it," he said, shaking his head. "I'm going back to the barracks."

Stengel walked over to him and placed his hand on Reyak's thick shoulder. "You can't back out now. We need you. You've been in it this far, you've got to stay. We must do it together, just as we started out to."

The others did not say anything, but they all looked at Reyak. He knew by their silence that they agreed with Stengel, so he shook his head in acquiescence and told them he would stay.

Although it must have seemed very much longer to everyone involved, only ten minutes had elapsed between the time they had dropped Drechsler in the glare of the searchlights and the moment they once again started across the yard toward his barracks.

They planned to enter the same way—four from the front door—and three from the rear—and the scene would be almost exactly like the one that had been enacted earlier. The only difference was that Fritz Franke had secured a small rope and fashioned it into a kind of dog's leash. He told the men that it would be the best way to handle Drechsler, to get it around his neck and tighten it enough so that the man could not scream. Helmut Fischer also had a handkerchief he planned to stuff in Drechsler's mouth to accomplish the same purpose.

When the four men entered the front door, Drechsler was still sitting on the edge of his bunk. He looked up with alarm. The back door swung open and the other three men came running down the aisle. Drechsler yelled frantically, "Wait, wait... please no more, tomorrow, give me till tomorrow." But the men did not wait—they did not attempt to answer—as they swooped down on him.

The fight began all over again. Drechsler was weaker, but from the way he fought back it was scarcely evident. The men grabbed at Drechsler, trying to get Franke's rope around his neck, but he burst loose and dove for the aisle, slamming into Stengel and sending him sprawling across the aisle and over one of the bunks on the other side. The other six were on him again, however, and he stumbled. They wrestled him to the floor, punching and kicking at the same time. Fischer tried to put the handkerchief in Drechsler's mouth, but Drechsler immediately spit it out and began screaming. As Fischer tried again, Drechsler bit down heavily and caught Fischer's thumb. Fischer screamed out in pain, but Drechsler kept his teeth tightly clamped on the thumb. Stengel had picked himself up and was back in the fight, and he reached out quickly and grabbed Drechsler by the neck, gouging his thumb and forefinger deeply in behind the Adam's apple until Drechsler finally released Fischer's thumb. Drechsler struggled furiously to get up, but a well-aimed and powerful kick plowed into his groin, literally crushing to pulp one of his testicles. Drechsler's scream of agony tapered off into a low gurgling moan and his entire body went limp. He was not even aware that Fritz Franke was slipping the leash around his neck.

Waves of consciousness pushed some of the blackness out of the way and Drechsler tried to scream but the pain and the shock, coupled with Franke's tightening of the rope, stifled the cry and he lapsed back into the black void each time.

As the men got Drechsler up, they saw that Reyak was already standing at the door, holding it open. The spectators had gathered again outside but the six men ignored them as they hurried out of the building carrying Drechsler. Franke had the leash in one hand and Drechsler's arm in his other hand. Another man held Drechsler tightly by the hair, the others grasping every available limb. The six men half ran and partially stumbled under the weight of Drechsler's body. They turned right as soon as they hit the yard and headed straight for the shower room, about sixty feet away. Every few steps Franke would loosen the rope to let Drechsler have some air, a strangely paradoxical charity, but as soon as Drechsler revived slightly and made his now feeble attempts to shout, the rope was tightened to cut off the air.

Reyak let the door slam and walked over to the group that had gathered. "You'd better get of here now," he told them.

"You, too," one of the group said and placed a restraining hand on Reyak's arm. "They don't need you anymore." The man looked at Reyak and then across the shower room. "Don't go in there. You've done your part. Don't take any more chances." The group began to leave but Reyak stood where he was. His fellow conspirators were already in the shower room. He heard what sounded like a bench being knocked over, and then he began to walk slowly toward the shower room.

Inside, the men had propped Drechsler up under the crude noose that hung from a rafter. Two of them had jumped up on a bench and the other four passed the unconscious Drechsler up to them. One of the men on the bench held Drechsler while another slipped the noose around his neck and tightened it. Drechsler was beyond any form of resistance. When the noose was secure, the two men jumped down and one of them kicked the bench out from under Drechsler.

When Bernhard Reyak reached the door of the shower room, two of the men were already coming out. One of them said,

"It's over. It's finished now." Reyak walked past the two men into the shower room. He looked at Drechsler swaying gently from the noose, his feet about a foot from the floor, his arms dangling loosely at his sides, his face contorted into a grotesque mask, the rope looking incredibly tight around his neck. Someone grabbed Reyak by the arm and said, "Let's get out of here." They thoughtfully turned out the light and left.

Werner Drechsler was probably not legally dead at that moment, but for all practical purposes he was very dead. In a few minutes it would be ten o'clock; Werner Dreschler had lasted not quite six and one-half hours at Papago Park.

7

Preliminary Investigations

AT 5:30 the next morning, the whistles blasted out reveille, and all over the camp the men groggily scrambled about getting ready for formation. It appeared to be just another normal day at Papago Park. But between the time the prisoners arose and the time they were marched off to the mess halls for breakfast, no one used the shower room of Company 5 in Compound 4. In the compound it was common knowledge that Drechsler's blood-soaked body was still hanging there. And it did not take long for word to filter out of Compound 4 to the other compounds, even to the German officers' isolated section.

A U.S. army guard discovered the body at about 6:30 and rushed out to inform the camp's provost marshal, Captain Cecil Parshall, who was in his quarters shaving when the news was revealed to him about five minutes later. Captain Parshall threw on his clothes and went immediately to Compound 4 with a small entourage of officers and men from his office. When he saw the body, he muttered something to himself and then ordered a guard posted at the door to keep anyone from entering the shower room and possibly disturbing whatever evidence there might be in the room. Captain Parshall notified everybody who needed to be concerned, from the medical officers to the camp commander, thereby giving rise to a steady stream of visitors to the shower room through most of the morning. Finally, Drechsler's body was cut down, placed in an ambulance, and taken to a mortuary in Phoenix. Photographs had been taken and examinations were made while the body was still hanging, but any evidence as to who might have done the deed was nonexistent. For identification purposes, Captain Hebblewaithe attempted to take fingerprints, but it was not at all easy because Drechsler's hands were curled into fists and rigor mortis had already set in. He managed to get three fingerprints, enough to meet legal requirements, before giving up.

The prisoners were sent off to work as if nothing had happened while army authorities at the camp got together to draw up plans of what to do next. The camp commander wanted a report immediately drawn up to forward to the Ninth Services Command at Fort Douglas, Utah, and the Provost Marshal General's office in Washington and ordered Captain Parshall to start a thorough investigation of the murder to find out exactly who was responsible for it. Parshall set the investigation in motion that morning and groups of his men wandered through the empty barracks in Compound 4, looking for anything that might be even remotely associated with the crime. All they found were neatly made bunks, with the exception, of course, of Werner Drechsler's, which was still in the state of disarray that it had been left in the night before. Everything else in the barracks was in neat and proper order, so much so it was as if the prisoners had prepared to stand a detailed inspection.

All day at work, Helmut Fischer was concerned about his

finger; besides being painful, it could be incriminating, he knew, if investigating authorities happened to see it. It was bruised and deeply gashed and still bore teeth marks. It looked unmistakably as if someone had bitten it. When Fischer returned from work, the entire compound was called out before supper for a special formation. Fischer took his assigned place in the third row. An American lieutenant and a sergeant began to inspect the prisoners. The lieutenant started with the first row and stood before each man, looking carefully at the man's face and neck and then ordered him to hold out his hands, which the lieutenant roughly turned so he could inspect both sides. When the two Americans neared the far end of the second row of prisoners, Fischer moved quickly and quietly up to the first row, and equally as stealthily a man from each of the first two rows moved back a row. Fischer stood there, eyes frozen straight ahead, waiting to hear the shout that would tell him he had been caught. But there was nothing but silence, broken methodically by the raspy voice of the lieutenant saying, "Put out your hands...Put out your hands..." as he made his way through the ranks of prisoners.

When the inspection was over, Captain Parshall and his investigators were no better off than they had been before. They had found nothing to link any of the prisoners with the violence that had occurred the night before. As Fischer went off to the mess hall later, he told Guenther Kuelsen, who had been in the first row, how he had avoided detection, and they both laughed loudly. Fritz Franke knew how it had happened because he was the man who took Fischer's place in the third row and was therefore inspected twice, which brought about another round of laughter. Bernhard Reyak and Rolf Wizuy had also observed the operation from their places in the fourth row, and later that night they made it a point to congratulate Fischer on his ingenuity. The men knew, of course, that they were far from being home free and that the investigation was really just beginning. But the omen was good.

A great many prisoners knew who had taken part in the

execution, and the seven men were nervously counting on them not to break down and reveal their desperate secret. At least their hope was reinforced by orders from the noncommissioned officers barracks to the effect that absolutely no one in the compound was to admit to knowing a thing about what had happened to Werner Drechsler. The prisoners should need no reminder of the importance of their silence in the matter; after all, the fate of Werner Drechsler stood as a striking example of a person who talked too much to the wrong people.

Captain Parshall's questioning began with the prisoners in Drechsler's barracks, but it produced absolutely nothing. No one had even heard a noise in the night, they claimed. Parshall had several informants in Compound 3, but the men were in the wrong compound to know who had actually taken part in the murder. They promised to keep their ears open but thought it would be unlikely that in their compound they would hear anything more specific.

One other prisoner in Compound 1 was in fear of his own life, Parshall knew, because his fellow prisoners suspected him of being too friendly with the American authorities and because the man had made the mistake of saying he did not really care for Hitler and Naziism. Word had come back from no less than Fregattenkapitan Wattenburg himself that the man was in serious trouble, and that if he associated in any way with the Americans, he would be handled accordingly. Needless to say, the man was reluctant to say anything to the investigators and, in reality, did not actually have anything substantial to tell them, though, after a little pressure, and with the promise that he would be moved to a camp for other anti-Nazis if he cooperated, the man related that the story in the camp was that Drechsler had been a traitor and had been done away with by those who knew of Drechsler's activities in Washington. The man's information was nothing that Parshall did not already know, and it showed that his best sources were going to be of no help at all.

The laborious task of questioning prisoners went on for several days, but it was as fruitless as it was tedious. Nobody knew a thing, and Parshall had no leads himself to go on. The camp commander, impatient for something to break, appointed a committee of officers to conduct the investigation, with Parshall staying on as one of the members. The committee, however, was no more successful than the original investigating team. Pressure was now coming both from Ninth Services Command headquarters and from Washington—it was made clear that the authorities wanted this thing solved and those responsible brought to trial. But after two weeks the officers at Papago Park were no closer to a solution than they had been on the morning of March 13.

The seven prisoners were, after two weeks, beginning to feel relatively secure; the authorities seemed nowhere close to associating them with the crime. True, they had been interrogated, but it had been only briefly in comparison to other prisoners, especially those in Drechsler's barracks. Then, just as they began to feel the investigation was letting up, the commanding general of the Ninth Services Command took up the so far unsuccessful case and sent down to Papago Park his top investigating officer, Lieutenant Colonel Gerald L. Church, chief of intelligence for the command's Security Intelligence Division.

Colonel Church was ordered to convene a board of officers to conduct a complete investigation of the case. So, with Major Herman J. Zabel as his assistant, Major Francis P. Walsh of the Judge Advocate General Corps as recorder, Sergeant Carl F. Blank as interpreter, and Sergeant Michael Donohue, the colonel flew to Phoenix to launch the investigation.

After conferring with the previous investigators at Papago Park, the board of officers flew to Washington to inquire into Drechsler's activities in the hope that they could link up some specific names who were involved with him. Unfortunately for the investigators, information was not forthcoming from the army, ostensibly because documented information of that sort did not exist—at least it was not in the hands of the army. Navy Intelligence was the least cooperative, saying, in effect, that they had no intention of helping the army. (Naval authorities remembered that the navy had previously told the army to be certain not to send Drechsler to a POW camp where other German submariners were held.) The navy was very unhappy with the way in which the army had handled Drechsler; in fact, naval officers allegedly told the investigators that the army by its actions had sent Drechsler to his death. Ultimately, the board of officers returned to Papago Park with only the list of Drechsler's crewmates from the U-118.

It was then decided by the investigating board to bring in a lie detector expert from Chicago, Leonard Keeler, and to interrogate under the lie detector anyone who even remotely appeared to have some information about the case. Their plan was to narrow down the suspects to those who failed or faltered on the lie detector and then to interrogate them intensely. Keeler was flown in from Chicago and a room was set up at Papago Park for the board to conduct their interrogations. Over 125 prisoners were scheduled for interrogation with the lie detector.

The first prisoners to be brought before the board were the members of Drechsler's barracks. They all said pretty much the same thing to the standard questions.

"Did you see or hear anything unusual on the night of March 12?"

"No."

"You were in the same barracks as Werner Drechsler, were you not?"

"Yes."

"And you heard nothing at all?"

"Well, I did hear something sometime during the night. It sounded like a man was sick or having a fit."

"Did you see who it was?"

"No."

"Did you try to help him, this man who you thought was sick?"

"No. Well, he stopped after a minute or so and I thought he was all right. I was really half asleep and just rolled over and went back to sleep."

Even the two men in the bunks on either side of Drechsler did not hear anything other than a momentary noise and both slept soundly through the night, they swore. In any case, it soon became clear that no one in Drechsler's barracks had actually seen the faces of the men who committed the crime and that they themselves had not actively participated in it.

The first real admission of any kind came from a prisoner of war named Alfred Friedrich, who lived in the same barracks as Otto Stengel.

"Do you know who killed Drechsler?"

"Yes, sir."

"Who did kill him?"

"I can't tell you that."

"Why won't you tell us?"

"If I tell you, I will be the same as Drechsler, a traitor."

"In other words, you say Drechsler was a traitor?"

"Yes, sir."

"Do you consider the hanging of Drechsler a legal murder?"

"I think so."

"How do you know he was a traitor without first letting him have a court hearing?"

"Because I heard from others that he spilled stuff at Fort Meade."

Friedrich was then asked if he would divulge the information about those who murdered Drechsler if Fregattenkapitan Wattenburg would give him permission to do so. At first he said that he would not, but with a little coaxing he finally agreed under the condition that Wattenburg personally advise him to do so. Wattenburg was then called as a witness before the board.

"Do you know anything about the murder of Werner Drechsler?"

"I don't know whether he was killed or whether he killed himself," Wattenburg said curtly.

Wattenburg was informed that one prisoner had agreed to give the names of those involved if he had Wattenburg's permission to do so. Wattenburg stoutly refused. "According to the convention of Geneva, for me to give such an authorization to a German soldier, it is not my task and I can't do it because I'm the representative of the prisoners of war and it is my duty to look after their health and welfare. I cannot do it."

Friedrich was then put on the list of men slated for recall and further intensive interrogation. The board had known there was no real possibility of obtaining Wattenburg's permission, but at the same time they wanted Wattenburg to know that they were making some headway and that it appeared some of the prisoners were weakening. They knew, too, that the information would pass back to all the prisoners scheduled to come up for interrogation and perhaps give the interrogators a certain psychological advantage in the investigations to come.

Drechsler's crewmates were next on the agenda, and they testified universally that they had no direct knowledge that Drechsler had ever been a traitor. They claimed that was the reason they did not have anything to do with the murder. The first to be questioned was the ranking noncommissioned officer of the U-118, Obermaat Werner Reinl.

"What time did you go to bed on Sunday night, March 12?"

"About nine or 9:15."

"What were you doing before you went to bed?"

"I was building a battleship."

Colonel Church cocked his head slightly and leaned across the table that separated him from Reinl, "A little model ship?"

"Yes."

After this beginning, Reinl's answers did not jibe with the lie detector, and his name was added to the list for intensive questioning.

Rudolf Weimer, another NCO from the U-118, provided some information about Drechsler's activities in Washington.

"Did anyone tell you at Stringtown that Drechsler was a traitor?"

"No, but while I was in Washington, an American naval officer told me that Drechsler talked quite a bit. The officer didn't say he was a traitor but that he talked."

"Did this officer tell you in order to induce you to talk?"

"Yes, one could look at it that way because he figured maybe I would talk myself."

"Did this American naval officer tell you what Drechsler told him?"

"No."

"Did he give you any idea what Drechsler said?"

"No. He just told me that Drechsler talked more than I did."

"Did you yourself believe that Drechsler was a traitor?"

"No. I don't believe that myself because on board the boat he was always a very good sailor. So it's hard to figure anything like that."

When Weimer was questioned about the night of the murder and his knowledge of it, he, like Reinl, failed the lie detector test.

The interrogation dragged on throughout the month of April, 1944; day in, day out, prisoners filed before the board, had the lie detection apparatus attached to them, and then were systematically inundated with questions. Colonel Church, Major Zabel, and Major Walsh poured over the testimony after each suspect was finished, picking up bits and pieces of information—a name here, a fact, an inconsistency—and of course the readings from the lie detector expert, which told them more than anything else. Those who were in some way involved were slowly weeded out, but there was still no evidence, and the investigators knew they would need a confession if they were to get this case to court.

Funkobermaat Friedrich Murza was caught up briefly in his testimony and let it slip that he, too, had had prior knowledge of Drechsler and his reputation. As the interrogators zeroed in on him, he began to reveal how he had come upon this information, which immediately placed him on the list of prime suspects because the lie detector showed that he was telling the truth about this matter, but that he was not when he was asked about having any part in the murder, which he had categorically denied.

"Did you see Prisoner of War Drechsler at the interrogation center in or near Washington?"

Murza moved uncomfortably in his chair. "I saw him but not under the name of Drechsler."

"Under what name did you know him?"

"Under the name of Niemmer. He was with me in the room."

"When did you first know it was Drechsler in the room with you?"

"In Stringtown, Oklahoma."

"How long was Drechsler in the room with you?"

"About three days."

"Did you talk to him at that time?"

"Yes."

"What did he say to you?"

"He came to my room and said he was Obermaat Niemmer."

"What else did he say?"

"Then he asked me where I came from and I asked him where he came from. Then he told me he was from the boat U-118."

"Did Drechsler ask you any questions?"

"He asked me certain questions about the U-boat that I was on, questions that had been asked me before, but questions which I could not answer and which I would not answer. These questions related to facts concerning the operation of my U-boat."

Murza paused but Colonel Church sensed that he had something more to say. "Go on."

"We talked at Stringtown about different things that happened at the interrogation center—in the rooms. And some others said that there was a fellow there that didn't act right. Then I also said, or explained, the kind of people that I was together with. Then it came to be known, or it came out, that this person always used a different rating. Then we talked about it, what this man looked like and then we came to the answer that this man's name was Drechsler. There can't be any mistake about it because they all mentioned the fact that he was wounded on the right knee. And we came to the conclusion that this was the same man."

It was nearing the end of April when Rolf Wizuy finally appeared before the interrogation board. He had heard about the lie detector being used and was, with good reason, quite disturbed about it. He failed the test miserably.

"Were you kept in a room alone or was there another prisoner of war with you at Fort Meade?"

"I was together with other prisoners of war."

"What are their names?"

"The first one was a noncommissioned officer by the name of Leimi."

"Was it Werner Drechsler?"

"I don't know whether it was or whether it wasn't but from what I heard in the camp, it was probably Drechsler."

"I will show you a picture of Drechsler and ask if that is the picture of the man that was with you at the interrogation center."

"At the interrogation center this man didn't have a beard, but it looks like him."

"Now, did this man ask you any questions?"

"No, we just held conversations between ourselves. Direct questioning, he never did that because he was just another prisoner of war like myself. We just had friendly conversations between ourselves."

"When did you first hear that Werner Drechsler was hung?"

"In the evening there was some excitement about this but we didn't know exactly what was wrong. But in the morning, I found out what was wrong."

"You went to the show that evening or afternoon, did you not?"

"Yes, I believe so."

"Who hung Prisoner of War Drechsler?"

"I don't know."

"Are you sure you don't know?"

"I don't know."

By the end of April, approximately twenty men were on the board's list of top suspects. Arrangements were being made to subject them to strenuous and continued interrogation until the case was broken apart. Among the twenty were Alfred Friedrich, Friedrich Murza, and Siegfried Elser, who, the board were convinced, knew who the actual murderers were and who also appeared to be good prospects for eventually relenting. Also Werner Reinl, Rudolf Weimer, and Drechsler's former friend Herman Polowzyk from the U-118 definitely knew more than they were telling, as did various others like Wizuy, Stengel, Fischer, Ludwig, Kuelsen, Franke, Reyak, Walter Nieswand, and Lothar Mandelkow.

The prime suspects were removed from their barracks and placed in the stockade at Papago Park. All of them knew at this point that they were in grave trouble, but they were still resolute and had no intention of letting down.

The investigating board discussed their next step. It was decided that the most effective move would be to transport the suspects to a secret camp outside Stockton, California, that was used primarily for secret interrogations and had a well-trained and well-equipped staff. The camp had been used mainly to interrogate Japanese prisoners of war as well as Japanese residents in the United States who were suspected of being in sympathy with the enemy. And the camp, despite all the secrecy about it and its methods, had a startling record of achievement in culling confessions and information wanted by various military authorities.

The investigating board was to accompany the suspects there and supervise the interrogations, at least formally. Major Walsh, however, would not be able to go along immediately. He had been ordered by Ninth Services Command to report to Florence, Arizona, to prosecute a case of arson involving an Italian prisoner of war. He was scheduled, however, to rejoin the board when the Florence trial was over. And so on May 3, the entire group was taken to Stockton; the prisoners had no idea whatsoever as to where they were going, but they did know it was not likely to be very pleasant.

At the secret camp, the prisoners were placed in cells on the second floor of a jail-like building. The cells were separate but were grouped to allow easy conversation, which was not without purpose because the cells were bugged and an operator manned the monitors downstairs 24 hours a day. The interrogations began immediately, structured so that the board would routinely call individual prisoners out for formal questioning but with no regularity and, in the interim, interrogations were conducted "informally" by the staff members of the camp. Captain Oscar Schmidt was the chief interrogator of the prisoners in these "informal" inquiries, and his findings were duly related to the investigating board. Schmidt's interrogations were varied and sporadic; they could come at any time of the day or night and they could be as short as a few minutes or as long as a day. Some were held in the camp; others involved blindfolding the prisoner and taking him outside the camp in an automobile. The exact methods employed in the interrogations were classified information; all that is really known about them is that they were carefully planned and designed for maximum effect.

The month of May, 1944, was a nightmare experience for the prisoners. They held out strongly, and even Colonel Church's board were having their doubts about ever breaking them down. But they did not really need to worry because the grueling mental and physical strain, the sleepless nights, the long and agonizing questioning, their fears, and the overall surrealistic nature of their existence were gradually taking their toll on the prisoners. The scraps of information were adding up and a picture was beginning to unfold. Then, in the last days of May and the first of June, it finally all fell irrevocably in place.

Gerhard Richter had been interrogated a number of times both in Papago Park and outside Stockton. In the beginning he was one of the least cooperative of the suspects; in fact, he was belligerent. Richter was reputed to be a member of the POW camp's gestapo, and he made it quite evident that he was a faithful Nazi. He did not do well on the lie detector, and he admitted having been in a room with Drechsler at the interrogation center at Fort Meade. He also lived in the same barracks at Papago Park as Otto Stengel. By the end of May, however, he was a weakened man, and as he stood before the investigating board, it was hard to imagine him as a once proud and militant Nazi. The same questions he had answered before about his conversations with Drechsler on the night of the murder were hurled at him again and again.

"Did you hear any conversation concerning the hanging of Werner Drechsler right after the soccer game?"

"Yes. It was talked about Drechsler's being a traitor." And then he began to fall apart. "Stengel remarked that the traitor should be hung; this conversation was about six o'clock that evening. At about ten or 10:30 that night Stengel came back into the barracks. Most of the men were in the barracks at the time getting ready to go to sleep and Stengel came to the corner of the barracks where I was at and said 'Do you know that the traitor is already hung?' and someone asked him who hung him. Stengel stated he didn't know the people by name but they were people who had been at Fort Meade with Drechsler."

"Who else in your barracks heard this?"

"According to my opinion, anybody that wasn't asleep."

"Richter, do you believe that Otto Stengel was one of the men who hung Drechsler?"

The prisoner hesitated for a very brief moment and then said, "I believe it is possible."

"Why do you believe that, Richter?"

"I believe it because Stengel brought the news so rapidly and in detail to the barracks."

"What you told the board before then were not true answers, is that correct?"

"Yes, they were lies. The reason I gave those answers was because I didn't want to involve Stengel in it because Stengel was married and had two kids."

The board dismissed Richter and told a guard to bring Alfred Friedrich in immediately. Friedrich was questioned in detail about Otto Stengel.

"Didn't Stengel tell the crowd that they were going to beat and hang a traitor?"

"He said the man was going to get the 'holy ghost' which in the navy meant that a man would be beaten and punished for his deeds."

"Then it was a fact, Friedrich, that you knew that somebody was going to be hung that Sunday afternoon, didn't you?"

"I heard that someone was going to get the 'holy ghost' and that the man was the traitor Drechsler. I assumed that he was going to be hung."

"When did Otto Stengel talk first about the Drechsler hanging?"

"The next day."

"Now, after you asked who had done it, what did Stengel say?"

"Stengel was talking about it and then I asked if he knew what had happened and Stengel then laughed and I assumed from the previous conversation that Stengel had been along. He said that he didn't know, but everybody in the line who overheard him assumed him to be present."

"Then Stengel at roll call told about the hanging, didn't he?"

"Stengel said that he had been present and saw how it had been done."

"Just tell the board in your own words what Stengel said."

"Some of the men complained that Drechsler was beaten and Stengel replied that the man had tried to defend himself and that as a traitor he even deserved more. And I assumed that Stengel had been present from the details he gave."

"Did he tell you Drechsler was struck in the nose and kicked in the body?"

"I didn't speak to Stengel about it personally."

"What did Stengel say about having his fingerprints taken?"

"Captain Hebblewaithe told me that fingerprints had been taken from the dead man's neck."

"Did Captain Hebblewaithe tell that to Stengel?"

"No, he told me that."

"Captain Hebblewaithe told you that?"

"Yes, and he told the rest of the company that fingerprints had been taken, and then Stengel remarked that he didn't have any gloves on . . . " Friedrich suddenly froze as he finished the sentence.

Colonel Church looked up quickly. "That he didn't have any gloves on?"

Friedrich paused before answering and then nodded his head. "Stengel said that he didn't have any gloves on."

"When was that statement made?"

"I don't remember exactly but it was later."

"It was after roll call?"

"Yes." Friedrich then attempted to soften what he had said by adding: "I assume that Stengel was present. Any man that gave the details the way he gave them had to be present but I can't state that he did do it."

Colonel Church motioned for the guard to take Friedrich back and after the prisoner was out of the room said, "Bring Stengel in now."

Stengel admitted to the board that he had been in the vicinity when the murder occurred but only as a spectator and that he was not able to recognize any of the men participating in it.

"When I arrived Drechsler was lying on the ground, on the gravel, and I noticed how somebody kicked him with his foot. Drechsler shouted and then he jumped up and goes onto the steps leading into the barracks."

"What men of these did you recognize?"

"I did not know these men but as far as their postures and looks were concerned, they looked like obermaats."

"Then what did you do?"

"All of a sudden the six men came out again. The six men went inside of Drechsler's barracks on one side and came out the other end. I was standing about half way along the fourth barracks. When they came out, they were carrying Drechsler with his head facing the ground. Two men carried one leg each and two men were posted on the middle of his body on each side and the last two men had a rope in their hands and Drechsler's neck was in that rope." Stengel then described how he, along with 200 to 300 other prisoners, walked up to the shower room to observe Drechsler's body.

When Colonel Church questioned him about fingerprints, Stengel was noticeably disturbed, but he admitted nothing. Stengel was sent back to his cell, but word was passed to Captain Schmidt to bear down on him because the board were now convinced that Otto Stengel was one of their men.

8

Breakthrough

THE informal interrogators were already bearing down on Funkobermaat Murza and Obermaat Elser, to whom it was made clear that, because of their ranks, they might very well be held responsible and punished accordingly—that is, if they did not cooperate.

Friedrich Murza was the highest ranking of the suspects. To the investigating board, it appeared that if anyone had an overall knowledge of the murder, it had to be Murza. They knew by late May that he was implicated, but to what extent they were still uncertain. Captain Schmidt had been informally interrogating him off and on for almost 24 hours when Murza was finally called back before the board at eight o'clock on the evening of June 1. Murza was a tired, drained, and fearful man as he stood before Colonel Church.

"Let the record show that Major Zabel is acting as recorder; Major Francis P. Walsh is absent on official business. Prisoner of War Murza, you are being recalled as a witness before this board. You are reminded that you are still under oath as a witness and that you were sworn as a witness before this board on 21 April 1944 at the prisoner of war camp, Papago Park, Phoenix, Arizona. . . . The board wants to examine you further on events which took place on the night of 12 March 1944. To refresh your memory, this was a Sunday and it was the date upon which Prisoner of War Werner Drechsler was hanged. Do you remember that day distinctly?"

"Yes."

"What time on that day did you first hear that Werner Drechsler had come to Papago Park?"

"It was about four o'clock when I came out of the movie."

"From whom did you hear this news?"

"From Maschinenmaat Wiedermann. He got the news first because he had something wrong with his knee and as a wounded man he was transported from the movie house to the barracks. He got back first."

"Was Maschinenmaat Wiedermann a member of the U-boat 118?"

"Yes."

Murza went on to admit that after he learned of Drechsler's arrival he talked with the noncommissioned officers of the U-118 about Drechsler. "I told the men that I had been together with Drechsler at the interrogation camp near Washington, D.C., and told them that he had introduced himself as 'Nimmer,' and we said it took a lot of nerve to send him to this camp. That was all that was said. I only told them that I was together with him at the interrogation camp."

"Did anyone of the group say what should be done with Drechsler because he was a traitor?"

"No, that was not discussed right then."

"Then after supper you went to the soccer field in Compound 4?"

"Yes, it is in the compound."

"What conversation did you have about Drechsler at the soccer game?"

"We did not talk about it at the soccer game."

"Did you see Drechsler at the soccer field?"

"Only when he came out of the mess hall did I see Drechsler."

"What was said about Drechsler when you saw him coming out of the mess hall?"

"I said, 'That is him.'"

"Who did you say that to?"

"I said it to all of the men who were sitting with me."

"What did you say exactly—'Is that Drechsler?'"

"I said, 'That is Drechsler!'"

Murza then explained that he did not discuss Drechsler again until he was told by Guenther Bleise to report to the compound spokeman's office later that evening.

"And who was there when you got there?"

"There were already six or seven men there."

"And who were they?"

"There were a few men from the 1st Company in the office whose names I do not know."

"What were the names of the men that you do know?"

Murza stared blankly ahead. "The men I knew were all members of the 2nd Company. Then he added wearily, "Guenther Bleise, Ludwig, Wizuy, Elser, and Mandelkow."

"Were any of the members of the crew of the U-boat [118] there?"

"I believe Werner Reinl was there but I cannot definitely make that statement. Hermann Polowzyk, he was there."

"What others were there besides the ones that have been mentioned?"

"There were still other men from the 1st and 3rd Companies whose names I don't know."

"Did anyone come in after you got there?"

"There were several more after I entered the office. I don't know—I was sitting there and they came more and more."

"What are their names?"

"I believe Heinrich Ludwig arrived after I did and also Mandelkow and Nieswand."

"Are you sure that all of those people that you have mentioned were there?"

"Yes, I am sure."

His voice somewhat weakened by this time, Murza went on to describe in detail the meeting in Franz Hox's office. He had told Hox what he knew about Drechsler and added, "All told the same story: Ludwig, Bleise, Nieswand, Elser, Wizuy, and Mandelkow."

"And then what happened?"

"Nothing happened. We just left the office."

"Where did you go?"

"Two groups formed outside."

"Go ahead."

"In the first group there were Elser, Bleise, and Mandelkow. Nobody else was in this group. In the second group there were eight men. There were Wizuy, Ludwig, Nieswand, and Polowzyk."

"Who were the other men besides these four?"

"I don't know the men by name."

"And then what happened?"

"In both groups there was talk about Drechsler. I said the man should be beaten up. I made the remark and the other three men agreed. We only discussed that for a moment and then went over and joined the second group and in the second group they said that a complete job should be done."

"And what did they mean by that?"

"Probably that he should be hanged."

"Who said that?"

"I don't remember who made this remark because while we four were joining this group they were already parting and going to their barracks."

Step by step, the actual scene of the night of March 12 was

Otto Stengel, the only one of the seven who was married, served on the U-352, the second German sub sunk by an American warship in World War II. He and his wife, Anna, had two children.

Guenther Kuelsen, who was 19 years old in 1942, proudly poses in his uniform just before he left to join the crew of the U-615. Soon after, he embarked on his first and only war cruise.

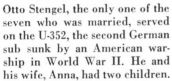

Otto Stengel, in knickers and marked with an "X," marches down a Munich street in 1939 with other naval recruits.

Otto Stengel, indicated by arrow, poses with fellow trainees in a foxhole in 1940. He saw action, however, only from the bowels of a submarine.

Official U.S. Navy photo.

The U-118 takes a depth charge just aft of its conning tower on June 12, 1943. Another charge can be seen (just below the tower) about to hit the water. The two men running on deck were the first out of the conning tower hatch. Only 16 of the boat's crew of 58 survived—among them, Werner Drechsler.

Prisoner of War Werner Drechsler, left, arrives at the U.S. naval base at Norfolk, Virginia, on June 19, 1943. Wounded seriously in the right knee, he is helped by fellow prisoner Herman Polowzyk—his friend, at least in 1943.

Werner Drechsler is processed at the naval hospital in Norfolk. The beard, a respected symbol of the U-boatman, would be shaved off later, but not before he had spent quite a bit of time at his next camp, the interrogation center at Fort Meade, Maryland.

Helmut Fischer, 22, of the U-615   Fritz Franke, 21,

Guenther Kuelsen, 22, of the U-615

Captain George A. Towle
was Roman Catholic chap-
lain at Leavenworth in 1945.
For eight months he spent
part of each day with the
seven prisoners and was a
close friend.

Heinrich Ludwig, 25, of the U-199

of the U-615   Bernhard Reyak, 21, of the U-615

Otto Stengel, 26, of the U-352

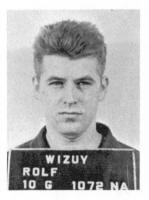 

Major Francis P. Walsh pros-
ecuted the seven. It was his
only murder case. He was
pleased with the verdict but
not with the severity of the
sentence.

Rolf Wizuy, 23, of the U-615

U.S. Army photo.

On the morning of March 13, 1944, someone haphazardly made up Werner Drechsler's bunk (marked with "X"). The other prisoners in the barracks denied knowledge of what had happened during the night.

U.S. Army photo.

The large bloodstain, two feet in diameter, in front of Drechsler's cot testifies to the violence of the fight on the night of March 12, 1944.

U.S. Army photo.

Exterior view of the shower room of Compound 4 at Papago Park—the execution chamber for Werner Drechsler. Between one and two hundred prisoners filed past the windows on the night of March 12, 1944, to view the hanging body.

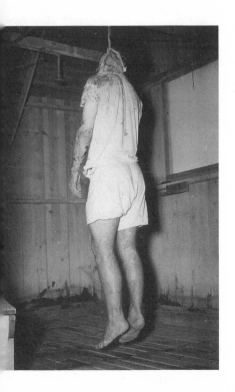

Werner Drechsler was hung less than six and one-half hours after his arrival at the prisoner of war camp at Papago Park in Phoenix, Arizona. No one in the U.S. Army knows (or will admit) why he was ever sent to that particular camp.

U.S. Army photo.

U.S. Army photo courtesy Fort Leavenworth Public Information Office.

Richard P. Merr

The United States Disciplinary Barracks at Fort Leavenworth, Kansas, is dominated by an eight-wing "castle," the basement of which was the last home of the condemned German prisoners. The old salvage warehouse, which served as the execution chamber, is the building with the white roof in the lower left corner.

The "seven" were buried at this wooded, out-of-the-way site at Fort Leavenworth. The simple headstones bear only their names, ranks, and dates of birth and death.

revealed, and all the fragments of information that had been gathered from previous interrogations finally fell into place. Murza labored on, reconstructing the events and the people in answer to the relentless probing of Colonel Church, who scented success. Murza described how he had returned to his barracks with Siegfried Elser to change his shoes while Elser changed clothes.

"And then what happened?"

"The others came out of their barracks."

"All of these people that you've mentioned?"

"Yes, all came out. I don't know whether Bleise came out because he worked as a salesman in the canteen and he should have been in the canteen at that time."

"Did you see Guenther Bleise later?"

"No, I didn't see Bleise any more that day."

"Were all of the men you mentioned before in the second group there?"

"All the men of the second group returned too. Several more joined us whose names I don't know. But I know that Rudolf Weimer was one of them."

"And what other ones joined that you knew?"

"Several men, they were the same men who had been at Hox's office but I don't know their names."

"And then where did you go?"

"We went to the 5th Company. The entire group went there."

"And where did you go?"

"We went to the last barracks of the 5th Company."

"Was that the barracks that Drechsler was in?"

"Yes."

"Then what did you do?"

"We went inside the barracks."

"All of these men went inside the barracks?"

Murza shook his head slowly. "About half of the men went inside the barracks and got Drechsler."

"Which ones went inside?"

"Wizuy, Ludwig, and Nieswand," Murza appeared to be drifting off into his own thoughts and he was speaking rather slowly. "And some men from the 1st Company. About five or six men went in the barracks the first time."

"Did you go in the barracks the first time?"

Murza snapped back to the reality of the situation. "No." Then he went on to describe how he and Siegfried Elser stood off in the distance and watched how the men dragged Drechsler from the barracks, how Drechsler resisted and how, under the glare of the spotlights, the men dropped him and disappeared into the darkness. A short while later, the same men reentered Drechsler's barracks and a few minutes after that emerged carrying Drechsler. By name he identified three of the men again—Wizuy, Ludwig and Nieswand. "They carried the body and ran to the washroom and they went very fast. We couldn't observe any more as everybody parted."

"Where did you go?"

"I went back to my barracks."

"Who went with you?"

"Elser went back with me."

"How many prisoners of war had gathered there during this time?"

"There was a big crowd. Due to the screaming many men came. There might have been 100 or even more."

"To go back a little bit, were these men wearing gloves when they brought Drechsler out of the barracks the last time?"

Murza breathed deeply before answering. "Yes, they wore gloves."

"And did they have gloves when they ran with Drechsler to the washroom?"

"Yes."

"Are you sure of that?"

"Yes."

"You are sure of that? You swear that under oath?"

"Yes."

Colonel Church sat back in his chair. It was all out in the open now, but he was not going to let it drop there. "I am going to ask you to tell the whole story in your own words again for the record here."

"Yes, sir, where do you want me to start?" Murza said drearily.

Murza began to repeat the whole story from the point when he first learned that Drechsler had arrived in camp. The description droned on until he reached the part where the body was being carried to the shower room. Colonel Church asked him again, "What men carrying Drechsler did you yourself see and recognize?"

"Fischer and Wizuy."

The colonel looked up quickly. "What is Fischer's first name?"

"I believe his first name is Helmut."

"Was the light sufficient so that you could distinctly recognize the faces of both Wizuy and Fischer?"

"It was about ten o'clock and it was dark but there are two street lamps and I'm sure that I recognized Fischer and also Wizuy."

Colonel Church pressed for more names. "Who were the five or six who went in the first time?"

"I cannot say for sure."

"Where did they come from?"

"They came from a group."

"The same group you were with near Drechsler's barracks that later parted from you and went up to Drechsler's barracks?"

"Yes."

"What were their names?"

"Fischer, Wizuy, Mandelkow, Nieswand, Ludwig, Polow-zyk, and there were several others whose names I don't know."

The recorder, Major Zabel, passed a note to Colonel Church, who scanned it and then looked back at Murza. "Did Weimer go in at the same time when this other group went in or before?"

"He went in before with another man. None of the group had been in Drechsler's barracks previously."

The recorder then asked: "He did not come out prior to the removal of Drechsler?"

"Weimer returned before the others went in the first time."

"What did Weimer say when he returned?" Colonel Church asked.

"I wasn't standing there so I didn't overhear the conversation, but I did hear it said that Drechsler was asleep so they didn't try to bring him out."

"How do you know it was actually Drechsler that was carried out later?"

"Because the talk previous to that time was about Drechsler and it was Drechsler that was supposed to be carried out."

"Carried out to be hung?"

"That he was supposed to be hung I didn't hear. The only thing I heard was 'Everything is understood,' and 'We will do a complete job.'"

"And who made that statement?"

"'Everything is clear,' Hox said that, those were the last words before we left the office; and it was Wizuy who said 'We will do a complete job.'"

"He said that before they went to change their clothes?"

"Yes."

Colonel Church paused and began going through the papers on the table before him. There was a long, empty silence before the colonel looked back up. "Any statements that you told us before you told in your own words what happened and that conflict with this last story are not true, is that correct?"

"A lot of what I was telling at Papago Park was a lie. Everything I was telling before I told my story in narrative form was correct except that I gave wrong names. I said at one time that I was not walking with the group from the open space in the 3rd Company toward Drechsler's barracks. I change my statement now that I did walk with this group for a little way."

"Was the list of names that you testified to as being in Hox's office correct?"

"The names I stated were correct, but I don't remember all of the names who were there."

"Are the names of the men that you gave us in the two groups after you left Hox's office correct?"

"The names of these men are correct also."

"And the names that you have now given us of Wizuy and Fischer, who carried Drechsler out, are correct?"

"I did not mention Fischer and Wizuy previously but they are correct."

"Is the statement that you gave to this board under oath at Papago Park when you said you knew nothing about the hanging of Drechsler a lie?"

"I have lied in part."

"You lied when you said you didn't know who hanged Drechsler?"

"Yes, I did."

"And you lied when you said you did not know any more than what you told us at Papago Park?"

"Yes, I was lying."

Colonel Church sat back in his chair and said, "That will be all for now."

It was 11:30 at night when Funkobermaat Friedrich Murza was led out of the interrogation room and escorted back to his cell. He was not just a worn and tired man; he was physically, mentally, and emotionally decimated by the ordeal of the last 3½ hours. In abject silence he collapsed into his cot.

Colonel Church and Major Zabel conferred for a short time after Murza had been removed; for the first time in over two months they could say that they had turned the corner in what was one of the most difficult cases they had ever encountered. They now had the direct implication of three men in the actual hanging—Otto Stengel, Rolf Wizuy, and Helmut Fischer—and the possible but still uncorroborated association of a number of others, such as Walter Nieswand, Herman Polowzyk, Lothar Mandelkow, Heinrich Ludwig, and Rudolf Weimer. And in the last few minutes of June 1, 1944, both officers knew that it was only a matter of time before they would have the necessary confessions.

While Friedrich Murza was telling his story to Colonel Church and the investigation board, other interrogators were hard at work on Otto Stengel. For that matter, they had been at it all day. And the long, relentless interrogation proved to be too much for Otto Stengel. In the early morning hours of June 2, while the secret camp at Stockton was still covered with darkness, he finally yielded and told the interrogators: "It's enough. I want to see the major. I'll give an oath."

A lieutenant who had been participating in the interrogation went to fetch Major Zabel, and both officers appeared very shortly in the small interrogation room.

"I would like to go before the board," Stengel told the major. "I'm ready to tell my part."

It took about fifteen minutes to get Colonel Church and reconvene the board, and when they did, they had their first confession. Stengel admitted that he had directly participated in the beating and hanging of Drechsler and then described in detail the crime itself and what his actual role was, but the only other person he identified was Rolf Wizuy, who, Stengel confessed, was equally involved in all aspects of the murder. Stengel claimed Wizuy was the only other man he knew by name; therefore he could not help in identifying the others. The board listened intently to his confession until he finally ended it with a slightly disoriented but deeply motivated justification.

"I want to say furthermore I had believed that the matter could be delayed until I could present myself to the authorities in Germany. But now I see I must make these statements here. Frankly, I was a bit afraid to before.

"I have always said in my room that I am a soldier and now I have to tell the truth. And if I am put before a court martial, then I wish to say something in my defense because in every German heart it feels bad that one sees such a man turn traitor who has so many men on his conscience, even men of my own folks. Some of my folks have lost their homes and my woman cousin has lost her life in a bombing attack.

"If I am put before a court martial I will be standing before soldiers who will have an understanding of this matter."

When it was over, Colonel Church directed that Stengel be taken to an isolated cell and provided with a pen and paper so that he could record in his own handwriting a complete confession. Stengel unhappily but with resignation agreed to comply and was led out of the room. It was somewhere around 4:30 in the morning.

Things were happening fast now. Word was passed to Captain Schmidt to intensify the interrogation of Rolf Wizuy. The order of suspects slated for questioning by the board was juggled to accommodate their new findings, and everyone was in a state of restrained excitement. Wizuy was again brought before the board early in the morning of June 2, but despite a detailed and deeply disconcerting interrogation, he refused to yield, holding to his earlier story. Wizuy, however, sensed that the board already knew, and he thought that others had probably broken down and implicated him. He was immediately remanded back to the custody of Captain Schmidt. The captain and others under him continued to interrogate Wizuy throughout the day and into the night.

After Wizuy had testified before the board on the morning of

June 2, Colonel Church called for Obermaat Siegfried Elser. Elser, too, showed sings of the ordeal, and he also sensed that everything was ominously closing in around him.

Perhaps because of his feelings, Elser had made up his mind to cooperate. He was reminded he was still under oath and was then questioned about his activities on the day and evening of March 12, 1944. In many ways he corroborated the story of Friedrich Murza, but in some ways he contradicted it.

"Obermaat Weimer went in the barracks with another man, I don't remember the name of that other man, and after a short time he returned and stated that Drechsler had gone to sleep. Thereupon I suggested that the matter be postponed until the next day, and I retired from the group. I thought that the others would have some understanding for my suggestion and retire too, but I noticed that the other men kept standing there; they were not only the men who had been in the office of Hox but all the other people who had joined the group in the meantime. There were about forty men in that group. I soon found out that the discussion was that we should take Drechsler out with force. I then saw five men who moved in the direction of Drechsler's barracks."

"On April 22, 1944, at Papago Park you testified before this board in answer to a question—the question was: 'Did you talk about this hanging before Drechsler was hung?' You answered: 'I don't know. I didn't know Drechsler personally. I don't believe I heard anything that evening. I found out about it in the morning.' Was that testimony you gave at that time a lie?"

"Yes."

"You also testified in answer to the question: 'Do you know Franz Hox?' Answer: 'Yes he was our compound spokesman.' And the question: 'Did you talk to him about it?' Answer: 'No.' And was that answer 'No' a lie?"

Elser appeared confused and groped for an answer. "I cannot remember whether I said 'No' at that time."

"If you did say 'No,' was it a lie?"

Elser nodded his head affirmatively and mumbled, "Yes."

"Did you go to your barracks with Murza after you left Hox's office?"

"I can't remember, but in any case I went to the washroom, but whether I went back to my barracks I don't remember for sure."

"Did you get your gloves at that time?"

"I don't remember exactly when I got the gloves. I believe I got the gloves at the time which passed between the first two men and the second men entering the barracks of Drechsler."

"And after you got your gloves you went back to where the group was talking about hanging Drechsler?"

"Yes."

"And who was in the group at that time when you went back?"

"Funkobermaat Murza, Wizuy, Paul Buchholz, and Ludwig. There were still other men I know but I cannot remember their names."

"And did they all have gloves too?"

"I don't know."

"Who did you see with gloves besides yourself?"

"I can't state that I saw anybody with gloves but I suppose that the largest part had gloves."

"Why did you get your gloves?"

"Because there were agreements about that and I didn't want to exclude myself." Elser now appeared noticeably upset by the line of questioning.

"What was the agreement?"

"The agreement was that gloves should be taken along."

Major Zabel interrupted quickly: "For what purpose?"

"In order to hang Drechsler."

The major continued: "Isn't it a fact then that you got your gloves for the purpose of helping to hang Drechsler?"

"No," Elser answered emphatically.

"Then why did you get the gloves?"

"I personally could not do a thing like that and I personally was not in favor of Drechsler's hanging."

"Was it your intention to administer a beating to Drechsler?"

"Yes, I had the intention of getting Drechsler out and have him report, and my intention was to try to convince the others to get Drechsler out of the compound but to tell them before would have been without purpose because they were all too excited." Elser hesitated for a split second. "They were not excited but they had the opinion that Drechsler should be hanged."

"Who had that opinion?" Colonel Church asked.

"The largest part of the men who were standing there."

"All right, name some of them," Major Zabel said sharply.

Elser screwed up his face in exasperation. "Murza, Wizuy, Ludwig, the other names I can't state but I stated previously that Buchholz was in it too."

"Did Wizuy and Murza say that Drechsler should be hung?"

"Yes."

"Did Murza and Wizuy have gloves?"

"I couldn't tell but I assume so. The same thing is for the other three men."

"Why do you assume it?"

"I got mine even not having the intention inside to help them hang him. I got my gloves and I assume that the others got their gloves because they had the intention to hang Drechsler."

"Did Murza, Buchholz, Ludwig, and Wizuy go in a group to Drechsler's barracks?"

"Murza did not go to Drechsler's barracks."

Major Zabel interrupted again. "When was it when you discussed with the others about punishing Drechsler?"

"That was after the discussion in Hox's office."

"Then it was decided to administer a beating to Drechsler?"

"That Drechsler should be moved out of the compound."

"And also to punish him, isn't that right?"

"Yes."

"You were personally willing to participate in the punishment by beating Drechsler?"

"Yes."

"You suggested that they beat him?"

"I suggested that he should be gotten out of the barracks and that he should be questioned."

"You were personally willing to participate in that particular action of beating Drechsler, weren't you?"

"Yes."

"That action miscarried, didn't it?"

"No."

"Instead of Drechsler's being only beaten, he was also hung?"

"Yes."

"You being a participant, a planner of that particular action, you are also a participant in the hanging of Drechsler?"

Visibly shaken, Elser shouted, "No."

"You are the ranking noncommissioned officer, aren't you?"

"Murza outranks me."

"But you are a noncommissioned officer?"

"Yes."

"The gefreiters are willing to follow your lead, isn't that right?"

"No, it is different while being prisoners."

Colonel Church looked over at Major Zabel and nodded and then turned back to Elser, "That will be all for now." It was 11:45 in the evening when Elser was taken back to his cell.

Captain Schmidt's interrogation of Rolf Wizuy had continued off and on throughout the night and was now moving into the morning hours. Finally, at a little before eight in the morning, a weary and trembling Rolf Wizuy told Captain Schmidt that he was ready to make a statement and was taken before the interrogation board.

Wizuy told his story in complete detail, beginning with the time he first heard about Drechsler's arrival in the camp all the way through to the act of washing his gloves after the hanging was accomplished. He admitted that it was his idea all along that Drechsler should be hanged because he personally knew Drechsler was a traitor. When it was determined that they could do it, he was accompanied into Drechsler's barracks by four of his crewmates, whom he named—Helmut Fischer, Guenther Kuelsen, Fritz Franke, and Bernhard Reyak—as well as two other men, Henrich Ludwig and Otto Stengel, all of whom aided in subduing Drechsler and in one way or another helped to hang him. After his testimony, Wizuy was taken off to a cell by himself so that he could write out his confession for the board.

Later that day, Heinrich Ludwig also admitted his participation in the murder, and before the board he implicated the same persons Rolf Wizuy had mentioned earlier. He added no new names to Wizuy's list. He dated his handwritten confession June 3, 1944, and resigned himself to whatever fate lay ahead of him.

The other confessions did not come as quickly, however; in fact, they were not signed for another five days. But on June 8, the obvious futility of it all was too much for them and each finally relented—Franke first, then Kuelsen and Reyak, and last Fischer. The interrogations of other prisoners continued despite the confessions now of seven men, each of whose admissions essentially corroborated the others. The army did not want to leave anyone out who might also have been directly involved and who had thus far escaped detection. They continued to work on Friedrich Murza, Siegfried Elser, Guenther Bleise, Paul Buchholz, Lothar Mandelkow, Walter Nieswand, Hermann Polowzyk, Werner Reinl, Hermann Wiedemann, Rudolf Weimer and a few others. But the army was unable to attach any of them directly to the physical action of the crime, although it still held out for the guilt of the two noncommissioned officers, Friedrich Murza and Siegfried Elser, because of their rank and the motivating force the army felt that they had on the actual act of murder.

On June 20, 1944, the investigating board adjourned. The record of hearings and interrogations were transcribed and sent on to the Ninth Services Command at Fort Douglas for review and forwarding to the Department of War in Washington, along with a succinct summary of their findings and recommendations.

The findings of the board are that the board has carefully reviewed and considered the evidence adduced at the various hearings and sets forth as follows:

1. That Werner Drechsler was a German prison of war at the time of his death, and was duly confined at the prisoner of war camp, Papago Park, Arizona.

2. That German Prisoner of War Drechsler came to his death by strangulation on the night of Sunday, March 12, 1944, at about the hour of 9:30 p.m.

3. That said death by strangulation was caused by said Prisoner of War Werner Drechsler having been murdered by hanging by the following German prisoners of war: Otto Stengel, Rolf Wizuy, Heinrich Ludwig, Helmut Fischer, Fritz Franke, Bernhard Reyak, and Guenther Kuelsen.

4. That German Prisoners of War Siegfried Elser and Friedrich Murza aided, assisted, counseled and advised the above named murderers of Prisoner of War Drechsler prior to such murder and therefore, in the opinion of this board, should be charged and tried as accessories before the fact.

The board recommends that the following named prisoners of war be charged with and tried for the willful and premeditated murder of Prisoner of War Werner Drechsler: Otto Stengel, Rolf Wizuy, Heinrich Ludwig, Helmut Fischer, Fritz Franke, Bernhard Reyak, and Guenther Kuelsen; and that the following named prisoners of war be charged with and tried for the murder of Prisoner of War Werner Drechsler as accessories before the fact: Siegfried Elser and Friedrich Murza.

The findings and recommendations were signed by Colonel Church, Major Zabel, and Major Walsh.

9

Interrogations

Major Walsh learned of the investigating board's success while he was still in Florence, Arizona, prosecuting the arson case of an Italian prisoner of war. He returned to Stockton to help tie the whole thing together after the signed confessions had already been written out and to prepare the documents to be forwarded to Fort Douglas. Soon after that, he was informed that he had been assigned to prosecute the seven men who had confessed. After a brief reflection, he realized he would be handling the largest case of his life — all seven were being charged with first degree murder, and conviction could carry the penalty of death by hanging.

Walsh, in his forties, had had a successful civil practice in San Francisco before the war broke out, but his past experiences were going to be of little value in the challenge that now confronted him. Major Walsh had never tried a criminal case before entering the army, and this was to be his first murder trial.

The case itself presented two legal problems — the use of the lie detector and the various methods employed in the "informal" interrogations that had eventually produced the confessions on which Major Walsh planned to base his prosecution. He and his staff immediately plunged into research, from which would come the actual construction of their case against the seven men. In their research, Major Walsh came across a case in Oklahoma that had a striking but disturbing similarity to the murder case he was about to try. A soldier had been brought before a court martial board, charged with rape. A great amount of pressure and coercion had been used to procure a confession from him, and the prosecution based its case solely on that confession. The man was found guilty, but a higher court had overruled the decision because of the methods used to obtain the confession.

The only way to add credence to the confessions Major Walsh now had, he believed, was to send an investigating officer out to each accused and give the accused the opportunity to reconsider his confession. This was required by the Articles of War to insure that all the rights of the defendant had actually been honored, but it also gave Major Walsh the opportunity to base the central thrust of his case on these subsequent investigations in which he was giving the accused the chance to refute or amend their statements in light of their rights, which in essence would assure that all of the rights of the defendants had been afforded to them. First Lieutenant Harry A. Baldwin, a Judge Advocate General officer from Fort Douglas, was assigned the job of investigating officer.

The seven prisoners of war were taken out of Stockton and incarcerated at different army facilities in California. It was the first time that they had been geographically isolated since they had arrived at Stringtown almost nine months earlier. Otto Stengel had been taken to Dibble General Hospital in Menlo Park immediately after his confession, where he was operated on for appendicitis. He remained there for over a month, and it was at the hospital that Lieutenant Baldwin met him to investigate the charges. Rolf Wizuy was held at the Hammond General Hospital in Modesto. Heinrich Ludwig was at the DeWitt General Hospital in Auburn; and Fischer, Franke, Kuelsen, and Reyak were being held separately at a rehabilitation center in Turlock.

The seven men actually had almost a month to think over their confessions and recuperate from the incredible ordeal of their interrogations before Lieutenant Baldwin arrived to investigate the testimony. But all of them felt it was futile at this point to do anything about the confessions. They knew that the U.S. army had them unquestionably in terms of committing the murder, that there was no way out of that, and that their entire defense was in their motivation and the justification of their actions. Now that it was all out in the open, they were not ashamed; rather, they were proud of having done their duty.

Lieutenant Baldwin drove to Dibble General Hospital on July 3. Otto Stengel had already been informed of his pending arrival and why he was visiting. By this date, Stengel was ambulatory, and it was he who was brought to the room where Lieutenant Baldwin sat with two staff sergeants, Melvin G. Obujen as reporter and Paul Held as interpreter. It was a little after 11:50 in the morning when he was unhappily led into the room.

"I am investigating the hanging of Prisoner of War Werner Drechsler," the lieutenant began, "which occurred on or about 12 or 13 March 1944 in Compound 4, Papago Park, Phoenix, Arizona. Under Article of War 70, and as a German prisoner of war, you are entitled to the protection of the Articles of War. A thorough and impartial investigation must be made before trial. I am not the prosecutor, nor do I represent the prosecution. I am not your counsel. I am here merely to inquire into the truth of the charges, and to recommend what disposition should be made in the interest of justice and discipline. I am not here for the purpose of securing any military information."

Lieutenant Baldwin then read the charge and specification of the charge to Stengel, who sat impassively, looking quite bored by the whole proceeding. He became much more alert, however, when the lieutenant read the list of witnesses against him, both American and German.

"Now, Prisoner of War Otto Stengel, under Article of War 70 you are entitled to hear the evidence against you, if you wish. You have the right to examine any of those witnesses whose names I just read to you, if they are available, and you understand I will examine them for you, if you wish. Do you want to examine any of the witnesses or have me examine any of them for you?"

"I understand, and I do not desire to examine any of the witnesses or have you examine any of them for me."

Lieutenant Baldwin raised his eyebrows slightly at the coldness in Stengel's voice but then went back to the business at hand.

"You have the right to remain silent at this time and say nothing, or you have the right to present anything in your own behalf in defense or mitigation. You have the right to make a statement in any form, subject, however, to its being used against you in the future. Do you understand?"

"Yes."

"Explain to me what you understand by what I have just told you."

Stengel appeared visibly irritated. "I want to make the same statements as I made before to Colonel Church and the other officers, exactly the same and nothing else. I do not understand how all these people can be witnesses against me. For the time being I want to hear only the statement of Friedrich."

Lieutenant Baldwin decided to adjourn the investigation at this point. It was time for lunch and the lieutenant felt his inquiry was on the verge of getting out of control. But at one o'clock, Stengel was brought back to continue the investigation.

Lieutenant Baldwin began again. "Prisoner of War Otto Stengel, do you understand all that was explained to you before we adjourned this noon?"

"Yes."

"Do you wish to make a statement at this time?"

"I have nothing to add. I just want to state what I have told the fact finding board previously. I have told Colonel Church why I committed the crime, and I know nothing more. I have acted as a German soldier would do. Drechsler was a traitor and a German soldier does not like a traitor."

"I will at this time read to you Article of War 24, and ask you if you want to repeat to me what you previously stated to Colonel Church at the previous investigation:

"Article of War 24—Compulsory Self-Incrimination Prohibited. —No witness before a military court, commission, court of inquiry, or board or before any officer conducting an investigation, or before any officer, military or civil, designated to take a deposition to be read in evidence before a military court, commission, court of inquiry, or board, or before an officer conducting an investigation, shall be compelled to incriminate himself or to answer any questions not material to the issue when such answer might tend to degrade him.

"Do you understand that?"

"Yes."

"What does it mean?"

"According to Article 24 I am permitted to refuse an answer which has nothing to do with the matter, or which may incriminate myself. I can refuse to answer by referring expressly to Article 24."

"I will now read to you a paragraph from Article of War 70:

"Article of War 70—Charges: Action upon.—No charge will be referred to a General Court Martial for trial until after a thorough and impartial investigation thereof shall have been made. This investigation will include inquiries as to the truth of the matter set forth in said charges, form of charges, and what disposition of the case should be made in the interest of justice and discipline. At such investigation full opportunity shall be given to the accused to cross-examine witnesses against him if they are available and to

present anything he may desire in his own behalf, either in defense
or mitigation, and the investigating officer shall examine available
witnesses requested by the accused. If the charges are forwarded
after such investigation, they shall be accompanied by a statement
of the substance of the testimony taken on both sides.

"Do you understand what I have just read?"

"I understand everything clearly."

"Knowing your rights as I have explained them to you, do
you now wish to make a statement?"

Otto Stengel then gave his statement. It was long and ram-
bling and almost an hour had passed before he finished it, but
it was almost exactly the same as the statement he gave to
Colonel Church a month earlier.

When Stengel finally finished, Lieutenant Baldwin asked
him: "Is there anything further you want to say?"

"I want to add something in my own defense, as to why I
had participated in the crime. At first, I didn't think that I
would get involved in that crime, in spite of the fact that the
hatred against Drechsler was pretty intense, because he had
insulted Adolph Hitler and my government in the worst way
possible. A thing like that hadn't happened to me up to that
time. After two years, being a prisoner of war, I had
come upon somebody for the first time who had insulted
Adolph Hitler and my government, and before when I went
to the football field and heard he was a traitor I got mad,
and I wondered why the Americans sent a man like that to
the camp. We thought probably he had given the enemy
enough information, and now they wanted to get rid of
him. We said, 'The enemy likes treason, but the enemy has
no respect for the traitor either,' and when I joined these
other men I have mentioned I was enthusiastic about doing
my share in order to kill a traitor who had maybe thousands
of men on his conscience. He had on his conscience the
wives and children of the people of Germany, and thousands
of brave submarine men, and possibly he also had on his

conscience my woman cousin who was killed in a bombing attack on Berlin, and the sister of my wife who lost her home as airplanes had destroyed everything. Therefore, we agreed to do away with this scoundrel. We could not wait until Germany could judge him. Germany should be grateful to us for such action, for getting rid of such a bastard. That is all I have to say."

"I show you a document consisting of 23 sheets of paper written in pen and ink and ask you if you recognize it?"

"That is my handwriting."

"Is the signature on the last page thereof yours?"

"Yes. I made it myself."

"What is the date of this statement?"

"Second of June 1944."

"Was any person other than yourself present when you wrote out this statement and signed it?"

"I did it all alone in my room. Nobody was with me at that time."

"Are the facts stated therein true?"

"Yes, it is the full truth."

"When the list of witnesses against you was read from the charge sheet you said that was not all correct. Do you recall that?"

"Yes, I made such a statement before. What I had reference to was not the names of the witnesses, but the phraseology of the specification. It was stated that we had committed the crime deliberately, willfully, and with premeditation—especially premeditation I do not think is right."

"Why don't you think it is right?"

"I especially do not like the phraseology 'premeditation' because I did not have time to think things over clearly. There is proof to the fact that I was not there when preparations were made in the shower room of the 5th Company to hang Drechsler. Maybe premeditation applies to the other men who had participated. I came by accident upon these men and I only helped them because they seemed to need another man. Because if I had planned this thing and had thought this thing out I certainly wouldn't have joined this group of men without having my gloves on, as everyone else had gloves on but myself."

"Do you want to hear the testimony of any of the other witnesses, other than Friedrich?"

"No."

Lieutenant Baldwin then read the complete testimony of Alfred Friedrich. At the end he added: "Is there anything further you want to state at this time?"

"I want to state at this time that I had never talked to Friedrich at the football field. What Friedrich was telling about the fingerprints is correct. It happened on a Monday afternoon when I was telling this story to Friedrich. Could I possibly find out on what date Friedrich made the statement just read to me?"

"His statement was made on 31 May 1944."

"That is sufficient information for me. Friedrich had told me when I was together with him at the guardhouse at Papago Park: 'I hope that the murderers will come out soon because I want to go back to camp.' And he gave me his promise then he would never give away my name, and now in the testimony read to me I see he mentions my name many times."

"Do you want to make another statement?"

"No. Possibly I will get a chance to see Friedrich later on."

"And all the statements you have made to me this afternoon you have made under oath?"

"Yes."

At lunchtime the following day, Lieutenant Baldwin arrived at the Hammond General Hospital in Modesto to talk with Rolf Wizuy. Wizuy was firm, but he was much easier to deal with than Stengel. Lieutenant Baldwin went through the formalities of explaining his purpose and reading the appropriate Articles of War and ended with the usual. "Do you understand what I have just read to you?"

"Yes, I understand."

"Knowing your rights as I have explained them to you, do you wish to make a statement at this time?"

"I want to hear the statements of Hox and Obermaat Weimer, and then I want to make a statement of my own."

Lieutenant Baldwin read the testimony of the two men, and Wizuy sat facing him with a placid look on his face. It was obvious he was taking in every word.

When the lieutenant finished, he asked: "Are you satisfied, or is there some other statement you would like to hear?"

"I want also to hear the statement of Polowzyk."

The lieutenant then read the testimony of Hermann Polowzyk. When he put the papers down, he looked back at Wizuy and asked again, "Is there anything else?"

"I would like to know whether I can hear the statements made by my comrades Franke and Kuelsen?"

"You may." And the Lieutenant then read their statements.

"Are you now satisfied?"

"Yes."

"Do you want to make your statement under oath?"

"What is the difference if I make a statement under oath or without oath?"

"When you make a statement under oath you swear that what you state is the truth, the whole truth, and nothing but the truth. It is immaterial whether you make it under oath or without oath."

"I don't want to make any statement under oath. Among other things in my statement I want to describe the mood and the spirit and the eventual reasons which led up to this crime, and I want to make these statements to you now. Whether all these statements check is up to the job of the investigating officer." When Wizuy saw there was no response from the lieutenant, he began his statement.

"I had about four hours time since Drechsler came to camp to think over the case itself. We had talked about the case very little before, and we didn't have a plan before Drechsler arrived in camp. That Drechsler was a traitor I knew one hundred percent.

"There were no connections between us and the officers' camp, and we could not ask our officers what to do in that case. We asked Chief Quartermaster Hox and didn't get an answer, which gave us an indication as to exactly what we should do. There were different opinions in the camp as to how to deal with a case like that. About one hundred of the men in Compound 4 at Papago Park have gone through American interrogation centers. Some of them have been in San Francisco, and some of them in Washington. In these camps we were told we could be eliminated very easily. In other words, we were threatened with the following statement: 'We could be sent to a special camp and there we could be hanged.' From the time I left the interrogation center to the time Drechsler was hanged, I didn't give that statement any thought, but when Drechsler arrived in camp I assumed right away that a thing like that was possible. That is the reason we didn't consider the crime very long. I am sure that if there are over one hundred prisoners of war in a prisoner of war camp, and all of them have been told a thing like that—regarding the statement we could be eliminated very easily—that influences the general opinion in camp, especially when a traitor like Drechsler arrives in camp. Whether men are really killed in these camps we have no way of checking. Several men were missing from each submarine crew. It could have been easily possible that some of these men had been sent to these camps in order to be hanged. I am of the firm opinion that if the American armed forces assumes the right to deceive us in an interrogation camp, then the American government automatically has the obligation to tell us men, who had been in these interrogation camps, that these statements are not right. I am sure that if we had known that all prisoners

of war, whether they were good Germans or traitors, would
be sent back to Germany after the war, Drechsler would be
still alive today, and I wouldn't be standing in front of
an investigating officer. If we had known that for sure,
maybe we would have given Drechsler a thorough beating
so that he couldn't sit on his rear end for five days, but
we never would have hanged him—that is as far as I am
concerned.

"I want to make additional statements which could have led
other buddies of mine to participate in this crime without hesitation. Through these conversations with Drechsler, some of
the men in camp had a feeling he came into this camp because
he had to perform a certain task for the Americans, for he asked
for a short-wave receiver. Then he tried to get information regarding a number of traitors, and besides that he has told me
personally he would leave the camp the very next day. I myself
did not think he was sent to the camp because he had to perform a certain task for the Americans, but I thought that he was
sent to this camp by the Americans having the intention to see
him hanged by us. I also assumed that Drechsler didn't want
to continue to work for the Americans or that he knew too much.

"I want to add at this time that the crime probably will be considered by the court martial judges as a bloody deed, but I want
to state emphatically that we considered the crime as a military
action, and that we had to break the resistance of Drechsler in
order to accomplish the thing we had intended to."

"Is there anything further?"

"I want to think it over."

"Take your time."

But Rolf Wizuy really had nothing more to say. He admitted
that the statement he had written out at Stockton was, to his ac-
knowledge, correct and that he did not want to change it. Then
he was led back to his room; the inquiry had lasted approximately two hours.

By 6:45 that evening, Lieutenant Baldwin was at the Turlock

rehabilitation center. First on his list was Guenther Kuelsen, who was brought before the investigating officer shortly after the dinner meal had been served. Again the formalities were dispatched, and Kuelsen explained: "I am fully conscious of the fact that all the statements I make will be read before the judges. I will tell the truth, so I am not afraid that anything I might tell might be used against me in a bad sense. I know further that I don't have to talk at all if I do not desire to do so, and that I don't have to make any statements whatsoever if I don't feel like it. The names of the witnesses have been read to me, both American as well as German prisoners of war. I have previously made my statement, and what I say here will not change my previous statement. The men who did not participate in the crime itself could not have said anything against me personally."

"Knowing your rights as I have explained them to you, do you wish to make a statement at this time?"

"Yes."

"Do you want to make your statement under oath or not?"

"Everything I want to testify to is the full truth, and I am ready to take the oath."

"Will you proceed now to make the statement you indicated you desired to make?"

"I want to give a reason why I participated in that crime. One only can judge the situation I am in when one has lived through the sinking of a submarine as I have, and when one has further realized how much damage a man like Drechsler has done. I wanted to help my buddies Drechsler had harmed in the past, and I wanted to prevent Drechsler from rendering further services to the Americans.

"I could continue my statement, but I don't want to be over hasty. I would rather you give me a few minutes' time to think it over."

"That's agreeable. We will adjourn the hearing for five minutes in compliance with your request."

When he was ready, Kuelsen was reminded he was still under oath.

"I understand, yes, sir. I would like to hear the beginning of the statement I made a few minutes ago." It was read to him by the recorder.

"I will continue. I am a soldier and I am fully conscious of the fact that a man like Drechsler, who had once given an oath of allegiance to the German flag, and who has broken that oath of allegiance, is not worthy of living with German men in a German prisoner of war camp. This gave me a reason to participate in that case."

Then he added: "I want to know how far I, as a German prisoner of war, can be punished by the American authorities?"

The answer was to the point: "The Geneva Convention, Article 45, provides that prisoners of war shall be subject to the laws, regulations, and orders in force in the armies of the detaining power, and that any act of insubordination shall justify the adoption towards them of the measures provided by such laws, regulations, and orders."

"I understand this matter would be altogether different if I had done a thing like that to an American soldier, but I have done it to a German soldier, and I have to own up to this crime after my return to Germany."

"As a prisoner of war captured by the American forces, your conduct is governed by the Articles of War. The 92d Article of War prohibits murder, and the fact that you are not an American soldier does not excuse you from that Article."

"I cannot imagine how I can be under the American laws as a soldier. Things would be different if I had committed theft. I brought up this topic of conversation because I heard there were rumors that the officers of Papago Park, who conducted the first investigation, have said we only want the names of the men who had participated in the crime in order to have proof for a report to Germany through Red Cross channels."

"Is there anything further you wish to state?"

"No, sir. I stick to my previous statement."

Guenther Kuelsen went back to his cell at Turlock a confused, frustrated, and angry young man.

It was eight o'clock in the evening and Lieutenant Baldwin decided that was enough for the day. He had a full day facing him the next day. Baldwin hoped to finish with Fischer, Franke, and Reyak at Turlock and then move to DeWitt General Hospital to end his investigation with Heinrich Ludwig.

The day of July 5 began very early for the investigating officer and his staff. Before 8:30 they were prepared to proceed with Helmut Fischer.

Fischer articulately explained his justification for the murder of Drechsler but had nothing more to say about the crime. He asked to hear the statement of Franz Hox, and when it was read to him, he simply shrugged his shoulders. At this time, he said, he just had nothing more to say.

Fritz Franke followed Fischer; in fact, he passed him in the hall as Fischer was being taken back to his cell. The two men nodded in silence as they passed.

If Fischer had little to say, Franke had far less to add. His entire testimony lasted less than half an hour. Franke listened indifferently as the lieutenant read the Articles of War, and when he was finally asked if he had a statement to make, he answered coldly: "I have nothing to add."

The lieutenant continued. "I show you this document consisting of five pages written in pen and ink and ask if you recognize it?"

"I recognize it."

"In whose handwriting is it?"

"It is my handwriting."

"Is the signature on the last page thereof yours?"

"Yes, it is my signature."

And that was really all Fritz Franke had to say. He did not want to hear anyone else's testimony nor would he say any more himself. He gave the distinct impression that all he wanted was to be taken back to his cell.

Bernhard Reyak was brought in next. Unlike Fischer and Franke, however, he wanted to say quite a bit. After listening to Lieutenant Baldwin go through all of the same preliminaries, his first statement was: "If possible, I would like to hear the testimony of all witnesses who had said that I was present in the shower room when Drechsler's head was actually in the noose."

"No one said you were there when his head was put in the noose," Lieutenant Baldwin said.

Reyak then went on to give a complete description of the events of the evening. He admitted taking part in the beating of Drechsler but swore that he was not present at the actual hanging, although he said that that was actually their purpose in entering Drechsler's barracks and attacking him.

"Did you have gloves on?" the lieutenant asked.

"I had gloves with me. I carried them inside my shirt and never had a chance to put them on, because I never participated in the actual hanging."

"When did you get the gloves?"

"We got the gloves in the beginning before we assembled in the open space."

"Why did you get your gloves?"

We had assembled previously and somebody, I don't remember who—I think it was Funkobermaat Murza—said we should be very careful because of fingerprints. For that reason I got my gloves."

Reyak kept looking at the lieutenant, as if to find some form of understanding. When none was forthcoming, however, he continued and gave a lengthy justification for his part in the execution, but it was no different from that of any of the five men who had testified before him. It was basically summed up in his last sentence to the investigating officer:

"We had to prevent him from doing further harm." Then he was finished, and he looked sadly defeated as he was escorted out of the room.

With one more defendant to go, Lieutenant Baldwin drove to Auburn, California, to end his assignment. Heinrich Ludwig was still at DeWitt General Hospital, and after his dinner on the night of July 5, he was brought in to face the investigating officer and his staff.

"I want to make a few statements in my defense and give a few reasons for eventual leniency," Ludwig told the lieutenant. He then agreed to make his statements under oath, looked up at the lieutenant coldly, and began.

"I was personally with Drechsler in the interrogation camp near Washington, D.C. I was in the same room with him for about ten days, and he tried to ask me all kinds of questions concerning secret matters of my submarine, and what I had told him he repeated to the American authorities. I was interrogated at this interrogation camp near Washington by an English officer, and every time I returned from an interrogation it happened that a few minutes later Drechsler was called out of the room. He returned about ten or fifteen minutes later. He told me himself several times. He said when he was called away the officers questioned him as to what I had told him [Drechsler] about the interrogation conducted by that English officer. The time interval between my interrogation and the time Drechsler was called was about five minutes. Further, Drechsler introduced himself under the wrong name and also a higher rank, which he was not entitled to."

"Where was this that he assumed this false name and false rank?"

"That was in the interrogation camp in Washington. When this man came to our camp at Papago Park at Phoenix, Arizona, we found out about it right away. We were all very excited in the first moment and we decided we couldn't have a man like that with us because he was a traitor. I think we only fulfilled our duty to Germany by hanging Drechsler. The American authorities who sent this man to Papago Park must have known that this man was a traitor, and must have further known that something would happen to that man. For that reason the man shouldn't have been sent to the camp." Ludwig paused and then added: "I would like to hear the statement of Nieswand."

The testimony of Prisoner of War Walter Nieswand was read to Ludwig by the investigating officer.

"That is all I am interested in," Ludwig said.

"I show you a document consisting of seven sheets of paper written in pen and ink, and ask you if you recognize it?"

"That is my statement in the Drechsler case."

"In whose handwriting is it?"

"That is in my handwriting."

"Is the signature on the last page your signature?"

"Yes, that is my signature."

"Was that signature made by yourself?"

"Yes, it was."

"What is the date of that statement?"

"June 3, 1944."

"Was any person other than yourself present when you wrote out this statement?"

"I was alone."

"Are all the facts stated therein true?"

"Yes."

"Is there anything else you wish to say at this time?"

"That is all."

As Ludwig left the room, the lieutenant breathed a sigh of relief. It had been a long, hard day, but his investigation was now complete. He piled all of his papers back into a briefcase and left to present his report to Major Walsh.

10

Court Martial

S PECIAL Orders No. 168 came through from the headquarters of the Ninth Service Command, Fort Douglas, Utah, on July 11, 1944, appointing a general court martial board and directing it to meet August 15, 1944, at the POW camp at Florence, Arizona, for the trial of Helmut Fischer, Fritz Franke, Guenther Kuelsen, Heinrich Ludwig, Bernhard Reyak, Otto Stengel, and Rolf Wizuy. The orders, signed by Colonel John H. Wilson, chief of staff of the Ninth Service Command, were processed and distributed immediately, although they would not be officially served on the seven men until the end of July.

Somewhere in the decision-making apparatus of the army it was decided to drop the second recommendation of Colonel Church's board of investigation, and hence the charges against Friedrich Murza and Siegfried Elser were rescinded. The two noncommissioned officers were released from any responsibility they had in the murder and were returned to the status of ordinary prisoners of war. The reason for dropping the charges was not recorded; the two men simply did not have to stand trial.

As ordered, the court martial convened on August 15, at 9:08 A.M. Colonel Cassius Poust was appointed president and law member of the court martial board, in effect the judge in the case. Colonel Poust, from Sycamore, Illinois, was an able and stern jurist, who had an extensive background in both civil and criminal law before entering the army in World War II. The twelve other officers assigned to the board, whose responsibilities were roughly equivalent to the jury in a civil trial, were drawn from various branches of the regular army and listed according to their rank: Colonel Clayton J. Herman (Infantry), Colonel Bertram I. Lawrence (Infantry), Colonel Callie H. Palmer (Cavalry), Colonel Joseph H. Whiteley (Medical Corps), Lt. Colonel William H. Wertz (Coast Artillery Corps), Major Robert R. Taylor (Army of the United States), Major Curtis H. Wienker (Infantry), Captain James C. Reilly (Quartermaster Corps), Captain Norman W. Edward (Ordinance), Captain Ross J. Thomas (Quartermaster Corp), Captain Clarence Evans (Military Police), and Captain Thomas H. Carrick (Chemical Warfare Service). In essence, they comprised a diverse grouping of professional military men, brought together as a jury to hear testimony and render a verdict on the crime of murder allegedly committed by seven German prisoners of war. It was that particular point—that it was a *crime*—that the seven men, even as they were led into the courtroom, could still not comprehend. They faced the thirteen uniformed officers, not as a judicial body, but as the military authorities of a country with which they were still at war. As they looked around the room at all the men in alien uniforms, even their own defense counsel, at the strange insignias and ensigns, at the flag of the United States standing next to the bench, they felt to a man that they were sorely in the enemy camp.

The prosecutor of the case, Major Francis P. Walsh, from Fort Douglas, Utah, was well prepared to present the government's case. He had brought with him as assistant trial judge advocate Captain Robert O. Hillis, who served with him on the staff of the Judge Advocate General's office of the Ninth Service Command. Major William H. Taylor, a JAG officer, was appointed defense counsel for all seven defendants, and his assistant was Major Harold A. Furst, another army law officer. Captain Oscar S. Schmidt, whom the seven defendants remembered with very little affection from their various interrogations over the last four months, was sworn in as the official court interpreter. A private, Erwin J. Gruenebaum, also was sworn in, to interpret the proceedings of the trial from English to German for the seven accused.

The swearing in took only a few minutes, and the seven defendants sat uneasily through it; they had not, so to speak, gotten their sea legs yet. Finally, each defendant was asked to stand and Major Walsh asked him who he wished to have as counsel. Each stated that Major Taylor and Major Furst would be satisfactory.

The prosecutor then approached the court martial board, looked first at Colonel Poust, and read the charges against the seven defendants. When Major Walsh finished, Private Gruenebaum interpreted the charges in German and the seven looked at each other without surprise and then back at the prosecutor.

"Do you at this time desire to challenge any member of the court for cause?" Major Walsh asked.

Each defendant answered no.

"Do you desire to challenge any member of the court peremptorily?" Major Walsh turned quickly to the interpreter, "Will you please explain carefully to the accused that where it is a joint trial they are only allowed one peremptory challenge. Only one challenge collectively for all of them."

When Private Gruenebaum finished explaining this in German, the court ordered Helmut Fischer to stand.

Major Walsh spoke to him directly. "Do you understand what is meant by the word *challenge,* and do you understand the answer you made that you do not desire to make any challenge to any member of the court?"

"I do not know any of the members of the court and therefore I have nothing to say against them."

Colonel Poust leaned forward across the table. "The matter of personal acquaintance is not material. The question is, do you desire to challenge or not?"

"No, I do not," Fischer answered curtly.

Major Walsh's question was then read to each of the other six defendants, and each declined to challenge. When Major Walsh finished, Colonel Poust addressed the others in the courtroom:

"As president of the court, I advise all persons in the courtroom that this is a secret proceeding. No person present has the right to disclose any of the proceedings of this court outside of this room. Major Pickard is responsible for the care of the accused, and the guards of his command are, at such time as action is necessary, to retain the accused in custody and prevent any unauthorized persons from communication with them or entering the courtroom except witnesses as they are called for by the trial judge advocate or counsel for the defense." When he finished, Colonel Poust nodded to the prosecutor to begin the trial.

Major Walsh faced the seven defendants. "Prisoners of War Helmut Fischer, Fritz Franke, Guenther Kuelsen, Heinrich Ludwig, Bernhard Reyak, Otto Stengel, Rolf Wizuy, I will now read the charge and specification under which you are about to be tried."

Turning to the court interpreter, he said. "Will you translate that to them please, Captain Schmidt?"

The charge and specification were then read in English by the prosecutor and subsequently in German by Captain

Schmidt. The court martial that had seemed so far away only a few months earlier was now officially under way.

"At this time, may it please the court," Major Walsh said, "for the purpose of the record I might state this, and counsel for the accused Major Taylor will agree with me, that on 27 July 1944, Major Taylor, a German interpreter, and myself personally contacted each of six accused, with the exception of Heinrich Ludwig, served the charges upon them, and the charges were fully explained to them at that time. On 28 July 1944 I personally served the charges on accused Heinrich Ludwig and the charges were fully explained to him."

Major Walsh then asked Helmut Fischer to stand. "Prisoner of War Helmut Fischer, how do you plead to the specification of the charge?"

"Not guilty."

"How do you plead to the charge?"

"Not guilty."

The same two questions were asked to each of the other defendants, and without trepidation each gave identical answers. There was almost the trace of satisfaction in their voices as each firmly disclaimed his guilt.

At ten o'clock the court took a five-minute recess, during which time Major Taylor, through his interpreter, Private Gruenebaum, explained to the seven defendants the stipulations that they had signed the previous day and that were to be introduced as exhibits when the trial reconvened. The stipulations were basically designed to ascertain that certain facts in the case were self-evident and that both the prosecution and defense counsel agreed that they did not need to be presented formally at the trial. In this case, the stipulations simply bore witness to the fact that the seven accused were officially incarcerated and were present at the POW camp at Papago Park, Arizona, on the date of the crime.

The seven men, their lawyer, and the interpreter had not left the table in the courtroom, and they were still sitting there when the members of the board began filing back into the room. The accused appeared to have relaxed a little since the start of the trial, or at least to have become somewhat accustomed to the austere surroundings.

Colonel Poust called the court to order and added, "Let the record show that all persons present prior to recess are now present." Major Walsh then called on each of the defendants individually and showed them the stipulation, which had been written in both English and German. Each man verified his signature and the stipulations were entered as exhibits by the prosecution.

"At this time, may it please the court, the prosecution desires to call its first witness, 1st Lieutenant Thomas V. Jackson."

Lieutenant Jackson was the assistant post engineer at Papago Park. He had brought with him various plans and drawings of the POW camp at Papago Park as well as of certain buildings within the camp, which the prosecution wanted entered as exhibits. Floor plans of the barracks that Werner Drechsler lived in during his brief stay at Papago Park and the shower room where he died were received in evidence and marked as exhibits. The seven men sat through the testimony with no apparent interest as the actual scene of the crime was described for the court in laborious detail. Lieutenant Jackson's testimony lasted until 10:55, when he was excused by the court, which then took another five-minute recess. The defendants, under guard, left the room and outside talked among themselves about the trial. So little had occurred that there really wasn't much they could say; the trial seemed civilized enough, more so than they had expected, but their hopes as to its outcome were not by any means encouraged. Captain Schmidt came out into the hall and told them to put out their cigarettes because the court was being called back into session. The seven men looked at him with contempt but said nothing.

Major Walsh called the prosecution's second witness. "Will you state to the court your full name, rank, organization, and station?"

"Captain Cecil S. Parshall, Prisoner of War Camp, Papago Park, Arizona."

The seven men knew Captain Parshall from camp; they had not had much personal experience of him, but they were aware of his reputation as a strong yet fair military professional. Their most vivid recollection of him was on the morning of March 13. Although, for obvious reasons, they had made every effort to stay out of his way, the captain had seemed to appear everywhere they turned that morning in Compound 4.

"What are your duties there?" Major Walsh continued.

"At the present time, assistant director of internal security. and provost marshal."

"What were your duties on 12 and 13 March 1944?"

"Provost marshal, sir."

The defendants knew Captain Parshall was not a young man for his rank and that he had probably been around the military for quite some time, but they did not know how far from the ordinary he really was. Captain Parshall, born in Texas before the turn of the century, was, as he put it "two quarters Texan, one quarter German, and one quarter American Indian." He enlisted in the army and went to France with General John J. Pershing's American Expeditionary Force, assigned to the 1st brigade of the 1st Division. He fought through the bloody battles of Cantigny and the Marne and was awarded the Silver Star for bravery and two Purple Hearts—one when he was gassed in the front lines and the other when he was shot and wounded by a German officer whom he stopped to talk to.

Parshall reenlisted in the Army in the 1920s and was stationed on the Mexican border with the 1st Cavalry Division. On a three-month furlough in Mexico, he received a rather staggering promotion—from sergeant in the U.S. army to general in the army of a Mexican revolutionary leader named Escobar. On one of their sorties they captured a Mexican bank, which, according to Parshall, contained about $16 million in gold. Escobar quickly tired of the revolution and fled to Canada with most of the gold, and Parshall made his way back across the Rio Grande after putting his share, about $350,000, in a pouch and dropping it into a hiding place in the river. Reported to the U.S. authorities by the Mexican government, Parshall was court-martialed and received a five-year suspended sentence.

The U.S. army general who passed sentence told Parshall: "The army shouldn't turn away men who carry out their missions. I hope you reenlist." The next day Parshall did and, replete with a brand new 201 file, resumed his army career. Now, ironically enough, Parshall was testifying against seven men who were being tried for an action they felt was not only their mission but their national duty.

Later, Parshall served as an undercover agent for the army in the Canal Zone. Then, he left the army again and, on a forged Mexican passport to protect his U.S. citizenship, went to Spain to fight with the Loyalist forces up to and including the retreat from Guadalajara. Captain Parshall was indeed a man not unacquainted with court martials, military reasoning, or taking action on his own.

From his testimony and his bearing at the trial, however, no one would guess the diversity of his controversial background, least of all the seven defendants who listened intently to his testimony.

"Did anything unusual occur on 12 or 13 March 1944 that you remember?" Major Walsh asked.

"Yes, sir. On 13 March 1944, at approximately 6:45 in the morning, I was notified by Lieutenant Ginieres that there was trouble in Compound 4."

"What did you do then?"

"I immediately proceeded to Compound 4."

"What did you observe there?"

"I found a man hanging by the neck in the shower room proper. He was dressed in American issue of American underwear, shorts, and shirt. He was hanging by the neck by a tent rope looped three times, caught and fastened to the rafters of the bath house, one end around his neck as I recall it, facing east approximately twelve inches from the duck boards in the bathroom."

"Did you observe the condition of the body?"

"I did."

"Will you state exactly what you observed?"

"Tongue protruding through his teeth, lips slightly drawn back, his tongue swollen several times its size and black, multiple bruises about the head and body."

The seven defendants were unmoved by the description, though they appeared to be listening with interest. On one occasion, Helmut Fischer whispered a question to the interpreter, Private Gruenebaum, as to why they were going into this in such lucid detail. The interpreter passed the question on to their counsel, who scribbled a brief note, "It's just routine," and passed it back to Private Gruenebaum.

Captain Parshall identified the rope used in the hanging, and it was placed in evidence by the prosecution. Then the captain proceeded to explain to the court that he did not cut down the body and that he placed a guard on the shower room with instructions not to let anyone enter until the camp's commanding officer arrived. After that, he went directly to Werner Drechsler's barracks.

"When you arrived at the barracks building, what did you observe?"

"I entered the building from the north entrance—the building faces north and south—as I entered I found a pool of blood smeared approximately two and one-half feet in diameter in the middle of the aisle opposite the second cot on the end."

The barracks were empty, Captain Parshall went on to explain, because the prisoners had already gone about their day's duties. He placed a guard on that building as well and then left the immediate area.

On cross-examination, the defense had only two questions—to establish the facts that Captain Parshall could not positively identify the rope that was entered as an exhibit and that he could not swear that the blood he observed on the floor came from any one individual.

The prosecution then called Captain Leland Hebblewaithe to the stand. The court martial, which had been progressing rapidly, with few objections and interruptions, had been tediously routine. The appearance of Captain Hebblewaithe, Papago Park's classification and identification officer, did not portend any great enlivenment of the proceedings. His purpose was simply to prove that the man killed was Werner Drechsler and was correctly identified. Captain Hebblewaithe related to the court how he had taken charge of and classified 350 new prisoners on March 12, and that, according to his records, Werner Drechsler was one of them, although he could not remember personally processing him through, any more than he could remember any other individual prisoner he had classified that day. Drechsler's Form No. 2, his personnel record with a photograph and fingerprints, was introduced and marked as an exhibit.

It was nearing the lunch hour, and most of the seven defendants listened apathetically as Captain Hebblewaithe's testimony droned on. Helmut Fischer appeared to be the most acutely interested of the seven, and Rolf Wizuy and Otto Stengel displayed a rather tense nervousness. The other four showed little feeling one way or the other. Even the prosecutor, Major Walsh, was beginning to show signs of the weight of the tedious pace of the trial, but he continued his methodical probing.

"Did you see Werner Drechsler again that day?"

"I did not."

"When did you next see him again, if at all?"

"About 07:00 on the morning of the 13th of March 1944, Major McIndoo . . ."

"I don't want to know about anyone else. I asked you when you next saw German Prisoner of War Werner Drechsler."

"Approximately 07:30, March 13, 1944, hanging in the barracks in Compound 4."

Major Walsh took a few steps away from the witness and turned to face the defendants. He gazed at them absently for a few moments but continued to ask questions of the witness. Then he turned abruptly back to the witness: "State to the court what you first did after you arrived."

"First thing, I took the photograph of the body hanging on the second rafter, about three or four feet from the wall. I took three shots at different angles."

"I asked you what you did first."

"Took the photographs, sir."

"Captain, I hand you prosecution's exhibit 12 and ask you to state to the court what it is."

"It is the body of prisoner Drechsler suspended from the rafter."

"That is not the body."

Captain Hebblewaithe, with a noticeable wave of exasperation, corrected himself. "That is a picture of the body."

After Captain Hebblewaithe testified as to how he and a sergeant from the medical corps cut down Drechsler's body and had it sent out of the compound in an ambulance, Colonel Poust interrupted the questioning to recess for lunch.

It was after lunch that Captain Hebblewaithe would reveal under cross-examination that he knew a little bit more about Werner Drechsler than appeared to be the case from the meager amount of information in Drechsler's file. The court reconvened at 1:30 P.M., and Captain Hebblewaithe was recalled to the stand. He was still under examination by the prosecution, but Major Walsh wrapped up his questioning quickly after the captain gave the court a grimly graphic description of Drechsler's body.

"The right side of his face was bruised and from all indications, his nose from the righthand side was broken. He had bad bruises on the left side and his testicles were practically beaten to a pulp."

The defense counsel approached the witness stand and began a routine probing of Captain Hebblewaithe, mostly in regard to the credibility of the captain's identification of the rope used to hang Drechsler. Then he suddenly changed his tack.

"You did have some knowledge or information on prisoner Werner Drechsler before the date of the hanging, did you not?"

"I did, sir."

"What type of information?"

"In checking the Form 2s to make out the roster when these men arrived and for that entire group, the roster was made out prior to Monday morning."

"What was this group that you got in? What was their history, do you know?"

"I had never seen them before they came in. I was only accountable for making out their roster and the information I had on the Form 2 assigning them to the camp."

Major Taylor paused, glanced quickly over at the court martial board, and then bore down on Captain Hebblewaithe. "Had you ever seen Drechsler at another camp?"

"I had never seen Drechsler before, sir."

"Do you know whether or not he had ever aided the United States in giving information?"

"I heard that later, sir."

Major Walsh, who had been staring down at the pad of yellow paper on the table in front of him, looked up at the witness, and then leaned over to whisper something to his assistant prosecutor, Captain Hillis.

"What did you hear?" Major Taylor continued.

"I heard that he aided in getting information for the authorities."

"Were you present at any time at an interrogation camp in Washington?"

"Yes, I was, sir."

"At that time did you question any of the accused here before this court?"

Captain Hebblewaithe looked over at the defendants and slowly shook his head. "Not to my knowledge."

"Did you know the deceased, Prisoner of War Drechsler, at that time?"

"No."

"Did you make a remark to another officer at the time you heard of the hanging of Prisoner of War Werner Drechsler, that he had done the American government a lot of good?"

Major Walsh rose from his chair. "Objection on the ground that it is incompetent, irrelevant, and immaterial."

The law member of the court, Colonel Poust, turned to the defense counsel, "Was that after the deceased had been hung?"

"Immediately after the hanging."

"In what way would his conversation after the commission of the crime be competent?"

"It might have some bearing on the status of Drechsler as a traitor."

Colonel Poust cocked his head slightly and ended this line of questioning abruptly. "Objection sustained."

The competency of the testimony in regard to the trial at hand was a legal question that, in light of its presentation, probably was ruled on properly by the president of the court martial board, but it was a starkly significant revelation that the army authorities, even some at Papago Park, were not nearly so ignorant of Werner Drechsler's past history and affiliations as one might be led to believe by their choice in assigning him to Compound 4 at Papago Park prisoner-of-war camp. And Captain Hebblewaithe admitted knowing it at about seven o'clock on the morning of March 13, approximately fifteen minutes after the body had been discovered.

At a few minutes before two o'clock, Captain Hebblewaithe stepped down, and the prosecution called its next witness, Sergeant Fred R. Bornstein. The sergeant had been in charge of the ambulance detail that had picked up Werner Drechsler on the day of his death and delivered him to Compound 4. Bornstein related briefly his conversations with Drechsler in the ambulance and then told the court of his activities the next morning, which mainly consisted of helping Captain Hebblewaithe in cutting down the body and later transporting it to a mortuary in Phoenix. All in all, Sergeant Bornstein had little to add to the previous testimony, and the court martial lapsed back into the dreariness of routine.

Major Walsh's next witness was Captain Claude C. Stafford, the medical corps officer who had performed an autopsy on Drechsler's body on March 13, to determine the cause of death. Captain Stafford had left his surgery practice in Pismo Beach, California, in September, 1942, to join the army and had ended up as chief of surgical service at Papago Park. He explained to the court that he had been ordered to conduct an autopsy that Monday afternoon and had done so at a mortuary in Phoenix. He submitted a copy of the autopsy findings, which were entered as a prosecution exhibit. The findings provide a good description of Werner Drechsler as well as his battered condition, unnerving perhaps in its dramatic use of the present tense, but obviously beneficial to the court for its purposes.

REPORT OF AUTOPSY, 13 MARCH 1944
DECEASED: Werner Max Henry Drechsler, Cpl, ISN-5G-61-NA, German Prisoner of War.

Well developed and well nourished white young male. His face is covered with blood. His tongue is markedly swollen, and the anterior portion protrudes from the mouth. There are multiple bruises throughout his face and nose. His nose is fractured. There are bruises over an upper portion of his right shoulder. There are multiple bruises on his back and right upper thorax. Ante-mortem skin burns completely encircle his neck in three well marked rings. There are lacerations of fingers, left hand, dirt is ground into lacerations. There are bruises on his scrotum. Multiple knotty swellings on both legs below knees, indicating severe ante-mortem blows. Post-mortem pendant blueness on both legs and feet. No gross evidence of fracture, except on nose. Muscles are large and well developed. There is evidence of bruises on scalp by subaponeurotic hematomas. Both lungs are normal, there is no excess fluid in the thorax. Liver, heart, stomach intestines (color), spleen and both kidneys normal in size, weight and texture. Diffuse, soft swelling on entire anterior neck. Superficial veins of brain are congested. No evidence of skull fracture; no fracture of neck. Appendix was fibriotic with fecolith 1½ cc from tip.

DIAGNOSIS:
1. Strangulation
2. Bruises, multiple, generalized
3. Fracture, simple, complete, nasal alae

At 2:25 P.M., Colonel Poust recessed the court for five minutes. Captain Stafford, who had completed his testimony, left the courtroom; the others filed out into the hall, with the exception of the seven defendants, who were led into a waiting room off to the side.

When the members of the court resumed their seats, the prosecution called the last of its medical witnesses, Captain Max Marks. He had briefly examined Drechsler's body while it was still hanging from the rafter in Compound 4 and had later assisted Captain Stafford in the autopsy. His testimony was basically a corroboration of Captain Stafford's findings, not contested by the defense.

The continued descriptions of the body, in all their grisly detail, appeared to have little effect on the seven defendants, who seemed outwardly unmoved by the testimony.

The next witness for the prosecution brought a sign of recognition from the seven defendants, a remembrance of difficult days that were far from happy, but it ignited an interest in them that had been nonexistent during the preceding portion of the trial. The witness was Lieutenant Colonel Gerald L. Church, who headed the investigating team that had broken open the Drechsler case and produced signed confessions from all seven defendants. Since January 1, 1944, Colonel Church had served as chief of the intelligence branch of the Ninth Service Command's Security Intelligence Division. On March 29, Colonel Church, on orders from the commanding general of the Ninth Service Command at Fort Douglas, Utah, convened an investigative board consisting of himself, Major Herman Zabel, and the prosecutor, Major Walsh, to unravel the Drechsler murder case. A solution had eluded two investigating bodies before them, but in a little over two months from the day the board began its investigation, the case was solved.

The entire case of the prosecution rested on the weight of the statements that Colonel Church's board had produced and the defense based a good portion of its case on the methods used to gain them.

As Colonel Church took the witness stand, the eyes of all seven defendants followed him. Major Walsh's questions were well planned and methodically presented to achieve the maximum effect of this tremendously important part of his case. He first established the authority and jurisdiction of the investigating board in the Drechsler case and then plunged directly into the investigation itself.

"In your investigation of that occurrence, did you interrogate certain German prisoners of war?"

"The board did, yes."

"Where was that investigation conducted?"

"You mean all the places the board went?"

"Where did you first begin your interrogation?"

"Papago Park."

"Colonel, I wish you would, independently of me or any suggestion from me, examine this courtroom. Look around you and see if there is, in the courtroom now, any of the individuals whom you interrogated during the course of your investigation."

The colonel looked slowly around the courtroom; his eyes paused on the seven young Germans and then returned quickly to the face of the prosecutor. "Yes, sir. There are."

"Can you tell this court who the individuals are to whom you just referred?" Colonel Church said that he could, and Major Walsh continued. "I wish that you would do so. Point them out to the court, giving the court their names."

Colonel Church stood up from the witness stand and walked over to the table where the seven defendants sat. He pointed at each one individually, and as he did, he rattled off their names crisply: "Fischer, Franke, Kuelsen, Ludwig, Reyak, Stengel, and Wizuy."

Major Walsh motioned for him to return tò the witness stand and then continued his questioning.

"Did you interrogate them yourself?"

"Some of them. I had better explain. They appeared before the board as witnesses and some of the questions were asked by me personally."

"When these men—for instance, Fischer—came before the board, did you tell him anything before he testified?"

"Yes, I did. He was first advised through an interpreter that he was being called as a witness before the board, was warned of his rights under the 24th Article of War."

Colonel Church paused and shifted slightly in his chair. "The 24th Article of War was first read to him in English and was translated by the interpreter; then the board questioned him to ascertain if he understood the meaning of the article. After being so advised, he was sworn as a witness."

"He testified before the board thereafter?"

"Yes."

"After the accused Fischer testified before the board, what developed?"

"After he testified, I told him in English, which was translated into German by the interpreter, that I was going to give him a pad of paper, a pen, and ink; that I wanted him to go to his room and write out the story he had just told the board, substantially as he had told the board, including all of the facts and circumstances within his knowledge, also including dates and times and places concerning the murder of Werner Drechsler. I told him to first date the paper on the first page and start it out something like this: 'This is the statement of Helmut Fischer, German naval serial number, prisoner of war serial number, concerning the hanging of Werner Drechsler.' Then I told him to number his pages consecutively and when he had finished to sign the statement."

Colonel Church spoke clearly and rapidly; his answers, well thought out beforehand, were clearly to the point.

"What did he do then?"

"He went up to his room with the pen and ink and paper and later came before the board again with the signed statement."

"Who was with him in his room, if you know?"

"He was conducted out of the room where he was being interrogated by a guard. The guard was instructed in his presence to take him to his room, see that he had pen and ink and paper. I did not see him write it myself."

"Do you recall when it was you next saw him?"

"The 9th of June 1944."

"Do you recall the date when you gave the accused, Fischer, pen and ink?"

"The 8th of June 1944."

"On the 9th of June 1944, did the accused, Helmut Fischer, give you anything?"

"He gave me a statement, written in the German language."

"What did you do with the German language statement?"

Helmut Fischer was listening intently to the proceedings, picking up much of it in English but also paying close attention to the interpreter's translation, as if he did not want to miss a single word.

"I first . . ." Colonel Church began, then paused and looked over at the members of the court martial board. "Incidentally the board was in session when he came in with the statement and he was reminded he was still under oath as a witness and reminded again of his rights under the 24th Article of War. Then he presented his statement. He was questioned as to whether or not it was his statement in his own handwriting and if that was his signature. He answered in the affirmative to both questions. Then he was asked if he minded appending a statement to it, the gist of which was that it was a free and voluntary statement concerning the murder of Werner Drechsler. He objected to the term 'prisoner of war' Werner Drechsler and insisted that it be changed to 'traitor' Drechsler. I told him through the interpreter that it was his statement and he could put anything in it he wished. That was done and he signed the statement and it was received by the board."

The other six defendants looked at Fischer with expressions of obvious pleasure when they heard his correction of Drechsler's title read into the record, but Fischer never took his eyes from the witness stand and was unaware of their silent acknowledgment.

"Did you witness the signature of Helmut Fischer to that document."

"Yes."

"Did anyone else?"

"Major Zabel and Sergeant Donohue."

"Was a translation made of the German statement of the accused, Fischer, at your direction?"

"It was, by the official interpreter for the board, Sergeant Blank."

"I hand you an item marked prosecution's exhibit number 20 and ask you what it is."

"It's the statement of Helmut Fischer about which I have already testified."

Major Walsh paused, then began anew with the exact line of questioning in regard to defendant Fritz Franke. Colonel Church's answers were almost identical with his preceding testimony. The same line was followed for Guenther Kuelsen and Bernhard Reyak, and then Colonel Poust called with a five-minute recess.

At 3:30 P.M. the court reconvened and Colonel Church, reminded that he was still under oath, took the witness stand again. The questions were now presented in regard to Otto Stengel and brought much the same answers from Colonel Church, with one or two notable exceptions.

For example, Colonel Church said, "Prisoner of War Stengel testified more than once before the board."

"Did the accused, Otto Stengel, testify to the same facts on each occasion he appeared before the board?" Major Walsh asked.

"No, sir."

Colonel Church then testified that Stengel went off to write his confession after his last appearance before the board. The date the board received the signed statement, was June 7, two days earlier than the preceding four statements were received, one day earlier than they were written, and actually five days after it had been written.

The testimony in regard to the two remaining accused, Heinrich Ludwig and Rolf Wizuy, was routine, although they, too, had signed their confessions earlier, June 3, the day after Stengel signed his.

Major Walsh ended his questioning of the witness with a general question, the answer to which was to introduce a series of enigmas about the military security in the case, that would weave through the remainder of the trial and for all intents and purposes remain unresolved when the court martial was finished.

"Colonel, where were these exhibits, numbers 20 through 26 inclusive, received by the board?"

"At a secret military installation in the state of California," the Colonel answered.

Major Walsh then turned the witness over to the defense for cross-examination. Major Taylor took a last quick look at his notes before approaching the witness. From the testimony just given, it all appeared very simple, a neat and orderly package with no frayed or ragged edges. The suspect appeared before the investigating board, was informed of his rights; confessed, went off to write a statement of confession, appended to it a paragraph disclaiming that any coercion was used to obtain the confession, signed it, and then was led back to await his trial. All this did occur, but the problem was that it was not such a smooth and clean operation; in fact, the package was seriously marred with an overall tawdriness that even the classifications of wartime secrecy could not completely conceal. It was the task of the defense to put the package in proper perspective, and Major Taylor was aware that much of his case depended on the validity and voluntary nature of the statements that each of his clients had signed.

"Colonel, were the accused who stand before this court interrogated at any time and any place prior to the time you mentioned they appeared before your board?"

"The board interrogated part of them previously."

"By part of them, to which ones do you refer?"

"Otto Stengel, Rolf Wizuy, Heinrich Ludwig."

"In the previous interrogation you refer to in which these

three were interrogated, were any other prisoners of war who are not now here as accused interrogated?"

"Many others, yes."

"A total of about how many were interrogated altogether?"

"It will have to be an estimate, but I believe between 150 and 200 persons—not all prisoners of war."

"Over approximately what period of time did the interrogation of this large number of witnesses run?"

"About two and a half months."

"To start with, did you have or the board have any evidence as to anyone being involved in the crime?"

"No."

"Were any of the accused here and present interrogated by any other officer or person outside of your own board?"

Major Walsh objected to the question on the grounds that it was not proper cross-examination concerning the matter that had been developed on direct examination, and the objection was sustained by Colonel Poust.

The defense counsel then addressed the court martial board directly, facing Colonel Poust but pointing at the prosecutor. "He has definitely opened the scope of investigation insofar as he said this board was appointed to investigate charges of a crime which was committed. I am merely going further into the background of this investigation to show just how these confessions arose."

"The questions are objectionable," Colonel Poust answered. "Objection sustained. You will find other interrogatory means."

Major Taylor returned to the witness. "Can you testify as to the date that is on the statement?"

"I can testify as to the date that is on the statement."

"What is the date on the statement?"

"Objection," Major Walsh said quickly, "on the ground that the statement itself is the best evidence."

"Objection overruled." Colonel Poust nodded toward the defense counsel to proceed with the questioning.

"When did he appear before your board?"

"On June 2nd, 1944."

"That is the date he prepared the statement?"

"That is the date which the statement bears. I did not receive the statement from Prisoner of War Stengel himself."

"On how many occasions did the board of investigators interrogate Prisoner of War Otto Stengel?"

"Probably a dozen times. That is an estimate."

"How did the board arrive at a point where statements were asked of the seven accused whom you have testified statements were made by?"

The immediate objection of the prosecution was sustained with equal immediacy.

"In what manner did the board eliminate some hundred other witnesses from the proceedings at the time these . . ."

"Objection."

"Sustained."

The two counsels continued to test and argue the line of questioning, with Colonel Poust as arbitrator, but Major Taylor finally succeeded in at least getting to certain volatile questions with the court's approval.

"To your knowledge, had accused Prisoner of War Stengel been questioned prior to the time he made the statement that he wished to confess?"

"Yes, sir."

"To your knowledge, had coercion or violence ever been used?"

"Not within my presence."

"Do you have any information as to the use of coercion outside of your presence?"

"I have some information."

"Would you tell the court at this time what that information is?"

Colonel Church paused. "He had been interrogated at considerable length by other persons than the board."

"Do you know what individual did the interrogating you have spoken of?"

"Objection. The line of questioning is not proper examination."

Colonel Poust looked from the prosecutor's table to the witness stand. "Objection overruled. Colonel Church, pay strict attention to the questions. Don't presume to hearsay or anything of the sort. If you can't answer it of your own knowledge, say so."

"I cannot answer of my own knowledge," Colonel Church said, speaking directly to the court martial board president.

The defense began again. "Do you know of the methods used in the interrogation you have referred to?"

"I cannot answer that of my own knowledge. But there is something that occurred to me. May I tell it now?"

Before the defense could answer, however, Colonel Poust addressed the witness. "If you were present, you may testify what was said and done in your presence but the court does not want hearsay or secondhand information."

The witness nodded his head in agreement. "Three of the defendants were, I guess you would call it, interrogated. If I may describe it to the court?"

Colonel Poust again interjected, "First, give the time and place and who was present."

"It was at Papago Park during the latter part of April and the first part of May 1944. The examination was conducted by Leonard Keeler, the lie detector expert, at which time the lie detector was applied to three of the defendants at various times and questions were asked them."

"In your presence?" Colonel Poust asked.

"In my presence."

There was a pause, but Colonel Poust did not continue his questioning from the bench. Then, the defense counsel went back to his original line of inquiry: "The first statement obtained from the seven accused who are present in this court was that of Otto Stengel, was it not?"

"Yes, that's right."

Colonel Poust interrupted again and spoke directly to the defense counsel. "Are you talking about prosecution's exhibit number 24?"

"Yes," Major Taylor answered and then turned back to the witness. "Were any questions asked any of the other six accused which were based upon the fact that Otto Stengel had already signed the statement he made?"

The prosecution objected on the grounds that the question should be confined to a particular individual and not refer to a group, and the objection was sustained.

"In the hearing which you have testified was conducted on the eighth of June, at which time the majority of the accused were questioned as witnesses, was the statement made by the accused Stengel in any way made the basis for questioning."

"The objection was sustained," Colonel Poust said wearily before the witness could answer.

Major Taylor, however, continued this line of questioning until the defense, for some unknown reason, firmly established in Colonel Church's testimony that Otto Stengel's confession was *not* used as a basis for inducing the other six defendants to confess. Colonel Church, in fact, summed it up flatly with his last answer before the court recessed: "I don't recall a single statement that was used in that way. To the best of my recollection one of the accused stated that he would advise the others that he had already confessed but the board declined his offer."

At 4:30 P.M. the court was called back in session, but the defense had no further questions to ask Colonel Church, who then was excused and left the courtroom. The prosecution swore in its next witness, Major Herman J. Zabel, Colonel Church's assistant in the investigation. Major Zabel, a stern and rugged army career man, had been born in Germany and still spoke with a pronounced German accent. The seven defendants stared sullenly at him as he sat in the witness chair.

Major Zabel was walked through the same identification

procedure as Colonel Church; he stepped to the defendant's table and pointed out each man by name, testifying that he had participated in the interrogation of them as a member of Colonel Church's investigating team. The questioning of Major Zabel was essentially a substantiation of the preceding testimony of Colonel Church and was apparently designed for nothing beyond that. Before Major Zabel had completed his testimony, however, Colonel Poust recessed the court for supper, informing all present in the courtroom that the trial would reconvene at 7:00 P.M. that evening.

The prisoners were taken back to their cells, fed, and given a few minutes to themselves. Then they were returned to the court. It had been a long day and the strain was beginning to show in their faces as they were silently led back into the courtroom.

Major Zabel resumed his seat on the witness stand and testified particularly to his role in appending the "free, voluntary, and without coercion" clause in the statements of the seven men. It was Major Zabel who had ghost-authored the clause for the first man to confess, Otto Stengel, and then had it translated into German for the prisoner to sign. Later, he performed the same service for Heinrich Ludwig. The major was then turned over to the defense for cross-examination.

"Had Prisoner of War Stengel been examined by the same board prior to the time he made the statement?" Major Taylor asked.

"He had."

"On how many occasions?"

"About five or six times during the investigation."

"To your knowledge, was he examined on any occasion other than when you, as a member of the board, were present?"

"I couldn't answer that. I would not know."

The defense then asked the same questions in regard to the

defendant Heinrich Ludwig and received identical answers
from Major Zabel.

"Did Stengel make reference to you, at the time he signed
the certificate, of any coercive action taken against him personally by anyone?"

"He did not."

Otto Stengel shifted uncomfortably in his seat but continued
to look straight at the witness.

"Do you know of any coercive methods used upon him or
any of the other prisoners?"

"I do not," Major Zabel answered quickly, too quickly
in fact to be stopped by the prosecution's objection to the
question.

"He answered it," Colonel Poust said, shaking his head.
"Let the answer stand."

Major Zabel was then replaced on the witness stand by
Sergeant Carl F. Blank, who had served as the official interpreter of the interrogation board. Sergeant Blank, through
a tedious and repetitive line of questioning, testified to the
authenticity of the statements of the seven defendants and to
his official translation of them at the order of Colonel Church.
When he finished, the defense waived cross-examination.

Major Walsh then addressed the bench: "May it please the
court, we have a witness flying in from Fort Douglas and
just received a telephone call from him. His plane was late
and he just arrived in Phoenix. I doubt that he will be down
here for two hours. With that witness and a short statement
from myself, the prosecution will rest."

"What about your statements?" Colonel Poust asked.
"Do you intend to introduce them in evidence?"

"We will make that offer at this time with the understanding that we will have supporting proof in evidence from the
witness from Fort Douglas."

The statements were then introduced individually and admitted into evidence by the president of the court martial

board. Each statement was read in English to the court. At 9:00 P.M. the court adjourned until 8:30 the following morning.

The seven defendants carried the burden of the day back to their cells and wondered just what would happen now. They were sure that they would be found guilty of the crime; it was the sentence that now occupied all of their thoughts. Their fate, they knew, would be decided on that singular issue.

11

Military Confessions

THE seven young German defendants were returned under guard to their cells in the maximum security section of the stockade at the Florence POW camp. Although they had done nothing but sit all day, they were exhausted, but between the sweltering heat of Arizona in August and the pressures of the court, the night of August 15 offered little enticement to sleep. The men who were segregated, each having his own cell, still could talk to each other. They all seemed to prefer, however, to be left alone, each with his own solitary thoughts of the trial and the sometimes hopeful, sometimes hopeless, speculations as to how it would all turn out.

The night was not much better for the attorneys; both the prosecution and defense had to prepare themselves for the next day in court as well as to assess what had already occurred. The lights in their quarters remained on well into the morning hours. When the prosecutor, Francis Walsh, finally did make it to bed, he slept soundly until the alarm clock roused him a few hours later, at six in the morning.

Outside of the grim atmosphere of Florence, the outlook for other Germans was not especially bright either. General Omar Bradley's armies had broken out of Normandy and were advancing into France. To the north, Field Marshal Bernard Montgomery's command, composed of British and Canadian troops, had surged out of Caen, where they had been pinned down, and were now converging on the German armies, which were retreating all along the western front. In the south, Rome had fallen to the combined forces of the United States and Canada and what was left of the German defenses had withdrawn into the Italian mountains. The Russian army on the eastern front was already at the border of East Prussia, and Rumania was only days away from capitulating to Russia. In Germany itself, the Stauffenburg plot on Hitler's life had been a dismal failure, and Hitler was still secure in his power but the people, under the constant and horrendous bombings of the Allied air forces, were becoming deeply demoralized and were feeling the first sure tremors of the German collapse. Even thousands of miles away and behind the barbed wire of an Arizona POW camp, the seven defendants had begun to sense the faltering of the German spirit in their homeland although they were loath to admit it. Guenther Kuelsen tried to buoy the flagging spirits of his family in a warm letter to his parents, written June 1, the day before Otto Stengel had confessed all of the details of the murder of Werner Drechsler.

Dear Parents,

Many thanks for your lovely letter with pictures, which I received today. It really made me very happy. I also received the packages, for which many thanks also—they arrived in good shape. As for Erich [Kuelsen's younger brother] being called up, I hope that he likes the training. Perhaps he will even enjoy it.

As for our morale, it is just as you say in your letter—as it was on the first day. We have confidence and *depend on you*. I have no special wishes now, only pictures of you and time off here to write.

My very best to all of you, yours,
Guenther

But as the morning sun moved into the sky over Florence on August 16, the morale of Guenther Kuelsen and his six comrades was a good deal worse than it was when they were first captured. Not that they were yielding in the steadfastness of their loyalty or of the beliefs in the honor and nobility of the duty they had carried out for their country by disposing of Werner Drechsler; on this they did not falter once. But their situation was not good, and they knew it.

They were awakened by an American guard at 5:30 A.M., and they slowly dressed in the same blue fatigues they had worn the day before and pulled on their heavy work boots. Breakfast was brought to each one in his cell at six, and at eight o'clock Major Pickard and a detail of guards arrived to lead them back to the courtroom.

The prosecution's witness, who had been flown in from Fort Douglas, was First Lieutenant Harry A. Baldwin, the officer appointed in early July, 1944, to carry out the investigation preparatory to placing charges against the seven defendants. He was a member of the same Judge Advocate General office as Major Walsh.

Colonel Poust called the court to order at 8:30 and noted for the record that all persons present at adjournment the day before were again present. Lieutenant Baldwin was sworn in as the first witness of the day and took his seat in the witness stand, facing Major Walsh.

"Lieutenant Baldwin, do you know the accused Helmut Fischer?" Major Walsh asked.

"I do, sir."

"Will you look around the court and, if he is present, point him out."

The lieutenant looked over at the defendants and pointed to the young man sitting at the right end of the defense table. "This is he."

"Is the accused Helmut Fischer one of the men who was included in your investigation?"

"Yes, sir."

"Will you state the circumstances under which you investigated Prisoner of War Helmut Fischer and the time and place?"

"I proceeded to the Rehabilitation Center at Turlock, California, on or about July 4, 1944, in connection with the investigation of the German prisoners of war."

"What did you do there?"

Lieutenant Baldwin did not answer immediately. He sat forward slightly in his chair and looked absently beyond the prosecutor, as if to gather his thoughts and put them into a logical sequence. Then he began. "I there examined Prisoner of War Fischer and stated to him that I was the investigating officer detailed to make the investigation in connection with the death of a German prisoner of war which occurred at Papago Park on or about 12 or 13 March 1944. I explained to Fischer that under the Articles of War, particularly the 70th Article of War, a thorough and impartial investigation was required prior to trial. I explained that as a German prisoner of war he was entitled to the protection of the Articles of War. I further explained that I was not the prosecution but that on the other hand I was not his counsel." The lieutenant paused but it was obvious he was not finished.

The members of the court martial board appeared to be listening intently to the lieutenant's narrative, more so than the seven defendants, who displayed changing attitudes of anticipation and boredom, mostly boredom.

The lieutenant continued: "I stated that I was not interested in securing military information. I then read to Fischer the charge and specification charging him and six other German prisoners of war with murder. I read the name of the accuser, the names of the witnesses against him. I then read and explained to him the 70th Article of War. I stated that under the 70th Article of War an impartial investigation was required before trial, that under the 70th Article of War he had certain rights. He was entitled to question the witnesses against him if they were available. I stated he could make a statement if he desired in any form he wished, either in extenuation or mitigation, that such a statement might be used against him. I told him that at that time he could remain silent. I then asked him to explain to me what he understood by my explanation to him. I then read and explained to him Article of War 24 and then asked him to explain Article of War 24 if he understood it."

Lieutenant Baldwin also testified to the presence at the investigation of an interpreter, Staff Sergeant Paul Held, who translated the entire proceedings for the accused and the investigator. Major Walsh introduced as evidence, and without objection from the defense, the official report of Lieutenant Baldwin's investigation, which was then entered as a prosecution exhibit. The same line of questioning and testimony was repeated with regard to each of the other six defendants, and the whole procedure kept Lieutenant Baldwin on the stand for the prosecution for about forty minutes. Then Major Walsh turned the witness over to the defense for cross-examination.

Major Taylor had only two questions for the witness.

"Lieutenant, is it a fact that during the course of, or after, your conference and investigation of Prisoner of War and accused, Guenther Kuelsen, on or about July 4, 1944, he desired to make an additional statement?"

"The statement was recorded."

"Is it not a fact that he desired to add to his statement as recorded, a statement to the effect that anyone would have to be on a sinking submarine to know the attitude of such a person toward a traitor who divulged military information to the enemy?"

"As I recall it, he desired to make such a statement and it was recorded."

Major Walsh then took the witness stand himself and under questioning by his assistant prosecutor, Captain Hillis, testified to the fact and circumstances of his serving the charges on the seven defendants. The charges had been served individually on each in the presence of the defense counsel and an interpreter. Each defendant had been asked to sign an acknowledgment, written in both German and English, to the effect that he had been advised of his rights under paragraph 1, Article 62, of the Geneva Convention, which provides that the accused has the right to qualified counsel of his own choice as well as the services of a qualified interpreter. The signed acknowledgments were then introduced as evidence and marked for prosecution exhibits. Then the prosecution read aloud to the court the seven reports of the investigations conducted by Lieutenant Baldwin.

At 11:00 A.M. the prosecution rested its case.

Major Taylor rose from his chair and addressed the president of the court martial board. "At this time the defense moves for a recess until 1:30 this afternoon."

Colonel Poust nodded. "We will now recess until 1:30 this afternoon. All persons are again reminded that this is a secret proceeding."

When the court martial reconvened after lunch, Major Taylor waived an opening statement to the court and called his first witness, Staff Sergeant Paul Held. The case for the defense was to be built around only two witnesses and the testimony of three of the defendants — Otto Stengel, Helmut Fischer and Rolf Wizuy — in the form of unsworn statements.

The sole objective of the defense was to discredit the legality of the seven confessions.

Sergeant Held took his seat on the witness stand. Major Taylor stood before him, ready to begin the case for the defense.

"Will you state to the court your name, grade, organization, and station?"

"Paul Held, staff sergeant. I cannot reveal my organization by order of the War Department. I am sworn to secrecy."

"Sergeant what were your duties on or about May 31st and June 1st, 1944?"

"Sir, I was an interpreter."

"Where were you assigned?"

"I was working at a prisoner of war processing station and besides that at a secret installation which I cannot reveal."

"Were you assigned especially to any board of officers or to any individual officers at that time?"

"I was assigned to a board of officers as interpreter."

"Who composed the board?"

"Colonel Church, Major Walsh, and Major Zabel."

"Were you present at the hearings for the purpose of interrogation of the suspected prisoners of war?"

"Yes, sir. Sometimes I acted in my capacity of interpreter."

"During the course of hearings and interrogations, were you present at the interrogation of Prisoner of War Otto Stengel?"

"I was for a very short while but I interpreted all the board procedure, sir."

"Do you recognize Prisoner of War Stengel as being present in the court?"

"Yes, sir. He is the second from the left," the sergeant said, as he pointed at Otto Stengel.

"Were you present at an interrogation of Prisoner of War Otto Stengel on or about June 1st, 1944?"

"Yes, sir. I was."

"At that time what officer conducted the interrogation?"

"One of the officers of the board. I could not remember his name."

"Were you present when Captain Schmidt conducted the interrogation?"

Major Walsh looked up quickly. "Objection on the ground that it is a leading question."

Colonel Poust directed his answer to the defense counsel rather than Major Walsh. "Objection sustained. Assuming that Captain Schmidt did some investigation and some questioning, first ask if he did any and then inquire into it."

"Did Captain Schmidt conduct any interrogation at which you were present?"

"Same objection," the prosecutor interjected.

"Objection overruled." Colonel Poust nodded to the witness to answer the question.

"Yes, sir."

"As near as you can recall, on or about what date was that?"

"I can't remember the date, sir."

"At that interrogation, who was present besides yourself and Captain Schmidt?"

"Nobody else."

"Aside from interrogations, what other means were used in questioning Prisoner of War Stengel?"

"Nothing as far as I can remember, sir. I was only there for a very short time."

"Did you leave the interrogation before Prisoner of War Stengel and Captain Schmidt left?"

"No, sir. I came in at the end. Very late in the evening, around 9:30."

Sergeant Held was not proving to be a tremendously cooperative witness, but at the same time he was caught up in a conflict. He had been sworn to secrecy in regard to his

function and the actual methods involved with wartime interrogations, and he was being asked under oath questions
that could have a bearing on the life or death of seven
young men. The court martial board could not, at least
did not, require him to reveal those things that had been
classified secret for reasons of national security, even if they
did have direct bearing on the trial at hand.

"Do you know how long Captain Schmidt had been with
Prisoner of War Stengel?" Major Taylor continued.

"I could not say."

"Did you notice anything about the manner of Prisoner
of War Stengel's being dressed?"

"I remember, sir, that he had an overcoat."

"An overcoat, what was the temperature of the weather
at that time?"

"Very cool, sir."

"Was the heat on in the room?"

"No, sir."

"Did you notice whether or not Prisoner of War Stengel
was sweating?"

"I don't remember, sir."

"Did you see any third degree methods used while you
were there?"

"No, sir."

"Did you hear of any third degree methods being used?"

"No, sir."

Major Walsh stood up behind the prosecution's table.
"May it please the court, at this time I am going to object
to the line of examination. It appears this is an attack on
confessions already introduced in evidence. If that is the
purpose at this time, it is highly improper."

Colonel Poust overruled the objection.

"How long were you present on the occasion near June 1
at which time Prisoner of War Stengel and Captain Schmidt
were present?"

"Approximately fifteen minutes."

"Did you have any knowledge of when Prisoner of War Stengel went to this interrogation?"

"I do not know, sir."

"Were you waiting outside the room in which the interrogation was made?"

Major Walsh objected to the question, and Colonel Poust turned to the defense counsel. "Try not to ask leading questions. He is your witness."

"Where were you, sergeant, prior to going to the place where this interrogation was held?"

"I don't remember. Probably in an office or some place else."

"How did you obtain information which called you to this interrogation?"

"It is very hard to tell. Maybe I passed the room. I don't remember."

"Did you receive an order to report there?"

"No, sir."

"Did you go of your own volition?"

"Yes, sir."

"Why did you go?"

"I don't remember."

The defense counsel turned his back on the witness and walked back to the table where his assistant, Major Furst, was sitting. He whispered briefly to his colleague and then returned to the witness.

"To your knowledge, was Captain Schmidt the interrogating officer at any other occasion than the one you testified to?"

"Yes, sir, the interrogation of Prisoner of War Fritz Franke, Prisoner of War Helmut Fischer, and Prisoner of War Rolf Wizuy."

"Were you present during the whole time the prisoners of war you mentioned were being interrogated?"

The sergeant shifted in his chair before answering. "Franke and Fischer—I was there all the time, in fact, as long as Captain Schmidt. Prisoner of War Wizuy—only a few minutes, maybe fifteen minutes."

"Did you in the case of the interrogation of Fischer at which you were present, observe any methods other than mere interrogation?"

"No, sir."

"How was Prisoner of War Fischer dressed at the time of his interrogation?"

"In his undershirt and shorts."

"Where was the interrogation held?"

"I referred to that in the beginning. I cannot reveal the identity of the place the interrogation was conducted."

Major Taylor did not appear to be getting too far with his witness in regard to the methods used in the interrogations, so he proceeded to another matter that reflected on the legality of the confessions.

"Referring again to the interrogations made of Prisoners of War Otto Stengel, Wizuy, Fischer, and Franke, were they warned of their rights under the Articles of War before being questioned or not?"

"Yes, under Article 24."

"Was this done in each case?"

"Yes, sir."

"Were you present when the interrogation of Otto Stengel started?"

"No. I don't know, sir, whether you refer now to the interrogations conducted by Captain Schmidt or by the board."

"I had referred to those conducted by Captain Schmidt."

"As I mentioned before, I was not there in the beginning with Prisoners of War Stengel and Wizuy."

"Could you say whether or not Prisoners of War Stengel and Wizuy had been warned of their rights?"

"I could not state so."

"In the case of Captain Schmidt's interrogation of Prisoners of War Franke and Fischer, were you present at the initial stage of the hearing?"

"No. I started to talk to these two men last mentioned myself. I did not draw their attention to Article 24, but it was done before the board. We had only an initial discussion but before each board discussion started, we talked at length in English and German, explanation and everything."

"In the interrogations at which you were present, when Captain Schmidt conducted the questioning of Prisoners of War Franke and Fischer, were the prisoners of war advised of their rights under the Articles of War?"

"Not in the beginning, sir."

Major Taylor paused for a moment before asking his next question. "At the time of the interrogation by Captain Schmidt of Prisoner of War Otto Stengel, did you observe his physical condition at the time you entered the room."

"His physical condition was good, sir."

Major Taylor turned wearily away from the witness and walked back to the defense counsel table. "No further questions."

The prosecution declined to cross-examine.

"I would like to call Captain Oscar Schmidt as a witness for the defense," Major Taylor said to the court.

Oscar Schmidt had all the requisites of a successful interrogator; ramrod straight, stern, cold, he exuded a strength that was immediately apparent. The seven defendants glared at Schmidt as he left the table where he was serving as official court interpreter and took his seat on the witness stand. In the eyes of several of them there was sheer hatred, because this was the man most responsible for dredging from them the admission of their crime.

Major Taylor glanced about the courtroom and then approached the witness. "State your name, rank, organization, and station."

"Oscar S. Schmidt, captain, Air Corps, unit is secret."

"Captain, have you seen the seven accused prisoners of war who sit in this courtroom before today?"

After a quick glance at the defendants, he said, "I have seen some of them."

"Which ones have you seen before?"

"Fischer," Captain Schmidt said and then stopped abruptly. "About the only one I don't recall seeing is Ludwig."

"Did you see Prisoner of War Wizuy before?"

From his end of the table, Rolf Wizuy stirred uncomfortably but continued to stare icily at the witness.

"Yes."

"Did you see Prisoner of War Stengel?"

"Yes."

Otto Stengel's eyes betrayed a strange mixture of hate and fear, almost a childlike sense of having been scorned and then embarrassed but helpless to do anything about it. Captain Schmidt looked directly at Stengel when he answered but showed not the slightest emotion; Stengel looked away under the sharp gaze.

"Do you recall an interrogation of Prisoner of War Otto Stengel held on or about the last day of May or the first day of June?"

The prosecution objected on the ground that it was a leading question, but Colonel Poust quickly overruled it.

"I can't recall any one individual interrogation. I have been working on it for about a year. I couldn't single out any one."

"How long have you been working on a case involving the death of Drechsler?"

"About a month."

Major Taylor persisted in his probing about the Stengel interrogation. "Do you recall an interrogation of Otto Stengel?"

"I remember having interrogated him." Captain Schmidt appeared mildly annoyed at the repeated question. "But I couldn't state the date or time or anything along that line."

"Did you see him, during an interrogation by yourself, dressed in an army overcoat?"

"I cannot answer that question, sir."

Colonel Poust interrupted quickly. "You will answer the question."

"I am not allowed to divulge interrogation methods," the witness answered, looking over at Colonel Poust.

"You will answer the question as to whether you saw him or not."

"I don't remember seeing him with an overcoat on."

"Did you use any forceful means," Major Taylor continued, "or third degree methods in any way or in any form?"

"What constitutes third degree methods?"

"Answer yes or no," Colonel Poust admonished the witness.

"I used ordinary interrogation methods."

"What are the ordinary interrogation methods that you refer to?"

"I am not allowed to divulge those methods."

Colonel Poust motioned for the defense counsel to approach the bench, and then spoke in a tone loud enough for the other members of the court to hear. "Ask him leading questions about what he did in this case."

Major Taylor returned to the witness. "Is it not a fact that you did use a method upon Prisoner of War Otto Stengel which involved the use of a gas mask upon Prisoner of War Otto Stengel?"

"Yes."

"Did you use a method that involved the use of an overcoat?"

"I think I did see an overcoat."

"In what manner was the gas mask used on Prisoner of War Otto Stengel?"

"I do not quite understand, sir."

"How was the use made of the gas mask?"

"It was put on his head and face and used in the ordinary manner."

"Was an onion used in the gas mask?"

"There was."

And that ended the questioning of Oscar Schmidt. He was, surprisingly, on the witness stand for only a few minutes, and the prosecution declined to cross-examine.

Major Taylor then approached the bench and spoke directly to Colonel Poust. "At this time the defense moves that the statement or confession of Prisoner of War Otto Stengel be stricken from the record."

Colonel Poust moved his head slowly from side to side as he answered: "Motion denied."

"The accused Prisoner of War Otto Stengel will be called as a witness," Major Taylor announced to the court.

Colonel Poust looked beyond the defense counsel at the seven defendants. "The accused will stand." Stengel stood immediately, but the other six looked at each other, not knowing whether to stand or remain seated. The assistant defense counsel motioned for all of them to rise and they did. Colonel Poust began: "Accused Helmut Fischer, Fritz Franke, Guenther Kuelsen, Heinrich Ludwig, Bernhard Reyak, Otto Stengel, and Rolf Wizuy, with respect to the specification and charge against each of you, you each may do any of the following: 1. remain silent; 2. make an unsworn statement; 3. testify as a witness. In the event that you, or any one of you, elect to remain silent, this court cannot indulge in any speculation whatsoever from your failure to take the stand in your own defense and no presumption of your guilt or innocence arises from your failure to testify."

Colonel Poust cleared his throat and looked again at the seven men standing. They appeared to be paying strict attention, but Colonel Poust knew they understood very little of what he was saying in English. "You may make an unsworn statement in denial, extenuation, or defense of the offense charged. You may not be cross-examined in such a statement, but the prosecution may rebut. This statement may either be oral or written or partly oral or partly written and may be made personally or by your counsel. Such consideration will be given your statement as the court deems warranted.

"You may take the stand and be sworn as a witness in your own defense. You may be cross-examined by the prosecution or by the court with great latitude on any of the matters material to the specification on which you have testified or as to your credibility in that cross-examination. This applies to each one of the accused.

"Having heard this explanation, do you still desire to take the stand as a witness?" Then, turning to the official court interpreter, "Captain Schmidt, you will translate to the prisoners."

The translation was made and each defendant was asked individually if he fully understood the meaning of Colonel Poust's explanation. Each replied in the affirmative.

At the special urging of the assistant defense counsel, Major Furst, Otto Stengel and his counsel agreed that he would not be called as a witness; instead he would make an unsworn statement.

In his blue POW fatigues, Otto Stengel looked strangely forlorn and out of place on the witness stand. He clasped his hands as if he were Indian-wrestling with himself, and his eyes scanned the room several times. Then Major Taylor began questioning him to draw out the unsworn statement.

"Prisoner of War Otto Stengel, were you interrogated on or about June 1st in connection with the death of Werner Drechsler?"

"I object," Major Walsh said, rising out of his chair. "This is not an unsworn statement within the meaning in the manual. It isn't the proper procedure. If the statement is elicited by questions from his counsel, it ceases to be a voluntary statement."

The defense counsel stepped over to the bench and directly addressed the president of the court martial board. "I have searched and so has assistant counsel, Major Furst, and we have found no authority in the manual against interrogatories being made."

Colonel Poust listened and then decided to grant the prosecution a ten-minute recess to produce authority supporting their objection. At the end of the recess, Major Walsh cited both the *Manual for Courts-Martial* and *Winthrop's Military Law and Precedents,* but neither specifically ruled out interrogatories and, therefore, Colonel Poust overruled the objection and signaled Major Taylor to proceed.

"Where did the interrogation take place?"

"In the secret camp. I do not know the name."

"What officer, if you know, was present?"

"A captain," Stengel said, looking over and nodding toward the court interpreter, Captain Schmidt, "who is acting as interpreter. . .the sergeant who appeared as a witness before him, a lieutenant, and two guards were present at the time."

"What was done to you during the course of the interrogation?"

"It commenced with a ride of four hours at a speed I have never experienced previously. I was driven in the car for a length of time and inside of the car was a steel bar and it moved back and forth. After the car stopped in a field, it was called to me in the car, 'Do you want to confess now?' I said no and then the terrific trip continued until at the end of it we arrived at the questioning camp."

Major Walsh again rose from his chair to object. "For the purpose of the record I am going to make a second objection. The manual specifically provides that the accused whether he has testified or not, can make an unsworn statement to the court in denial, explanation, or extenuation. None of this is in denial, explanation, or extenuation. I submit that all of this part of the statement up to now is absolutely incompetent and should not be allowed."

"Objection overruled," Colonel Poust said and then turned to the witness and told him to proceed with his story.

"An officer was present, a lieutenant, and also the captain who is here, and I had to stand up in a corner quietly. Later on, a major came in the room and asked me if I wanted to confess and I said, 'No. I don't know.' Whereupon I was closed in the car again and a much worse trip started. It was in the afternoon late, at five o'clock, and I did not get anything to eat. After this trip, which lasted three hours, I was brought back and collapsed on the stairs coming back. Thereupon the American lieutenant and the guard dragged me to the questioning. I could not walk any more because the trip was too hard.

"At this time I always had appendectomy pains and I had a doctor with me in my room at all times. After that time I was dragged to the questioning, the major came in again and asked if I wanted to confess. I said, 'No, I don't know anything.' After that I was brought back in that car. The trip started again. It had become night but I was driven around and stopped in front of a restaurant. I was left in the car while the mosquitoes bit me and a captain, who is the interpreter, entered the restaurant. After approximately two hours, the captain came out again and we drove to the questioning camp at which I was awaited.

"I said again, 'I don't have anything to confess,' at which time three heavy coats were put on my shoulders and someone opened the steam heat. My shirt and underwear were torn and my sex organs were hanging out, at which time I was pushed toward the steam heat and burned myself. That was not enough. The American lieutenant went out to get a gas mask, which was put on my head. At that time the American captain said, or yelled at me, 'Will you confess now or will we give you some more of Dachau treatment?' I still said no, whereupon somebody got an onion and garlic which were smashed and put into the gas mask.

The lieutenant stood next to me and pushed me and jabbed me every time I closed my eyes.

"Suddenly the interpreter, the sergeant, stood behind me and yelled at me: 'Stand straight. Behind you stands a German Feldwebel.' I was not able to stand straight anymore. My legs were too weak because the three American coats were too heavy for me. This was not enough yet. The American lieutenant stepped next to me and closed the inlet holes of the gas mask. At that time he was looking at his watch to find out how long I could stand without air. The American captain said, 'Now you see how it is if slowly the air gets out. That is the way you did it to Drechsler.' When he had done this with me about eight times I collapsed unconscious.

"An American guard told me later that I had, while unconscious, called for my wife and children until the time someone poured water on my face. I was not altogether conscious yet and they lifted me up and already reached for the gas mask again. 'Do you want any more of that stuff?' yelled the captain. I said, 'No, it is enough for me. I want to talk to the major. I want to give an oath.' The sergeant said, 'You can't do it,' but another lieutenant said, 'If you want to give an oath, I will call for the major.' Thereupon the major was called and came to my room with the sergeant.

"I was afraid to tell all of it at this time and I only told part of it. I was threatened continually of being let out and shot. I said to the major, 'I would like to see the board,' and they went out to get Colonel Church. After about fifteen minutes Colonel Church arrived and I confessed about half.

"Finally, one led me back to my room. It was about 4:30 A.M. Only after two days I confessed all of it, the true matter, because I heard continually how innocent comrades were punished. I continually believed to be shot because I had shortly before seen of a shooting.

"I want to add something, too, which happened a few days

beforehand. An American doctor comes into my room and gives me three shots. I was like paralyzed and the American captain and the American interpreter were in my room sitting on a bench. He questioned me during that time about the case of Drechsler but I could only partly answer because I was part paralyzed. I do not know how long I was in the room because suddenly my eyes closed."

Seeing that Stengel had finally reached the end of his long narrative, Major Taylor moved back in front of the witness. "Were you advised of your rights before the start of this interrogation?"

"Yes, I believe in Papago Park."

Otto Stengel was then excused from the witness stand. He stepped down and made his way back to the defendant's table, squeezing past Rolf Wizuy and then dropping into his chair as if his legs had suddenly been cut out from under him.

Helmut Fischer was the next defendant called to make an unsworn statement. As soon as he was seated in the witness stand, the prosecutor without moving from his chair mentioned to the court that the prisoner of war spoke English quite well. Colonel Poust turned to the defense counsel and asked, "Is he going to speak English or German?"

"I suggest I ask him in English and if he understands we will proceed on that basis." Then, turning to Fischer, "Were you interrogated during the first part of June by Captain Schmidt?"

"Yes, sir."

"Where did the interrogation take place?"

"In Modesto, California."

"Who was present during the course of interrogation?"

"Captain Schmidt and Sergeant . . . ," Fischer paused and turned to his interpreter, Private Gruenebaum, and whispered something in German. The interpreter began to answer but before he could finish, Colonel Poust interrupted.

"Don't carry on any conversations in German. I think we had better continue the interrogation through the interpreter instead of in English." He nodded to Major Taylor to continue.

"What were you asked during the course of the interrogation?"

"I was asked if I could remember what happened at prisoner of war camp, Papago Park, Phoenix, Arizona on the 12th and 13th of March."

"Were you advised of anything pertaining to anyone who had confessed?"

"Yes. The written statements of the prisoners Franke and Kuelsen were shown to me."

"Was anything done during the course of interrogation other than questioning?"

"Yes."

"What was done?"

"Captain Schmidt ordered me to stand at attention."

"For how long a time did this continue?"

"It was from about 3:15 A.M. until 7:00 A.M."

"What happened then?"

"After that I was left standing alone with a guard."

"For how long?"

"Ten minutes."

"Was anything else done before you agreed to make a statement?"

"Yes," Fischer said, and then looked over first at Captain Schmidt and then at the six defendants who were staring up at him. Fischer was much more relaxed on the witness stand than Stengel had been, but at the same time he still displayed some effects of the tremendous pressure on him. He had a certain outward strength and his words were clear and to the point, but deep within his eyes there was a trembling uneasiness.

"I stood at attention the way I learned it as a German

sailor. Captain Schmidt said thereupon that I was on a U-boat and that I should put my hands across my body. Then I had to press my chin on my chest. After about half an hour, I had to cross my arms under the seat of my pants. The present interpreter," nodding toward Captain Schmidt, "stepped twice with his shoes on my crossed hands so that I bent over backwards with my body."

"How long did this go on?"

"In this position I stood under the continuous yelling of Captain Schmidt from about five o'clock until 6:30 in the morning."

"Were you asked any questions?"

"At first I was asked if I could remember what happened on the 12th and 13th of March. Then Captain Schmidt asked me if I knew the 'pig dog' Hox. At the same time he asked me if I knew something about a super Nazi, Wattenburg. I answered that I knew only a captain at sea Wattenburg and a Chief Quartermaster Hox. Further I was asked if I knew Dachau. I said no to the question, and then Captain Schmidt asked me if he should show me some things about Dachau. I said, 'No.' Thereupon the interpreter asked me if my undershirt and my shorts were bothering me. If they did bother me, I should denude myself."

At this point, Helmut Fischer appeared to lose some of the poise that he had so far maintained through the questioning, but it was only momentary and after a short glance around the courtroom he settled back in the witness chair and was ready to go on.

"What happened next?"

"After they left me alone at 7:00, I was in such a physical condition that my whole body was shaking."

"What was done then?"

"After the interpreter came back, he told me that all the others had confessed and there would be no further use."

"Were you advised of your rights before the interrogation you just described?"

"No."

Major Taylor turned abruptly and as he was walking back to the defense table looked over his shoulder at the court martial board and said, "That's all."

Fischer was excused from the witness stand, and Colonel Poust announced that the court would take a five-minute recess. Before the defendants left the courtroom, Major Taylor and the interpreter, Private Gruenebaum, spoke briefly with Rolf Wizuy, who simply sat there nodding his head in agreement with whatever it was they were saying. Then, the major went to confer with his associate, Major Furst, and the defendants and their guards filed out of the room.

After the recess, Rolf Wizuy was called to the witness stand. He appeared much younger than Fischer, even though he was over a year older, and he was noticeably nervous.

"Prisoner of War Wizuy," Major Taylor began, "were you interrogated during the first part of June 1944 by Captain Schmidt?"

"Yes."

"What happened during the course of this investigation?"

Wizuy's small, very mobile eyes were roaming all over the courtroom, but they finally came back to rest on the defense counsel. "I was taken out of my cell in the night on the first or second of June and put in a dark cell without a bed and with just what I had on."

"How long did this happen?"

"At about eight o'clock in the morning I received breakfast, and shortly thereafter I was called for questioning. Since I did not make any statement, I was sent back to my cell. Right after that I was taken out of the cell and put into a closed car. It was about 9:00 A.M. The car kept standing before the camp. I was taken out of this car and put into another car and then the trip started. They took it along a highway. It was stopped suddenly and I fell headlong inside the car. Then I was driven in curves through ditches. I fell all about in the car. The trip must have lasted about four hours. We stopped in front of a restaurant and two persons got out of the front seat and went into the restaurant. After that they finished the return trip to camp.

"I was taken out of the car and brought into an empty room. There were an American lieutenant, Captain Schmidt, the interpreter, a sergeant, and two guards. It was forbidden to me to speak and I was not allowed to ask anything. I had to stand in a corner at attention. Captain Schmidt stood behind me and drew my arms down. Then he took me by my shoulders and pressed my shoulder blades together.

"Then I noticed that the captain had been drinking. He smelled of alcohol. His eyes were bloodshot. He kicked me in the back of the knee to find out if I really stood at attention. I made it known to Captain Schmidt that I did not have anything to eat for twelve hours. Thereupon Captain Schmidt answered something like I was a superman and should be able to stand that. It continued until I would talk. This all took about one and a half hours.

"After that I was brought into another cell and allowed to sit down. I sat on the floor but was watched by a guard so that I could not fall asleep. Several times my eyes closed. In the morning at about eight Captain Schmidt came into my room with the interpreter, and he asked me if I wanted to confess. After that I was brought into another room and made the statements. That's all."

Major Taylor did not give Wizuy a moment to reflect on the story he had just related with what appeared to be a surprising degree of spontaneity. "What was the effect on you of the treatment you described?"

"I don't understand the sense of the question."

"What was the physical or mental effect of the treatment and the experience you have described just now upon yourself?"

Still not understanding the question, Wizuy answered anyway: "Captain Schmidt let me know that this condition would not change until I would talk. I did not have any help to make my rights as a prisoner of war of value."

"Were you warned of your rights before any questioning was made of you?"

"It was on the twentieth of April when I was called to questioning at Papago Park that I was apprised of my rights."

"Were you asked any questions relative to the death of Werner Drechsler at the time of the treatment by giving you the ride in the automobile and the other treatment in the room?"

"In the automobile I was not questioned."

"Were you questioned in the room that you were then taken to?"

"Yes, in the room I was asked who killed Drechsler."

"Were you warned or advised of your legal rights before that question was asked?"

"No."

"That's all," Major Taylor said, motioning for Wizuy to leave the witness stand.

The major then walked over to the court martial board and spoke directly to Colonel Poust. "The defense rests."

Not quite two hours had elapsed since the defense began its case at 1:30 that afternoon, and it was all over but for the closing arguments of both counsels.

12

Verdict

I N the dry desert heat outside the military courtroom at Florence, Arizona, life was going on pretty much as
usual. Few, if any, of the other prisoners knew of the trial that
was taking place. The camp at Florence, one of the oldest
World War II prisoner-of-war camps in the United States, had
been in operation since 1942. Its capacity of 3,000 prisoners
was not filled, but in 1944 it already had a considerably larger
population than the small neighboring town of Florence. The
prisoners went about their jobs despite the torrid mid-afternoon
heat, those working outside adding to a suntan unlike any they
had ever experienced in Germany. Inside the courtroom, it was
brutally hot; the electric fans did nothing more than blow the
hot air around.

After the defense rested its case, the court continued its proceedings without recess. Major Walsh announced that the
prosecution waived opening argument, and Major Taylor
stepped before the board to present his argument on behalf
of the seven defendants.

"If it please the court, the members of this court, the personnel of the prosecution and the personnel of the defense, as well as a great part of the personnel who have appeared here to testify before this court, are members of the armed forces of the United States. The seven accused in this case are all members of the armed forces of Germany, a power with which we are today at war. I mention this so that every member of the court may be apprised of the fact that our mental attitude must be absolutely unbiased by the fact of the history of this war or anything that has happened in this war. In considering this case, counsel, meaning myself, has acted entirely without any personal animus or feeling for the reason that the accused are enemies. Perhaps that puts upon us all an unusual burden, an unusual responsibility, because I believe it is hard for a human being to entirely divorce himself from the background of personal feelings and emotions. May I ask, however, that the members of the court, as I have, will treat the accused as American soldiers, as Americans, be they prisoners of war or not and not the soldiers of the power with which we are at war.

"The prosecution has, naturally, based its case upon certain written statements which can be termed for all legal intents or purposes, confessions. They were written statements, subscribed and sworn to by the accused, of certain facts known to the individuals as having happened. If the confessions in each case be taken as simple evidence in open court, then the question which I am about to refer to would not arise. But the court at every stage of their deliberation and consideration of whatever evidence has been introduced either by witnesses examined by the defense and witnesses brought to court by the prosecution or by the accused themselves, must carefully consider them because a principle of law is involved. I will briefly read from the *Manual of Courts-Martial,* 1928, Chapter 25, page 115, paragraph 3:

"An accused cannot be convicted legally upon his unsupported confession. A court may not consider the confession of an accused as evidence against him unless there be in the record other evidence, either direct or circumstantial, that the offense charged has probably been committed; in other words, there must be evidence of the corpus delicti other than the confession itself.

"I do not feel able to argue in view of the able manner in which the prosecution has proved the corpus delicti. It will, however, be recalled that the fingerprint expert brought to the court by the prosecution, could only identify the fingerprints of three fingers and two of them were smudged. It could be argued it was in that respect, so far as evidence of the rope, it was not absolutely proved beyond a reasonable doubt that these items were connected with the body of the deceased who is alleged to have died by the acts of the accused. I will read from the same paragraph in the manual:

> Usually such evidence is introduced before evidence of the confession; but a court may, in its discretion, admit the confession in evidence upon condition that it will be stricken out and disregarded in the event that the above requirements as to evidence of the corpus delicti is not met later.

"We have, if we admit that the corpus delicti is proved, reached the point of the confession itself. In other words, the confession itself is not proper evidence before this court if the corpus delicti is not proved beyond a reasonable doubt.

"The most important point in connection with my statement in referring to the confessions is this principle, and it is a principle of law universally and particularly in this case, found in the first sentence on page 116 of the manual:

> "It must appear that the confession was voluntary on the part of the accused. In the discretion of the court a prima facie showing to this effect may be required before evidence of the confession itself is received.

"Further in the manual on page 116, paragraph 4, it is stated:

"Facts indicating that a confession was induced by hope of benefit or fear of punishment or injury inspired by a person competent (or believed by the party confessing to be competent) to effectuate the hope or fear is, subject to the following observations, evidence that the confession was involuntary. Much depends on the nature of the benefit or of the punishment or injury, on the words used, and on the personality of the accused, and on the relations of the parties involved. Thus, a benefit, punishment, or injury of trivial importance to the accused need not be accepted as having induced a confession, especially where the confession involves a serious offense; casual remarks or indefinite expressions need not be regarded as having inspired hope or fear; and an intelligent, experienced, strong-minded soldier might not be influenced by words and circumstances which might influence an ignorant, dull-minded recruit.

"Let the court remember that these accused are within the power of our armed forces, are confined in stockades, they are constantly under fear of punishment at any time. It is apparent that a threat made to a prisoner of war might well have a stronger effect on a prisoner of war than it would to an intelligent soldier of our own army who knew his legal rights. It is true, the accused have been warned, at least in most cases, of their rights, prior to having been interrogated but I believe the court will see that the previous reading of their rights under the Articles as they apply could not give full confidence in the justice of treatment or the fact that they will receive justice and will not be punished at the will of the threatening officer. On examination Captain Schmidt definitely admitted that in the interrogation of one prisoner of war, one of the accused, Stengel, he did make use of a method which I now maintain is unauthorized, the use of a gas mask with an onion placed within it, and the use of an overcoat which has been further described by the prisoner himself in his unsworn statement. Such methods are not countenanced. The defense maintains that one obtained by duress or coercion is not a voluntary statement. The court cannot say it is a voluntary confession in that the accused's thoughts must have been influenced by what might happen to him if he had to go through it again.

"It was testified by another accused that he did have to go through it again, confessing because of his hesitancy to face a further ordeal of that kind. Several of the accused testified as to certain things done to them in the inducement of their confessions. The defense did make a motion for the striking of a confession. However, it would still seem proper that the matter should still be referred to the court in connection with the case as a whole if in the event the court should find that some coercive means did mentally or physically affect the voluntary nature of the making of the confessions can not be considered in determining the guilt or innocence of the accused. I plead with the court that if these methods were used in some cases, they could have been in all cases. In all probability, and beyond a reasonable doubt, perhaps they were used on all the accused.

"But even if the court ignores all evidence of the nature of the confessions and considers them full force and significance in connection with alleged acts which had to do with the death of Prisoner of War Drechsler, then the court will be to the point of considering the degree of the crime if the court so gets to that point. Homicide consists of more than one type or degree. The charges here accuse the accused of murder, first degree murder, in which Drechsler was murdered with 'malice aforethought.' As stated on page 162 of the manual, under discussion of Article of War 92, it is stated: 'Murder is the unlawful killing of a human being with malice aforethought.' Unlawful means without legal justification or excuse. Unlawful killing, it could be argued by the defense, that if the confessions are taken to mean that if these accused have committed the act they have described, such an act is excusable. In other words, the execution of a criminal is justified. If the court does not, after having taken the confessions at their full weight, consider that the nature and the method used and the background of this whole case does not justify them, a consideration of the meaning of malice aforethought should be definitely understood. Malice aforethought is generally defined as being unlawful killing without mitigating circumstances. Certainly there were mitigating circumstances. I am now considering the court as ignoring any consideration of validity or voidability of the confessions and in the consideration of the nature and degree of the offense, the question arises of mitigating circumstances.

"If the court carefully peruses the written statement of the accused, they will find they have described in words to the best of their ability as to why they did this act. They did this act to a man who was known by each one to be a traitor. He had sold information to a country with which his country was at war. Let us consider this analogy. American prisoners of war are in Germany and they in turn are joined by another American prisoner of war whom some of them had met in an interrogation center, and had been interrogated there by this American prisoner of war acting on behalf of the German government and he questioned them for military information. Perhaps he coupled these questions with promises of immunity and a softer way of living. They refuse because they are loyal Americans. They later found this same soldier, this American soldier, arrived at a prison camp. Perhaps the German government decided they had enough information out of him. American soldiers who had been questioned by him became suddenly so bitter that that very night, knowing he had so divulged information which perhaps contributed directly to the death of other American soldiers and sailors, killed him. Would it not be reasonable to suppose they would dispose of this man in some way? I see no other way than that the court consider that analogy. It is merely a reverse proposition.

"These men consider themselves soldiers. They do not appear

in uniform. They are prisoners of war. They were bitter, just as our soldiers would be bitter. They had seen ships sunk. They did their duty as they saw it. They executed this traitor, a man who might have further obtained information and divulged matters of military importance to the enemy. They stated that he had asked questions which would lead to the belief that he was obtaining information and in turn divulging it to the United States government. If the court comes to that point where it considers their guilt or innocence under the charge, it must definitely consider whether or not the mitigating circumstances shown are not sufficient to definitely remove the case from a definition of a killing with malice aforethought. May I ask each member of the court to carefully peruse the statements of these various accused that they may be familiar with the background and whole statements. May I ask that this court assume the solemn responsibility which is imposed upon it in consideration of this case which has international aspects.

"We could rightly pass it off on the ground that the death was merely that of another enemy of ours and not of importance to ourselves. This trial exists, however, because in this country we do try people who murder. In this country we do not inflict harsh punishment upon people, be they our people or prisoners of war. I ask you to look upon the accused and make your judgment which may not be harsh but will be fair and will be correct."

When Major Taylor concluded his argument, he walked slowly back to the defense table and sat down. He had put all that he could on the line; his job as far as this trial was concerned was finished. The defense had, during the trial, attacked the methods used to obtain the confessions, claiming they were invalid because the resulting confessions obviously were not made freely and voluntarily and instead had been forced from the accused. In the 1970's, it would be difficult, perhaps impossible, to find a jurist who would not be troubled by the questionability of the confessions that came to light. But this was 1944. The United States was still at war with Germany; it was a court martial; and the United States Supreme Court was many years away from ruling on the Miranda and Escobedo cases. Major Taylor was patently aware that his motion to have Otto Stengel's confession stricken had failed, and with its failure stood the admissibility of the seven statements. However, he felt that the point was of such importance that it required clear and emphatic reiteration in the defense's summation.

And if all this crumbled, if the defense's case were deemed worthless in the determination of the innocence or guilt of the seven accused, there was still the question of mitigating or extenuating circumstances, the defense argued. This, Major Taylor claimed, the court must take into consideration in determining the degree of murder and the extent of the seven men's guilt. In effect, if the case were lost, the sentence should be tempered because of the circumstances surrounding the crime.

Major Taylor leaned back in his chair to listen to the closing argument of the prosecution. The prosecutor, Major Walsh, looked briefly at the members of the court martial board, then glanced over at the seven young men in their dull blue fatigue uniforms who sat listlessly staring back at him.

"I will be brief. I wish simply to answer the arguments of opposing counsel. Gentlemen, there are thirteen high-ranking army officers who have been delegated to try one of the most dramatic cases that has ever come upon us in the annals of the United States Army. You, gentlemen, heard testimony whereby seven German prisoners of war went out one night and not only hung one of their comrades but beat him unmercifully and cruelly before they hung him. Gentlemen, evidence shows that Werner Drechsler came into Prisoner of War Camp, Papago Park, Phoenix, Arizona, at about 4:30 Sunday afternoon on the 12th of March 1944. Gentlemen, he was hung before ten o'clock of that night.

You know what was done to Werner Drechsler before he was hung. You, and each of you, and also the opposing counsel and myself are American army officers. We do not condone acts which are called acts of a traitor, but neither you nor any one can condone the treatment which was received by this poor boy before he was hung.

"Evidence shows conclusively that the poor boy was dragged out of his bed by the seven accused, taken outside, screaming all the while. They heard a guard coming and let him go. He was streaming with blood. Then what happened? As soon as the guard went away they went in again and took him out of his bed. They beat him up again and dragged him over to the washroom where, gentlemen, there was a noose already prepared for his neck. After the hanging, then they all went to bed and went to sleep. How can anyone argue that this was not cold-blooded, and premediated? Counsel has argued to you very ably that there is some question about the corpus delicti. Let us take you briefly through the proof that established the corpus delicti beyond a reasonable doubt and there is no contradictory testimony to dispute it.

"The testimony of Sergeant Bornstein, who testified without contradiction that he went to the Tempe railroad station and picked up Werner Drechsler and took him in the ambulance out to Compound 4. During the trip from Tempe to the prisoner of war camp, Papago Park, the unfortunate victim talked to Sergeant Bornstein and told him that he was Werner Drechsler. Werner Drechsler also showed him that he had a wound in his right knee. The next morning Sergeant Bornstein was one of the men who helped cut Werner Drechsler's body down and he testified that this man had a similar wound in his right knee and also that upon looking at his Form 2 he identified the picture of Werner Drechsler. You have that identification. You also have the second element of the corpus delicti, that is, the hanging of the victim in the washroom and he was discovered the next morning. Under the rules laid down by the United States District Courts, the Supreme Court and also the Judge Advocate General, we do not have to establish the corpus delicti beyond a reasonable doubt. It is only necessary that we prove that a crime has been committed. Let me read you one of the leading cases — *Murray* vs. *United States*, found in 228 Federal Reporter, page 1008:

"The corpus delicti, as relates to homicide, is composed of two elements: (a) The death of the person alleged to have been killed; (b) That some criminal agency caused such death.

"Of course, both of these elements must be established beyond a reasonable doubt. When the jury find these established, the next inquiry is as to the identity of the criminal agency; and this, too, must be established beyond a reasonable doubt, but is properly no part of the corpus delicti.

"Let us find out what our two elements of the corpus delicti show. One, the death. We have established that beyond a reasonable doubt, and there is no contradiction whatsoever in the testimony that Werner Drechsler was not killed. Second, we have a preponderance of evidence — in the testimony of Captain Hebblewaithe, Sergeant Bornstein, Captain Marks and Captain Stafford — that proves this man was murdered by strangulation. After establishing these two elements, we must prove who committed the crime. In this case gentlemen, you have seven confessions of those seven prisoners of war before you." Major Walsh paused and pointed at the seven seated men. "You have four of them, Franke, Kuelsen, Ludwig, and Reyak — four of them. Is there any evidence in this record that their confessions are not voluntary? No, for the simple reason that they were given voluntarily and you can read the statement at the end of each confession. If there was any question about coercion being used on those four, you would hear about it by an unsworn statement. You only have the confessions of three others which might be questioned.

"Take Otto Stengel. He should have been a novelist. He is one of the greatest storytellers I have ever heard. He can tell the most beautiful stories. But, gentlemen, in this case he told a beautiful story that points the finger right at him. Otto Stengel told his story at the interrogation center. Then he takes the stand and in an unsworn statement tells you how he was compelled to tell this beautiful story. I am not relying on that story. I am relying on the beautiful story he told the investigating officer. The story he told the investigating officer is much more perfect than the one related in his original statement. Was there any coercion in the statement made to the investigating officer? No. He was warned fully of his rights and he couldn't tell his story fast enough. He bragged about it. What was his excuse for hanging a German sailor? I wonder if he thought how he was an interloper — a man who had no part or dealings with Werner Drechsler. No. He came along this night and said, 'Boys, do you need any more help?' As a matter of fact, his story shows, and the stories of the other boys show, beyond any contradiction that he was the motivating force behind some of these boys. Then he tries to say that the story was forced out of him by brutal treatment. I will tell you who received the brutal treatment in this case: the poor victim who didn't have a chance. He didn't have a prayer. Was it his fault he was brought into this prisoner of war camp?

"I say this, that when a German soldier or sailor is brought into this country as a prisoner of war, he is subject to all the laws of the United States of America. One of the laws is this: you cannot beat him unmercifully and then take him over to a washroom, carried partly by the hair of his head, and hang him. Let us look at the point raised by the defense counsel that these men should be given consideration because they are German sailors. The answer is this: if they were German sailors as they say they are, they would not have hung Werner Drechsler the way they did. They would not have cruelly tortured him before they hung him.

"Going back to two other accused, Helmut Fischer and Rolf Wizuy, the defense counsel contends that there is some question about their statements, that they were obtained by the use of force. Gentlemen, when they told their stories to the investigating officer, was there any force used? No. They all willingly retold their stories and admitted complicity in the crime. Having that in mind, and your law member will also advise you, that any question about the invalidity of these three confessions is absolutely cured by the confessions and statements made before the investigating officer, Lieutenant Baldwin. I refer you at this time to the recent case of *Lyons* vs. *State of Oklahoma*, decided by the United States Supreme Court and found in Volume 64, Supreme Court Reporter, at page 1,208, a copy of which I have already furnished the law member.

"Let us go back to the statements made on the stand. Counsel in his argument depends very much upon these statements made by Stengel, Fischer, and Wizuy, to support his contention that these confessions — that the original confessions were obtained by force. Let me read what Winthrop has to say about unsworn statements, which is set out on page 300, *Winthrop's Military Law and Precedents*, second edition:

"While all due consideration is to be given to a statement properly presented, the statement is *not evidence* but a personal declaration or defense, and cannot legally be acted upon as evidence by either the court or the reviewing authority.

"Having that in mind, you cannot take into consideration as evidence any of the unsworn statements made by Prisoners of War Stengel, Wizuy, or Fischer in determining whether or not these confessions were voluntarily obtained through force or coercion. You have only one item of evidence in the testimony and that is the testimony of Sergeant Held and Captain Schmidt that Otto Stengel had an overcoat on and a gas mask. But, you can eliminate that and say that anything done in that interrogation center was wiped out and cured when these men went before an investigating officer and reaffirmed their stories again. Counsel would have you believe those three prisoners of war might have been forced to give their original confessions, then you would consider that all the rest of them were obtained through force. That is not the law and the law member will so advise you. Defense counsel is depending again on the unsworn statements given by these three prisoners of war. If that cannot be used as evidence, I say there is not one scintilla of evidence in this record to show that Wizuy, Reyak, Ludwig, Kuelsen, Franke, and Fischer were compelled to tell their stories. I will close now, gentlemen, and will ask you to read those confessions and see if a person so coerced could really tell those beautiful but gruesome stories contained in their statements."

At the conclusion of Major Walsh's closing argument, Colonel Poust announced that because neither the prosecution nor the defense had anything further to offer the court was now closed. All but the court martial board members left the courtroom. The twelve army officers then rendered their verdict; each member wrote on a piece of paper his finding, folded the paper twice, and passed it to Colonel Poust. When all of the votes were in, Colonel Poust opened them individually and read each verdict aloud; it was unanimous and duly recorded that "Under secret written ballot, all of the members present at the time the vote was taken concurring in each finding of guilty, the court finds the accused separately and individually, of the specification and charge: Guilty."

Each member of the court martial board, again by secret written ballot, submitted his verdict of sentence. Colonel Poust read the unanimous results of the vote. The court, "all of the members present at the time the vote was taken concurring, sentences the accused, separately and individually, as follows:

"Prisoner of War Helmut Fischer to be hanged by the neck until dead;

"Prisoner of War Fritz Franke to be hanged by the neck until dead;

"Prisoner of War Guenther Kuelsen to be hanged by the neck until dead;

"Prisoner of War Heinrich Ludwig to be hanged by the neck until dead;

"Prisoner of War Bernhard Reyak to be hanged by the neck until dead;

"Prisoner of War Otto Stengel to be hanged by the neck until dead;

"Prisoner of War Rolf Wizuy to be hanged by the neck until dead."

The court was then opened but Colonel Poust told all those present that the findings and sentences would not be announced. And so at exactly 6:21 P.M. on August 16, 1944, the two-day trial was officially closed. Seven young Germans had received the ultimate sentence, death, to be carried out in a more humane, perhaps, but grimly similar fashion to the way they themselves had meted out the death penalty to Werner Drechsler.

13

Board of Review

AFTER the court martial, the seven defendants were led back to the guardhouse at Florence, which was slated to be their home for the next five months. The defendants and their two counsels did not know the sentences that had been levied by Colonel Poust and the court martial board; all they knew was that they had lost their case. It was acceptable in those days to withhold announcement of the sentence, which is exactly what Colonel Poust opted to do, and because of the structure of the court martial procedure and the cloaking of it in military classification there was no way that the army could be forced to publicly reveal or officially announce what the sentences were while the case made its way through the channels of appeal.

The two majors who had defended the seven men went off about their duties in other cases; they were now freed from the Drechsler case and would not be involved in it in any way from that point on. They were, of course, curious about the sentences, and even though they had no way of knowing what the eventual outcome would be, they both doubted that the seven men would ever be executed.

The seven Germans, however, were not so optimistic. They assumed that they had been sentenced to die and that it would probably be carried out. They were not officially told of their impending doom but they heard about it informally within the first few days back at the guardhouse at Florence. All seven accepted it as truth, more as a confirmation of their own thoughts over the preceding month, but they also looked on it as a gross injustice. They simply could not fathom the reasoning of the authorities who had denied them their lives.

Major Walsh went back to his quarters afterward, not for any celebration however, and only accompanied by a generally empty, washed-out feeling now that the trial was finally over. He felt no joy, no satisfaction in the way it had turned out; deep within him he did not want to see seven young men, enemies or not, go to the gallows. It was not the verdict that bothered him—he knew they were guilty of murder, and a brutal murder at that, it was the sentence, so harsh and final, that loomed as a plague he would have to live with. He knew that he probably never again would be involved in a case of such magnitude, where the deaths of seven human beings would be the awful price of victory.

The imposition of the death penalty automatically opened two channels of appeal: first, an official review of the case by a reviewing authority and then by a separate review board; second, the transmittal of their findings and recommendations along with the original transcript of the trial to Washington for final approval by the President. Whether the sentences would be upheld as they made their way through these channels was another question, but the sentences at least could not be executed until these judicial checks and balances had been met. Therefore, there was still room for hope on the prisoners' part, although even they knew it was very tenuous. In addition, the seven men could have found encouragement in the fact that by the autumn of 1944 not a single German prisoner of war had been executed in the United States, although eight other Germans had been under sentence of death for some time; in fact, a prisoner of war had never been executed in the history of the United States.

The first step in the review procedure was to submit the entire case to the reviewing authority, that is, the general under whose command the court martial was held—in this case, Major General William E. Shedd, commanding general of the Ninth Service Command, headquartered at Fort Douglas, Utah. General Shedd reviewed the proceedings and on September 15, 1944, approved the sentence of each of the convicted prisoners and forwarded the record of trial to the review board for action under Article of War 48. General Shedd was sympathetic enough, however, to append to his report "the recommendation that the sentence of each accused be commuted to life imprisonment."

A three-man board of review was appointed, headed by Colonel Terry A. Lyon, a judge advocate, and including two other army officers, Earle Hepburn and Herman Moyse, also of the Judge Advocate General Corps. The board was convened at Fort Douglas but did not meet until November, 1944, after each officer had thoroughly gone over the record of the trial.

First to be established by the board was whether the applicable articles of the Geneva Convention had been properly complied with before and during the trial. It was pointed out that in accordance with Article 64 the seven accused had been advised before the trial of their right to have a qualified counsel as well as an interpreter, and that these officers were, in fact, provided to them throughout the course of the trial. Article 60 of the Geneva Convention required that notification of the decision to hold the trial be communicated to the protecting power, to be forwarded to the country whose armed forces the accused were members of. Compliance to this article was established by the presence in the record of a copy of a letter from the office of the Provost Marshal General in Washington, dated July 15, 1944, to the legation of Switzerland, which was acting as the protecting power and as diplomatic representative for German interests.

The letter contained the names of the accused, their status and place of imprisonment, the charge and specification, a quotation from Article of War 92 applicable to murder, the proposed date of the trial, the place where it was to be held, and the names of the defense counsel and the assistant defense counsel. Acknowledgment of the receipt of the letter was received from the Swiss legation on July 18, 1944, twenty-eight days before the trial was scheduled to begin. The review board concluded that there were no problems whatsoever with the tenets of the Geneva Convention; they had been observed scrupulously.

Colonel Lyon prepared a summary of the evidence that had been presented at the trial as well as a synopsis of each statement written by the seven accused. He began his summary with the consideration on behalf of the defense. Colonel Lyon noted: "None of the accused offered any testimony in contradiction of the evidence of their participation in the hanging of the deceased, contained in their confessions. Their explanation of their motives and their defense are found in these confessions, the general tenor of which has already been given. Because of the recommendation by the reviewing authority that the sentence be commuted to life imprisonment and in order that their views may be adequately presented, the theory advanced by each accused to justify his actions will be quoted."

The quotations Colonel Lyon referred to were taken mostly from the record of the declarations of the seven men to the court martial's investigating officer, Lieutenant Harry Baldwin. They were excerpted and typed up for the review board's reference, and all seven statements basically said the same thing. Perhaps the most concisely articulate was the explanation of Helmut Fischer. "The entire execution of Drechsler was really due to the fact that, as German soldiers, we have to fight for our country, we have to fight for our country even while prisoners of war. Drechsler was a traitor, and as such he didn't have a right to continue to live among us. Two or three days after the hanging it was said among German prisoners of war that American authorities also have to take a part of the blame, because they had knowledge that Drechsler was a traitor and sent him to our camp in spite of that fact. I took part in doing away with Drechsler because I had to act as a German soldier. I have nothing to say in my defense."

The "interloper," as Major Walsh had referred to Otto Stengel during the prosecution's closing argument at the trial, was equally imbued with a sense of duty despite the fact that he had no real evidence of the guilt of Werner Drechsler, other than the word of several prisoners who claimed they knew the man to be a traitor. Stengel spoke resolutely about his part in the crime, but it was tinged with emotion and predicated on a much more personal basis.

"I am a soldier, I acted out of my responsibility as a soldier when I committed the murder. Drechsler had been murdered; however, he had committed countless murders. My sister-in-law has been bombed out, my cousin — a woman — was killed during an air raid, and how many more women and children — even more so, how many brave U-boat soldiers were sent to their deaths by Drechsler. Should we prisoners of war wait until the war is finished in order to avenge the traitors of Germany? I love my Fatherland and cannot wait that long because until the end of this war Drechsler could have killed my wife and children also. I have committed a murder; however, I don't consider myself a murderer, but a conscientious German soldier."

Colonel Lyon was merely establishing and recording the motives of the seven men, and the review board was considering them without any judgment as to their validity in terms of mitigation or extenuation. (This would come later in the review board proceedings.) The review board then went directly into the only other point that the defense had raised, the question of coercion in connection with the confessions. In regard to this, Colonel Lyon recorded the following: "While no objection was made by any of the accused to the introduction of their respective confessions, the voluntary nature of some of them was questioned at least inferentially in the testimony adduced by the defense and in the unsworn statements made by three of the accused, and a motion to strike out the previously admitted confession of one, Stengel, was made by the defense counsel and overruled. The insinuation of improper pressure—which is in reality the only feature of the case in connection with which testimony was introduced by the defense and the unsworn statements were made—may not merit but does require consideration."

Colonel Lyon then summarized the testimony of prosecution witness, Colonel Gerald Church, and the two defense witnesses, Sergeant Held and Captain Schmidt. The unsworn statements of Stengel, Fischer, and Wizuy were also capsulized and recorded by the board of review.

All of the summaries the board needed for its deliberations and subsequent findings were now completed: compliance with the articles of the Geneva Convention, the evidence presented by the prosecution, and the case for the defense. Now it all had to be dissected and carefully scrutinized by the three-man review board, meeting in secret session and recording in detail their determinations in each pertinent aspect of the case, which would then be incorporated into the document of their proceedings, which they would entitle simply "Opinion of the Board of Review."

At about the same time in Washington, D.C., another series of secret and highly relevant deliberations were being conducted under tight security by the War Department and the State Department in regard to two other German prisoner-of-war murder cases. Although the two cases at this point did not directly touch upon the case being reviewed at Fort Douglas, Utah, the ramifications of what was going on in Washington had great significance in the eventual fate of Helmut Fischer, Fritz Franke, Guenther Kuelsen, Heinrich Ludwig, Bernhard Reyak, Otto Stengel, and Rolf Wizuy. In fact, over the next few months all seven were destined to become integral features in the diplomatic operation that was developing in Washington, although the German prisoners themselves were never to know about it.

The two murder cases under discussion were similar in many respects to the Drechsler case, differing in one notable aspect—that the review preceedings had been completed in both cases and the President of the United States, Franklin D. Roosevelt, had already confirmed the death sentences. The first case involved Walter Beyer, a compound spokesman at the Tonkawa, Oklahoma, POW camp, who—along with four other noncommissioned officers, Berthold Seidel, Hans Demme, Hans Schomer, and Willi Scholz—had accused another prisoner of war, Johannes Kunze, of being a traitor, called an assembly of the entire compound in camp's mess hall, found him guilty of treason, and beaten him to death on the spot. The other case involved Erich Gauss and Rudolph Straub, two German prisoners who had done away with another prisoner, Horst Guenther, for allegedly being unfair in the distribution of food at the branch POW camp in Aiken, South Carolina. After President Roosevelt had approved the death penalty, both cases became ensnarled in what turned out to be a red-tape-laden provision of the Geneva Convention. Article 66 requires that:

If the death penalty is pronounced against a prisoner of war, a communication setting forth in detail the nature and circumstances of the offense shall be sent as soon as possible to the representative of the Protecting Power, for transmission to the Power in whose armies the prisoner served.

The sentence shall not be executed before the expiration of a period of at least three months after this communication.

In the Beyer case, a letter was personally delivered to the Swiss legation's Department of German Interests by an officer from the Provost Marshal General's office, accompanied by a representative of the State Department. The letter set forth the charges and specifications against all five accused and contained notification of President Roosevelt's confirmation of the sentence. The communication, which was delivered on October 9, 1944, also stated that the three-month period required under Article 66 of the Geneva Convention would commence upon delivery of the letter. Receipt of the letter was acknowledged by the chief of the Division of Foreign Interests of the Swiss legation on the day it was delivered, but Swiss authorities turned around almost immediately on behalf of the German government and objected to the validity of the communication, which, they related, set forth only the charges and specifications and, therefore, did not meet the provisions of Article 66 because it did not set forth "in detail the nature and circumstances of the offense." The reaction of the Provost Marshal General's office was swift and predictable; they did not agree and would resist the objection, pointing out that clearance of the communication had been obtained from the army Judge Advocate General before delivery of the letter and that the communication had, in their opinion, met all the requirements of the Geneva Convention.

The State Department was not quite so sure, however, and a considerable amount of correspondence passed back and forth between its offices and the legation of Switzerland. It was finally agreed to by all parties that the three-month period

would begin with the date of delivery of a full copy of the record in the Beyer case, and the execution date of the five
Germans would be postponed accordingly. On October 25,
the full record of the case was delivered, but the Swiss again
protested, this time charging that nothing in the communication had defined that they were free to communicate the record to the German government.

As a result, another postponement of the executions was
granted, but on December 30, notification in writing was received by the Swiss legation that they were free to transmit a
copy of the full record to the German government, and that
as of that date the three-month waiting period would begin.

The Gauss and Straub case was similarly hamstrung by red
tape, and their execution dates were postponed. This case hung
in abeyance until negotiations with the Swiss in the Beyer case
were resolved, negotiations that, it turned out, were just beginning.

Meanwhile, the three-man review board at Fort Douglas was
still synopsizing and transcribing their findings in regard to the
conviction and sentence of Prisoners of War Fischer, Franke,
Kuelsen, Ludwig, Reyak, Stengel, and Wizuy.

With regard to the murder of Werner Drechsler, the review
board concluded: "The record discloses conclusively that all
seven of the accused, with clearly defined malice, deliberately
joined in the perpetration of a heartless, cold-blooded, premeditated murder, without legal justification or excuse. The crime, as
admitted by all, represents in its very worst aspect the attempt
of individuals to arrogate to themselves the right to pass judgment upon another without even the semblance of a hearing or
the right of explanation and, acting upon rumors and inferences,
to decree the forfeiture of that individual's life. Concluding, as
self-appointed judges, court and executioners, that Drechsler
was a traitor, six of the seven accused, with whom the seventh
subsequently not only willingly but voluntarily and 'enthusiastically' joined, determined that he was no longer worthy

to live and should be hanged. In furtherance of this determination every detail of the proposed lynching of the deceased was worked out."

The board of review went on to describe the efforts of the seven men in carrying out the murder, annotating the record to their satisfaction so that it proved that it was a premeditated action and that the perpetrators were well aware of the illegality of their operation. With regard to the criminal actions of the deed, the board concluded: "It needs no citation of authority to substantiate the conclusion that the action of the accused constituted murder as defined by Article of War 92 and as interpreted in paragraph 148 of the *Manual for Courts-Martial,* 1928, and that murder is a crime in the United States as well as in all other civilized nations."

This finding, of course, was not unexpected. Not once in the trial had the defense attempted to refute the fact that the seven men had participated in a crime; instead, the defense had based its case solely on the culpability of the accused and the methods employed to obtain their confessions.

The review board then took into consideration each of the defense's points and sequentially analyzed, or, perhaps more accurately, demolished, each in its turn.

"The right to try and punish the accused under the Articles of War can, of course, not be questioned. It is equally well established that prisoners of war must conform to the laws, regulations, and orders enforced in the 'enemy's' country (*Winthrop's Military Law and Precedents,* 2nd.ed., p. 792). In the United States of America, the infliction of punishment is restricted to duly constituted courts, commissions, and tribunals. Nowhere in our laws or in our jurisprudence, civil or military, is there any recognition of the right of any group of civilians or soldiers, unless acting as a tribunal, named according to law, to impose the penalty of death upon another and to execute its sentence. Certainly there is no occasion to grant this extraordinary and dangerous authority to prisoners of war."

The general tone of the review board's opinion was readily apparent; all that remained were the specifics. They were about to be dispatched.

"The contention that the accused were actuated by high motives of patriotism to commit what is in law a deliberate murder and that, therefore, their action should be excused or the seriousness of their offense should be minimized is without merit. It cannot be questioned that had their victim been an American soldier or civilian their crime would have been murder regardless of their sincere belief that the interests of their fatherland would be furthered by their action. The board sees no reason for applying a different principle where the victim is a fellow prisoner.

"In the present case there is a striking lack of excuse or justification, assuming that traitorous conduct justifies the summary execution of the offender by a self-appointed tribunal. No one knew that Drechsler had been guilty of improper conduct—rumors and inference were the sole sources from which the conspirators drew their conclusions. No opportunity to explain was afforded the deceased. Their informal conference with their fellow prisoner, Camp Spokesman Hox, drew no recommendation for extra-judicial punishment. Deceased's pleas for an opportunity to explain were unheeded. Instead of being a traitor to his country, deceased may have been an outstanding patriot, whose very actions may have been governed by secret instructions given him by his government. Yet he was hanged because seven men decided among themselves that he was a traitor. Such a flagrant violation of the law of the nation by which they were held as prisoners of war cannot be condoned.

"It is worthy to note that Article 2 of the Geneva Convention places upon the detaining power the duty to treat prisoners of war with humanity and to protect them particularly against acts of 'violence, insults and public curiosity.' This obligation applies to violence from their fellow prisoners as well as from the detaining power. The government would subject itself to warranted criticism were it to take the position that prisoners of war detained by it may with impunity do violence to any other prisoner of war so detained because of some real or fancied wrong."

So much for the motives of the accused. The review board would not, of course, find a scintilla of agreement with their findings from the seven convicted men. But the prisoners by this time took no relish in discussing either the justification of their actions or the reasoning of the enemy that had brought them to trial for the same actions. All such discussions caused only bitterness and frustration. Now, during the few times of the day when they were allowed to be together, they talked mostly of more personal things, their families and homes in Germany and the general life in their isolated state in the prisoner of war camp stockade.

Helmut Fischer was still the leader despite Otto Stengel's efforts to encroach upon this leadership. Stengel, perhaps because he was older than the others or maybe because of the role he played in the execution of Drechsler and the momentary authority he usurped in the darkness outside Drechsler's barracks when the others decided it was too risky to continue, now considered himself the leader and spokesman for the group. The others had not held it against him for having been the first to confess. In the secret camp in California they knew that it had been only a matter of time before they all had to break down, so it did not really matter who was the first. And they really did not resent Stengel's efforts at assuming leadership; instead they simply ignored them and went about their activities with the original order of command still intact. Some of the guards at Florence, and even later at Fort Leavenworth, often could not tell who actually was the leader because of the way Stengel talked, but those who knew the prisoners more intimately knew exactly where the power resided.

The men held little hope that the review of their case would change their status in any way, and their attitude probably stemmed from the sense of quiet doom that Fischer imparted to the rest of them. At the same time he also instilled in them the conviction of the rightfulness of their actions, and he thus was able to maintain their steadfastness and resilience throughout an otherwise bleak existence. The situaton bothered Stengel more than anyone else, but when he became too involved in talking about the injustice of it all, Fischer would effectively derail him with something like, "Tell us about your children, Otto. Better still, tell us about your wife."

In Fort Douglas, Colonel Lyon and the other two members of the review board were taking up the last element of the defense in the Drechsler murder case.

"A question requiring discussion is the admissibility of the confession made by accused Stengel, Fischer, and Wizuy. Those made by the other accused are not questioned. The Board of Review fully concurs in the action of the trial court in finding nothing in the record to overcome the convincing proof of the voluntary nature of the original confessions, placed in written form after the acknowledgment of guilt before the board by the seven accused, acting separately and individually, each of whom appended to his statement a certificate that it had been voluntarily written by him in his own handwriting 'without any offer of reward, threats, promises, or duress of any kind whatsoever' and of the subsequent confessions made individually more than three weeks later to the investigating officer, at which time each accused confirmed the correctness of his previous written confession.

"Ample opportunity was afforded to the accused to repudiate their original confessions when they appeared before the investigating officer, instead of which each admitted his guilt again. When the confessions were offered in evidence, no objection was raised to their admission.

"There is not the slightest suggestion in the records that either the board of officers or the investigating officer attempted to use or did use improper methods or resorted to threats, promises or duress of any kind."

Whether the foundation for this last statement lies in the definition of "improper methods" or simply in the fact that the questionable methods brought out at the trial emanated from Captain Schmidt, who was not a member of the investigating board, has never been explained, but for the review board to arrive at such a conclusion in light of the few, but still notable, instances of the applications of improper pressure brought out by the defense means that one of the two foundations had to underlie the board's reasoning. Their decision had to mean that the methods, which were secret and for the most part were withheld from the court martial board, were proper within the definition of "proper," at least in 1944; or that they were improper but that they were not employed by the board itself, to whom the confessions were made but instead by another party acting without the board's jurisdiction. The former appears as the more logical of the two — this *was* 1944 and the definition of "proper methods of interrogation" has changed considerably over the succeeding years. In any event, the review board was essentially saying that it had not been established that the investigating board had used any improper methods to secure the confessions, and with this conclusion the entire case for the defense evaporated.

The review board went on to explain: "Insofar as the record is concerned, the highest degree of care and consideration, probably unparalled in any record of trial of an American soldier, was shown in explaining their rights to the accused and in obtaining assurances from them that the statements were voluntarily made without coercion."

And then in regard to the testimony at the trial: "It is evident from the statement made by Colonel Church on cross-examination and the testimony of Sergeant Held and Captain Schmidt that the accused had been interrogated prior to their confessions to the board. In addition, Colonel Church had seen a lie dectector used in connection with the interrogation of three of the accused. On one occasion, Sergeant Held had seen Stengel wearing an overcoat during cold weather in an unheated room while being interrogated and on another occasion had seen Fischer in his undershirt and shorts while being interrogated. Captain Schmidt acknowledged that during the course of his interrogation of Stengel an overcoat had been used, and an onion had been used in a gas mask which had been put on Stengel's face, but he denied that any methods other than 'ordinary ones' had been used.

"There was no testimony," the review board went on to note, "to show that any of these methods induced the confession by Stengel and, in the opinion of the Board of Review, the inference that during the long drawn-out investigation that was conducted this accused was on one occasion subjected to treatment which, had it produced a confession, would have rendered that confession inadmissible, is more than offset by the declarations subsequently made by this accused. With respect to accused Fischer and Wizuy there is no testimony at all to indicate that their statements were produced by coercive methods."

Most of the testimony about interrogation methods, however, came out of the trial in the form of unsworn statements, which were not subject to cross-examination by the prosecution, though the statements did elaborate on the sparse testimony of the two defense witnesses. Still the review board dealt with the unsworn statements at greater length perhaps than any other single element before their consideration:

"We pass then to the unsworn statements made by accused Stengel, Fischer, and Wizuy. According to the *Manual for Courts-Martial,* 1928, such statements are not evidence, the accused may not be cross-examined thereon, and such consideration will be given to them as the court 'deems warranted.' They may be offered by the accused 'in denial, explanation or extenuation of the offenses charged,' and while they should not include what is properly argument, the court will not 'check a statement' on that ground if it is being made orally and personally by an accused. The unsworn statements made by the accused were neither in denial, explanation or extenuation of the charge of murder, but pertained solely to the alleged events preceding, at that time not definitely fixed, their first confessions."

The board of review cites *Winthrop's Military Law and Precedents,* 2nd ed.; the *Manual for Courts-Martial,* 1917; *Opinions of the Judge Advocate General,* 1912; *The British Manual of Military Law,* 5th ed., 1907; and *Ives' Treatise on Military Law,* 1879, in regard to unsworn statements. The major emphasis of these citations, however, applies to the fact that such statements are not evidence or testimony, but rather a personal declaration of defense on the part of the person making it. Such statement should, of course, be taken under consideration by the court, which also should attach to it as much importance as the court determines that it merits. This is the procedure the board of review followed — to arrive at the following conclusion:

"But, conceding that in the exercise of the extensive latitude allowed the court in receiving unsworn statements it was justified in overruling the objection of the prosecution to the acceptance of any unsworn remarks relative to the voluntary nature of the confessions, the court was then vested with the authority to determine what weight should be given to these statements. Had any doubt been created, the court was empowered to call additional witnesses. By its action the court unquestionably found that the unsworn declarations of the accused did not cast any such doubt. The Board of Review fully concurs in this conclusion and is of the opinion that the record establishes beyond any reasonable doubt that even though some of the accused may have been subjected to severe interrogation at some time prior to their appearance before the board of officers, their actual confessions were voluntarily made without any offer of reward, threats, promises or duress of any kind whatsoever, and were unaffected by any prior grilling they may have received."

The review board then added a substantiation that seems more the product of the military mind than of the world of jurisprudence: "To hold otherwise would be to consider as unworthy of belief Colonel Church and Major Zabel and to disregard the solemn certificates voluntarily signed by the accused."

On November 17, 1944, the Board of Review completed its examination of the trial of the seven German prisoners of war convicted of murdering Werner Drechsler. It found:

"The court was legally constituted and had jurisdiction of the persons and the offense. No errors injuriously affecting the substantial rights of the accused were committed during the trial. In the opinion of the Board of Review the record of trial is legally sufficient to support the findings of guilty and the sentences and to warrant confirmation of the sentences. A sentence of death or imprisonment for life is mandatory upon a conviction of murder in violation of Article of War 92."

The entire document, twenty-two pages long, the "Opinion of the Board of Review," was signed by each of the three board members and, along with the full record of trial, was forwarded to the Judge Advocate General in Washington. From there it would go to the Secretary of War for review and presentation to the President of the United States for confirmation. But it was destined to linger in the Secretary of War's office for over eight months, pending the outcome of the negotiations in the Beyer and Gauss cases, which were taking on a new and much more serious dimension.

For the seven Germans, the news of the review board's decision caused little more than a shrug outwardly and a slightly sick feeling inwardly. They expected it; they were being personally persecuted. They had no idea whatsoever of how prized a commodity they would become in the next few months to the same government that had just upheld their death sentences.

14

Death Cell

AFTER the review board's report was forwarded to Washington and the gist of it was transmitted to the authorities at Florence, the army began preparations to transfer the seven men to the United States Disciplinary Barracks at Fort Leavenworth, Kansas. The eight other German prisoners of war who were under the death penalty were already there, confined to maximum security. On January 27, the seven men were handcuffed in their cells and then, under heavy guard, led out of the stockade at Florence and put on a train for Fort Leavenworth. As the train made its way out of the desert and across the flat plains of the lower Midwest, the seven men often talked among themselves about what lay before them. They all agreed that their destination was undoubtedly the place where their sentences would eventually be carried out, although no one had officially told them that yet. What few hopes they had held for clemency had fled and now were replaced with an increased bitterness. Yet, in reality, there was still room for hope; the President had not signed the orders, nor apparently had he any immediate intention of doing so.

In Washington, the Department of War added the names of Helmut Fischer, Fritz Franke, Guenther Kuelsen, Heinrich Ludwig, Bernhard Reyak, Otto Stengel, and Rolf Wizuy to the purposefully styled confusion of communications between the United States and Germany, although it was made clear to Germany that, as was not the situation in the Beyer and Gauss cases, the sentences of the seven were as yet unconfirmed. In Washington, authorities were already resigned to the fact that this was going to be a touchy and complex affair because only a few weeks earlier the State Department had received a note, dated January 5, 1945, from the Swiss legation in the United States containing a message both the War Department and the State Department had feared but halfway expected. The note, the reproduction of a cable received from the German legation in Bern, categorically stated that certain members of the United States armed forces were being held under death sentences in Germany but that the German government had postponed their executions until information was received from the United States government as to whether it might be prepared to accept an exchange of the American prisoners for the five German prisoners of war in the Beyer case.

The Secretary of War, Henry L. Stimson, replied to the State Department almost immediately, recommending the dispatch of a strong protest to the German government on the grounds that the United States prisoners in Germany to which they were referring were condemned on trumped-up charges. The State Department relayed the communication to Germany through the Swiss legation but with little hope that anything would come of it. In the meantime, however, the U.S. government was not about to execute Walter Beyer, Berthold Seidel, Hans Demme, Willi Scholz, and Hans Schomer or Erich Gauss and Rudolf Straub; nor were the papers going to be presented to the President for confirmation of the death sentences of Helmut Fischer, Fritz Franke, Guenther Kuelsen, Heinrich Ludwig, Bernhard Reyak, Otto Stengel, and Rolf Wizuy. It appeared much would have to be negotiated and settled before anything happened to change the present impasse.

The train bearing the seven young Germans pulled into Kansas City, Missouri, on the morning of January 29. It was an overcast, cold, and altogether dismal day; a far cry from the warmth and sun of southern Arizona. The men were put in the back of an enclosed army truck for the twenty-five mile ride north to Leavenworth.

The truck had no windows and therefore the prisoners were denied the cold but starkly beautiful view of the hilly and barren farmland that lies between Kansas City and Fort Leavenworth; nor did they see the fort itself when the truck finally pulled up to the front gate. If they had, they probably would have been mildly surprised because Fort Leavenworth is not a typical army fort.

In fact, there is no gate as such; instead, there are simply two granite pillars. About forty yards behind them is a military police booth. Through the same gate practically every major military figure from John Pershing to Dwight Eisenhower had passed at one time or another in their careers; the same post had seen such diverse personalities as Buffalo Bill Cody, learning his trade as an Indian scout, and a young lieutenant named Scott Fitzgerald, sitting in the Officers' Club putting down the first draft of a novel that later would be titled *This Side of Paradise*.

The main gate enters upon a broad avenue lined with towering elm trees whose branches reach up to form a long, vaulted ceiling. On both sides the land slopes and rises like a gently rolling sea. It is a pastoral and peaceful setting. Further up the avenue, two small lakes flank the road, and beyond them the street is lined with stately old red-brick homes, whose large and imposing white porches look out on neatly trimmed lawns; the architecture is usually described as bastard colonial or Kansas colonial. The atmosphere seems much more appropriate to that of a small college town than to an army camp. Past the houses, the main road forks around a large bronze statue of Ulysses S. Grant, sculpted by Lorado Taft in 1889. Behind the statue stands a short but rugged stone wall with unmistakable slots for rifles and cannons; it is part of the fort's original blockhouse and an authentic relic from the year of the fort's founding, 1827. A little farther on is a pleasant park surrounding a large and ornate gazebo where officers and their wives or girl friends once listened to leisurely Sunday afternoon concerts in days much quieter than those of 1945. Then the road descends into a wooded ravine. To most visitors it appears that they have reached the opposite end of the fort without actually having seen anything that resembles a combat military post. But as the road angles up out of the ravine it makes a sharp left turn and suddenly confronts the massive granite wall of the U.S. Disciplinary Barracks. It was this same road that Fischer, Franke, Kuelsen, Ludwig, Reyak, Stengel, and Wizuy traveled in the darkness of the truck's van, past the prison's front gate and around to the west wall, where they entered through a barred gate large enough to handle truck traffic. When the back doors of the truck were opened, the men climbed out, still in handcuffs, and found themselves in the middle of the prison yard, surrounded by great stone walls. They knew immediately that this was a real, true-to-life prison and not a makeshift camp for ordinary prisoners of war.

Fischer looked around him and then turned to Fritz Franke, who was standing next to him. "It doesn't look too nice, does it?"

Franke's mouth curled slightly downward as he muttered, more to himself than to Fischer, "Shit."

An army sergeant yelled to them to shut up and told them that they were to remain silent as long as they were in formation.

"*Shit* is right," Fischer whispered back to Franke.

The men were processed in and then led to their cells in the basement of one of the wings of the central detention building. Each man had his own cell and they were all on the same side; they were assigned in alphabetical order and presumably in the order in which they would be executed: Fischer, Franke, Kuelsen, Ludwig, Reyak, Stengel, and Wizuy. The cells had bars on the front and sides and a heavy concrete wall at the back, so the men could see and talk to each other. Several times during the day they were let out into the corridor that separated them from the cells facing theirs, which were inhabited by the defendants in the Beyer and Gauss cases and Edgar Menschner. During these periods, they could exercise or merely walk around in the corridor. That was the limit of their world. They were not taken outside, either individually or as a group.

In the first few days at Fort Leavenworth the men talked to the prison commandant, Colonel Eley, as well as doctors and a psychiatrist, a representative from the Red Cross, and various others who were all part of the routine processing procedure. On their second day at the prison they each met two chaplains, Major John Sagar, the Protestant chaplain, and Captain George Towle, the Roman Catholic chaplain. Both chaplains talked to each of the prisoners, not for any ecumenical reasons but simply because none of the seven Germans had practiced any religion during the past several years. They exhibited no overwhelming desire to pick up the pieces of any particular religion now. Fischer, Kuelsen, and Reyak had been brought up as Roman Catholics; the other four were Protestants, all Lutheran with the exception of Otto Stengel, who belonged to the Evangelical faith. But even though the seven men felt at this point in their lives that they had nothing in common whatsoever with the two chaplains and had little need or desire for religious guidance the two chaplains had to offer, most of the men immediately sensed that this was their first touch in several years with a milder, more civilized world. It was a meeting with someone who did not represent war or violence or punishment, someone who wanted to talk about other things, their homes and families, their feelings and ideas on anything and everything—and in honesty kept telling them that they were there to help them in any way within their power. That in itself was something the men had not experienced in quite a while.

On his first visit, Chaplain Towle talked with each of the men individually, and told them flatly he wanted to do anything he could to help them.

"Can you get us out of here and back to Germany?" Fischer asked him.

"No, of course not."

"Then you can't help us." Fischer paused and then added, "God deserted me a long time ago, all of us. And it looks like he's even deserted Germany now. For me I don't want any part of it."

Chaplain Towle nodded, not in agreement but out of a desire to discontinue the argument. They talked for a few minutes longer, but Fischer was extremely bitter. The chaplain finally shrugged his shoulders and ended the meeting. "All right but if you do think of something I can do, let me know. Even if you just want to talk, I'm a good listener," he said as he stood up.

Fischer nodded but said nothing and Chaplain Towle motioned for the guard to let him out of the cell. In Franke's cell, it wasn't any better. "Is there anything you'd like to talk about?" the chaplain began.

"Not really."

"Where are you from?"

"Frankfurt. What does it matter? I'll never see it again anyway." Franke paused for a moment and then said: "Maybe there is something you can tell me. Why are we getting such a rotten, shitty deal by your country? Can you tell me that?"

"No. You had a trial. I can't really help you there."

"I didn't think so. I don't have anything else I want to talk about." Franke stretched out on his bunk and ignored the chaplain.

"All right, maybe later," Chaplain Towle said as he stood up.

It was much the same all the way down the line. Guenther Kuelsen was quiet and brooding; Heinrich Ludwig was as curt and as bitter as Fischer and Franke. Otto Stengel talked with the chaplain more than anyone else, but he was still evasive and guarded in what he had to say. Stengel was the only one who talked about his family on this first visit and told the chaplain briefly about his wife and two children. "You know, the boy I've never seen, and he's almost three years old now."

"You still might, you know. Nothing's final yet. Your case is still being considered in Washington."

"Do you *honestly* think there's a chance," Stengel asked flatly.

"I don't know. It's always possible. Anything's possible when you're dealing with fate."

Rolf Wizuy in the adjoining cell had obviously been listening to the conversation because he interjected, "Fate, horseshit," and then went back to staring at the floor.

The chaplain ignored the remark and continued, "I don't want to get your hopes up without reason, but . . . ."

"Don't worry, you won't," Stengel said and laughed shortly.

Rolf Wizuy was the last in line, and, as Chaplain Towle entered his cell, he could immediately see that Wizuy was nervous and frightened, yet this was not at all evidenced by what Wizuy had to say. He was bitter, uncooperative, and very unhappy with everything around him.

The chaplain finally left the basement of the disciplinary barracks with his own assurance that he would return the next day and with the knowledge that the seven men showed little concern whether he did or not.

Both chaplains continued to visit the seven men daily, and as the days wore on the cold façade of bitterness and contempt gradually relaxed, if not in regard to their captors at least as far as the two chaplains were concerned. The prisoners listened to the reports of the progress of the war, grim from their point of view, but the evidence was now so overwhelming that they could no longer merely cast it off as American propaganda. They had come to accept the two chaplains as honest bearers of the news, and the two men substantiated almost everything the prisoners had heard from other sources. Their letters from home did not shed any light on the course of the war because those writing the letters were still inundated with German propaganda, and anything that even remotely implied a German success was censored before the letter was delivered to the addressee. The news was not encouraging, but surprisingly it was not as detrimental to their morale as one might have expected. Perhaps the collapse of their own lives had prepared them to accept the collapse of their country, or maybe a steadily growing disenchantment with Adolph Hitler as a leader had reached a point in their minds that it now appeared inevitable that Hitler would take their country down with him. Whatever it was, they all begrudgingly conceded that Hitler was not all they had once thought him to be, although they steadfastly maintained that Germany as a country was as great as Hitler had said and as they so deeply had believed it was.

Chaplain Towle had quickly ascertained after his first meeting with the prisoners that Helmut Fischer was their leader and that Fischer had set the tone for their dismal conversations that first day. As he sat in his office assessing his meetings, the chaplain knew that if he was to get anywhere with any one of the seven, he would first have to be accepted by Fischer, and he would never be accepted by Fischer if they only talked about the two inflammatory subjects that always popped up—the war and their conviction for murder. So, with that in mind, he went about his daily calls on the prisoners, seven days a week.

Somewhere in the middle of February, a little over two weeks after the men had been brought to Fort Leavenworth, Fischer mentioned to the chaplain that the best part of their day was when they were allowed to congregate together in the corridor, but that it was never long enough.

"Maybe I can talk to the commandant's office about that," Chaplain Towle said. "Maybe he'll extend it a little."

"That would be good. Do you think he might do it?"

"I don't know, but I'll certainly ask." Chaplain Towle looked away for a moment. "Another thing occurred to me: we might have our sessions out there, together. Would you have any objections to that?"

"I don't think so. But I'd want to talk it over with the others first."

"Maybe we could get a table and sit around and talk together. That might be better for all of us, kind of a round-table discussion. What would you think of that?"

Fischer nodded his head. "I'll ask the others." He stood up and walked over to the bars that separated his cell from Fritz Franke's. Franke simply shrugged his shoulders in a gesture of almost total indifference when Fischer mentioned the idea. Heinrich Ludwig said he did not really care one way or the other, but the rest agreed that it was a good idea. Then Fischer looked back at the chaplain, "If you can do it, it'll be fine."

The next day the chaplain arrived with two guards carrying a table, which they set up in the corridor. Then another guard opened the cells and told the prisoners they would have to use their own chairs if they wanted to sit. Each man brought the single straightbacked chair from his cell, and they began what was to become their daily ritual: an hour-long discussion with Chaplain Towle as their moderator. From that day, most of the men accepted the chaplain as a friend, even if he was a friend in enemy's clothing.

The discussions each day varied from politics to the war to home to their capture at sea. They seldom became involved with religion or God, which matters, when they did come up, would generate acid bitterness in all seven of the men. Some of the talks were quite heated. Fischer liked to propound his theory that the United States made their biggest mistake by not joining with Germany to fight the hordes from the east, who, he felt, were the worst threat to his idea of the civilized world. All of the men had ideas as to how the war could have been won by Germany. Fritz Franke took little part in the discussions; what he did have to contribute was usually pessimistic or contentious. The others, even Heinrich Ludwig, at least to some degree, appeared to enjoy their meetings.

And as the days passed with no word on their fate the seven men were led to project that maybe they would not in fact be hanged. After all, the other condemned Germans still had not been executed despite the confirmation of their sentences. When they expressed this hope to the chaplain, he always smiled slightly and nodded his head, saying, "I hope you're right." After a while, he had difficulty envisioning the seven as murderers and would think of them mostly as "very likable young chaps, all of them."

Outside of the walls at Fort Leavenworth, not everyone shared Chaplain Towle's views on prisoners of war. The term "coddling" had crept into the everyday vocabulary of the American public, and it referred directly to the American treatment of foreign prisoners of war. Nationally syndicated commentators, especially Walter Winchell and Drew Pearson, leaped on the bandwagon and made it a *cause célèbre*. The people were outraged to hear that enemy prisoners of war were living not only better than the American fighting man but in many cases better than they themselves in their own country. The fact that the charge of coddling, in almost every case, was without foundation—quite a few journalists in 1945 neglected to stop and check their facts—did not alter the public's views.

It was the feelings of the times coming to light throughout the country. And despite the fact that the United States was rapidly winning the war, the anti-German and anti-Japanese emotions were as strong as, if not stronger than, ever before. Perhaps they are best summed up in the following entirely typical newspaper story from the *St. Louis Globe-Democrat:*

If the Army has a reasonable explanation of why Nazi prisoners are being transported about this country in private drawing rooms while servicemen and civilians are forced to stand in train aisles, a good many irate citizens would like to hear it.

The case brought to light in St. Louis last week gives point to the inquiry. On a train jammed with passengers, many of them servicemen and some disabled, a German prisoner being moved from Newport News, Virginia, to an Oklahoma hospital for treatment for an ailment contracted prior to the war, rode in luxurious state in a private drawing room and dined in comfort while the other passengers were forced to wait.

This was not an isolated case. Other complaints have been made recently of passengers being forced to give up reservations in order that an enemy prisoner might ride in comfort.

Presumably the Army's explanation is that this pampering of war prisoners is necessary to prevent their escape. If so, the explanation falls flat. Equal security for war prisoners could be provided in a baggage car, or even in a freight car. It is also quite possible that many of the prisoners can be treated in prison camps without moving them about the country.

There have been many criticisms of coddling war prisoners. Some of the charges no doubt are exaggerated, but we believe that soldiers and civilians alike agree that the Army should treat its captives as prisoners of war and not as pampered guests. Certainly they should not receive more consideration than the men they were shooting at only a few months ago.

In Washington a congressional committee launched a full-scale investigation into the charges. The House Committee on Military Affairs, under the chairmanship of Andrew J. May of Kentucky, conducted the investigation and found that the criticisms were for the most part unwarranted. But the inherent feelings of the American public, accustomed now to war for four years, were not going to be mollified that easily, and perhaps better than anywhere else they knew that fact in Washington.

The sensation and outrage brewing on the outside, of course, never touched the seven men talking to Chaplain Towle in the basement of Fort Leavenworth's castle, at least not directly. In fact, they knew nothing about it. Even if they had, it is certain that they would have felt little empathy with the outraged public.

Outside the basement cells at Fort Leavenworth, winter was giving way to spring, but this was another thing the seven men were scarcely aware of. Chaplain Towle gave them almost daily weather reports as a bit of conversation, but the change in the seasons actually meant very little to them in their situation. In March the first rains of spring started, and the warm Kansas sun testified to the fact that the long cold winter of 1944 was finally over.

On March 10, the War Department and the State Department in Washington agreed that they had better follow up on the proposed prisoner-of-war exchange. The German government had predictably ignored Secretary of War Stimson's protest, remaining silent on the whole issue, apparently awaiting a more definite response from Washington. On

March 10 the State Department complied by delivering a note to the Minister of Switzerland in Washington to the effect that the United States proposed an outright exchange on a head-for-head basis of eleven American prisoners sentenced to death by courts martial in Germany for eleven of the German prisoners of war under the death penalty as a result of United States' courts martial. Why the figure of eleven was used is still a mystery. Fifteen Germans were under sentence of death in the United States, and at least a similar number of Americans could be expected to receive the same fate in Germany.

At any rate, the communication was delivered to the German government by the Swiss. The note ended with a positive statement that said that the United States government agreed not to execute the Germans in question until another three-month notice of its intention to do so had expired, provided that the U.S. government received a similar promise from the German government to postpone their scheduled executions of American prisoners of war. Further, the note stipulated that a communication to this effect must be received by the United States no later than April 5, 1945. The confirmed executions in the Beyer and Gauss cases were postponed until April 5, pending the German answer.

Communications in Germany, however, were beginning to fall apart. The squeeze of the war on two fronts was crushing the life out of Germany. The great industrial Ruhr Valley was for all practical purposes in ruins. The bridge at Remagen had fallen and U.S. troops were already on the other side of the Rhine river. Patton's Third Army was streaming across the river with its sights set on Berlin, less than 300 miles away. The Russians were closing in from the eastern front, and within the Third Reich itself the whole system was quickly deteriorating. Hitler began the purge of his closest advisers, starting with Field Marshal Gerd von Rundstedt, and issued his moribund general order that all military and industrial installations would have to be destroyed so that they would not fall into the hands of the enemy. Such was the state of affairs in Germany when the Swiss attempted to communicate with German authorities about the proposed exchange of condemned prisoners of war. And the largest problem the Swiss had to surmount was actually finding those persons within the German government who could make that kind of a decision.

On March 30, the United States again communicated with the Swiss legation in Washington in regard to the proposal of March 10, stating that because no answer had yet been received by the United States and by reason of the disruption of communications in Germany and humanitarian considerations on the part of the United States, the period of time for Germany to reply was extended until May 1.

Finally, on April 12, the State Department received a communication from the Minister of Switzerland informing the United States that he was in receipt of a cablegram that said that the German government was prepared to exchange "fifteen American prisoners of war under sentence of death for an equal number of Germans under sentence of death." The figure now tallied exactly with the number of Germans scheduled for the gallows in the United States. The German government also agreed in its communiqué to postpone for the duration of the exchange negotiations the date of execution already imposed on the American prisoners of war and said that if any change of this directive was contemplated the protecting power would be duly informed in sufficient time to communicate with the United States.

The State Department relayed the communication to the War Department the following day, and both departments set about preparing a reply to the German proposal. A coordinated reply was drafted and sent to the Minister of Switzerland by the State Department on April 27. But apparently the United States was still having considerable difficulty with the mathematics of the situation because the communiqué began with a request for specific information in regard to "which nine of the fifteen German prisoners of war whose names were listed in the Department's communication, dated March 9, 1945, the German government wished to have exchanged." But it also outlined a proposal for the logistics of the exchange: "Upon receipt of this information, the United States government will immediately transport these prisoners as expeditiously as possible to a convenient point on the Swiss-French frontier, where they will be turned over to the Swiss government for exchange at the same time that the condemned American prisoners will be similarly turned over at the Swiss-German frontier."

The following day, April 28, the United States legation in Bern hastily sent a message back to Washington stating that they had been informed that because of the communications breakdown in Germany, the German legation in Switzerland was unable to communicate with the responsible authorities in Berlin in regard to the American proposal, and that the German legation had expressed the belief that the United States would, however, postpone their May 1 executions until the question of exchange was finally settled. It was also reported that the German legation at Bern considered the previous German assurances that they would not execute American prisoners of war while negotiations for their exchange were still underway sufficient promise to warrant a similar action on the part of the United States. A further telegram from the American legation in Switzerland received by the State Department clarified that the German High Command had assured, at least for the present anyway, that the death sentences against American prisoners of war would not be carried out.

Communications to Berlin had indeed broken down by late April, 1945. Himmler and Goering had already fled south out of the city. Everything in the city was chaos;

there was no responsible person left to communicate with. The allies were within the city limits, and Hitler was in his bunker. For Germany, the end of the Third Reich was only days away.

Adolph Hitler took his own life on April 30, but even that did not completely thwart the proposed exchange of prisoners. Members of the American legation in Bern met with representatives of the Swiss Foreign Office to discuss the still undelivered American proposal. The diplomats of both these offices agreed that because of the circumstances, it would probably be better to make no further efforts to deliver it. Their reasoning was based on the premise that the forwarding of the proposal to exchange on a man-for-man basis at the Swiss frontiers might possibly jeopardize the lives of the American prisoners in German custody because it would force the Germans to reply that they were physically unable to deliver the condemned prisoners of war into Switzerland. If they refrained from forcing Germany into this position by *not* transmitting the American proposal, it could be assumed that the exchange negotiations were still in progress and therefore the German assurances of no executions during that period would still be in effect. The American legation notified the State Department to this effect, and no further attempts were made to deliver the proposal.

While all this was happening, Helmut Fischer, Fritz Franke, Guenther Kuelsen, Heinrich Ludwig, Bernhard Reyak, Otto Stengel, and Rolf Wizuy spent their days in the vacuity of enforced routine. They read the few available books in German from the prison library, they played checkers and dominoes, wrote to their families even though there were great questions as to whether the letters would ever be delivered, and dragged their chairs out once a day for their meeting with Chaplain Towle.

Each day without word brought a new sense of hope and

with it a more acceptable adjustment to their confined existence. The food was not bad at all, they admitted; it was
actually the best they had eaten since becoming prisoners of
war. The menu was the same as that served to regular U.S.
soldiers on state-side duty, and it was infinitely better than
what was being served to their fellow prisoners of war in
camps outside Fort Leavenworth, who had the good fortune
not to be condemned to death but the ill luck to be rationed
to four ounces of meat per day that came principally from
the internal organs of the animal (including anything from
tripe to kidneys to pigs knuckles to fat back)—the news
media's charge of "coddling" notwithstanding.

As March gave way to April, the seven resigned themselves to the inevitable end of the war. They mentioned to
Chaplain Towle on various occasions that if they survived
until the war was over, they would probably get to go
home. And even though their allegiance to Germany had
not faltered, the thought of the war's ending began to create
ambivalent feelings in all of them.

Heinrich Ludwig observed glumly that "We'll probably
have to stand trial all over again there."

"But there it will just be a formality," Fischer corrected
him. "Even if we do lose the war, there is not a German in
our country who will see us as criminals. They would thank
us for what we did, you know that."

Ludwig agreed, but they all knew it was far too early to
begin making plans about returning to Germany. Any day
the orders from Washington could come through, and when
that happened, it would all be over. They were terribly
aware of their vulnerability.

On April 13, before Chaplain Towle arrived for his daily
session, the seven men learned that Franklin D. Roosevelt
had died the day before. It was a startling bit of news, and
they all wondered what the ramifications might be, in regard
not only to themselves but also perhaps to the course of the

war. Their conjectures were not a great deal different from those being discussed by Hitler and Goebbels in Berlin—perhaps this was the one stroke of fate Germany needed to turn the tide of the war. When Chaplain Towle arrived, they had a great number of questions ready for him.

"What do you think will happen to the war," Wizuy began, "now that Roosevelt's dead?"

"You've already heard, I take it," the chaplain said. "I thought I was bringing you some news."

Kuelsen repeated Rolf Wizuy's question.

"I don't think anything will come of it. It won't affect the war. It's very tragic, but I think everything will carry on as usual."

"Do you think the new President might go with Germany?" Fischer asked. "And join forces against Russia?"

"I don't think so. I don't really know, but it doesn't seem likely. You see it's different in the United States when the President dies, it's not like where only one man is in power."

"But what's the new President's feelings?" Fischer persisted.

"I don't know that, either. But it's all different here, you see."

Chaplain Towle and the men talked for over an hour, the chaplain well aware of their excitement about the possibility of a change as a result of Roosevelt's death. But there was really nothing he could tell them, and so for the most part he just listened to their ideas about the possible resurgence of Germany and how fortunate such a turn of events might be for everybody.

The next few days showed no change in the policies of the day, at least that they were aware of, and the only news they heard was that the war had not altered its course at all. If anything, it was moving more rapidly toward the final destruction of the Third Reich, so they gradually resigned themselves again to the collapse of their country and accepted with an odd mixture of bitterness and hope the uncertainty of their own fate.

Finally on May 8, 1945, they received the news that Adolph Hitler was dead and that Germany had unconditionally surrendered. They had survived until the end of the war, all of them realized, and that was encouraging. But they had mixed feelings about the outcome. There was the expected depression about the loss they had fought so hard to prevent from happening; there were fear and apprehension about what might happen to their relatives in Germany at the hands of the conquering armies, especially the Russian army; there was the hollow feeling that all they had ever really known in their way of life was now gone, presumably forever; and finally there was the grim realization that their patriotic and impetuous act against Werner Drechsler had been in vain. They talked with Chaplain Towle about these feelings and he could see that while they were sadly clinging to a hope, they were confused about everything that lay ahead of them. They told him that even now, with Germany defeated and in ruins, they were not sorry about what they had done. They had acted as they were supposed to as sailors in the German navy. Now that the war was over and Germany and the United States were no longer enemies, perhaps the authorities would view their act with more understanding eyes, they told the chaplain.

"What do you honestly think, chaplain?" Fischer asked.

Again Chaplain Towle was forced to tell them that he did not know and could not make even a reasonable prediction. In his own mind he wished very deeply that he did know; he was anxious for the whole thing to be resolved, and he felt there was something terribly inhuman about the long wait for a decision as to whether these young men would live or die.

In Washington, the first step in the decision-making process was made shortly after Germany surrendered. It was quickly determined that the American soldiers who were sentenced to death by the Germans had been safely recovered or that their recovery was a virtual certainty. The news was transmitted to the Department of War and made its way through channels to the office of the Provost Marshal General, the army branch responsible for all prisoners of war. The Provost Marshal General, Major General Archer L. Lerch, then forwarded a transmittal sheet to the Assistant Chief of Staff, G-1, with specific reference to the Beyer and Gauss cases, pointing out that the negotiations for the exchange of the condemned Germans for allegedly condemned Americans had failed by reason of the Allied military victory over Germany. In the Provost Marshal General's transmittal letter, it was recommended that the restrictions imposed by the Assistant Chief of Staff, G-1, against the execution of the individuals in the Beyer and Gauss cases and against the presentation to the President for confirmation of any unconfirmed death sentences of German prisoners be rescinded and that instructions be given to the Provost Marshal General to cause the death sentences of the Beyer and Gauss defendants to be executed.

Apparently the "humanitarian considerations" which had prompted the War Department earlier to postpone the executions applied only to the American prisoners of war in question. Now that they were safely recovered, there appeared to be no reason to hold off the executions in the United States. The days of bargaining were over, and it was certainly not anyone's fault that the exchange had not transpired before Germany fell. On the other hand, it was the fate of the fifteen unfortunate Germans that was to be determined because the negotiations were slower than the Allied war effort.

The Assistant Chief of Staff, G-1, returned the transmittal letter, routing it through the office of the Chief of Staff, with the direction that those prohibitions against the executions be removed and that necessary action be taken to carry out the confirmed death sentences on or after July 1, 1945, and to cause the death sentences imposed upon certain other German prisoners of war to be presented to the President for review and confirmation and, if confirmed, also to be carried out.

15

Execution

CHAPLAIN Towle was as unaware as everyone else at Fort Leavenworth of the decision that had been reached in Washington. Even the commandant of the disciplinary barracks, Colonel William S. Eley, did not learn of it until early July, and then only when the orders from the War Department unostentatiously appeared on his desk one morning directing him to carry out the sentences of the five defendants in the Beyer case. The fifteen prisoners in death row were not to know until one day before the execution date.

On July 3, while preparations for the building of the gallows were already underway at Fort Leavenworth, the unconfirmed death sentences of Edgar Menschner and Helmut Fischer, Fritz Franke, Guenther Kuelsen, Heinrich Ludwig, Bernhard Reyak, Otto Stengel, and Rolf Wizuy were sent to the White House for final presidential review. President Truman was personally to consider the cases after they were formally reviewed and presented to him by members of his legal staff. And Harry Truman was an incredibly busy man in the early days of July, 1945; he was still fighting the war in the Pacific and working at the peace arrangements of the Potsdam Conference, not to mention pondering such titanic questions as the dropping of atomic bombs on Hiroshima and Nagasaki.

The war in Europe had been over for almost two months, but the fervor of anti-German feeling had not slackened among the general population of the United States. The horrors of Auschwitz, Dachau, Buchenwald, and Belden-Belsen were now common knowledge; and the ghastly pictures of emaciated, half-dead prisoners who had somehow survived to be liberated by the American army and of those not so fortunate whose bodies were found stacked in huge piles like so much firewood illustrated the grotesque nightmare of the German treatment of Jews, gypsies, prisoners of war, and anyone else who happened to fall out of favor. The American people were enraged at the barbarism, and their opinions of the Germans were as bitter as they had been when the war first broke out. German-Americans felt the burden of their ancestry, and it was not uncommon for a brick to be thrown through the window of a German immigrant's house, even though the German-American might have had two sons still overseas fighting in the American army.

There had been some improvement in public information, however, and the charges of coddling German prisoners of war were no longer heralded in the country's newspapers and radio broadcasts. In fact, the newspapers were now writing stories like this one from the *Bayonne,* New Jersey, *Times:*

> Our so-called "coddling" of German war prisoners has saved the lives of many American prisoners in Germany, the International Red Cross reveals.
>
> A Swiss Red Cross official has stated that when Hitler ordered the execution of American and British aviators last March (1945), his officers disobeyed him because they knew that both Allied coun-

tries had lived up to the Geneva Convention covering treatment of prisoners of war. Thus 99 percent of American prisoners survived Hitler's intended vengeance.

This does not condone the Germans' unspeakable treatment of political, as distinct from military, prisoners. There was no Geneva Convention for Dachau, Buchenwald, and Maidanck. But it does vindicate the humane treatment of prisoners, in accordance with an honorable pledge, which apparently appealed to the remaining vestige of decency in the German army.

Although such statements may have soothed the anti-German POW sentiments, it did little to mellow the turbulent anti-German feeling throughout the country.

Without doubt, the most extreme example of anti-German sentiment was embodied in a young American army private named Clarence Bertucci. The young man, who had never been in combat, was assigned to guard duty at a temporary POW camp in Salina, Utah. One evening in the guard tower, he turned the tower's 30-caliber machine gun on the tents where the German POWs were sleeping and opened fire, raking one row after the other. When he finally stopped, eight Germans were dead and twenty were wounded. Bertucci calmly announced later that he hated Germans and therefore he had killed Germans. The actions of Private Bertucci were hardly typical, but they were fostered by the times and serve as a tragic but vivid testament to the feelings of the day.

Chaplain Towle was well aware of the undercurrent of mistrust and antipathy toward Germans in general. He carefully kept this from the seven men whom he talked to daily and as gracefully as possible ignored their questions as to what the American people thought about their being sentenced to death. Because the whole atmosphere was dreadfully suspicious, the chaplain made it a point to keep his own feelings about the likability of the seven young men and his concern at the severity of their sentence from the ears and minds of his superior officers and his own peers.

Through June and into the first week of July, the days began to drag for all of the condemned prisoners at Fort Leavenworth. Day after day went by with no word forthcoming. The men began to greet Chaplain Towle each day with the same line, "Any news yet?" but he would simply shake his head negatively and try to change the subject.

On July 6, all that changed. It was in the morning, somewhere around ten o'clock, when the heavy barred door to the corridor slid open and a lieutenant and two guards came briskly through it. They walked past several cells and stopped in front of Edgar Menschner's. All fifteen of the prisoners watched the three men in silence.

"Menschner?" the lieutenant called into the cell.

The prisoner was sitting on his bunk staring up at the lieutenant. "Yes, sir."

"Get your things; you're moving upstairs."

"What do you mean?" Menschner was startled.

"You're moving to a cell upstairs. You're a very lucky bastard. I've got orders to move you out of here. Your sentence was commuted by the President." The lieutenant paused and then added, "To twenty years."

Menschner stood up and walked slowly toward the door of his cell and looked through the bars deeply into the lieutenant's face. "Is it really true?" he asked.

"It's true. Get your stuff and let's get going." The lieutenant motioned to one of the guards to open the cell door.

The other prisoners in the first few moments of this astonishing revelation were awe-struck. They stared dumbly out of their cells at the three Americans. Then one of them shouted from his cell, "What about us? What are they going to do with us?"

The lieutenant looked down the row of cells to the vicinity of where the voice came from but said nothing in response.

"Is there any word on us?" It was the same voice. But there was still silence.

The lieutenant looked around uneasily and then finally said, "No, nothing on any of you yet. Only Menschner." He turned back quickly to Menschner, who was gathering up his bedding and his few other articles.

Menschner stepped out into the corridor, his arms full. "Can I say good-bye to my comrades?" he asked the lieutenant.

The lieutenant nodded and Menschner put his belongings down on the floor of the corridor. He went from cell to cell, shaking hands and listening to the congratulations each of his comrades exuberantly expressed. When he reached Otto Stengel's cell, he stopped and smiled. Stengel had become a close friend during their outings in the corridor, and the two men had talked at length many times. "I'll see you upstairs, Otto," Menschner said as they were shaking hands. "We'll all be upstairs together. It won't be long."

"We'll be up there," Stengel said, smiling too. "You wait for us, you son of a bitch. We'll be along. Don't go off and leave us." And they all laughed heartily.

Both chaplains, Captain Towle and Major Sagar, arrived together later that morning and were greeted by an enthusiastic and hopeful group of prisoners. The door to Menschner's now-empty cell was still open, but the chaplains had known well before they arrived that Menschner had moved out. The event of the morning was, of course, the prime topic of conversation. It was a sudden glimmering of something really substantial, and it had an enormous impact on the prisoners' morale. Fischer, Franke, Kuelsen, Ludwig, Reyak, Stengel, and Wizuy were especially optimistic in light of the fact that their sentences, like Menschner's, had not previously been confirmed, and now it appeared that there was a definite foundation for hope for a merciful hearing at the highest level of their appeal. The defendants in the Beyer and Gauss cases had no idea how, if at all, this would affect their confirmed sentences, but it certainly seemed to be a light in an otherwise dark time.

It was, however, a disturbing visit for the two chaplains because they could not fully share in the prisoners' enthusiasm; in fact, they could only pretend to take any part in it. Both of them knew that the date had already been set for the executions of the five defendants in the Beyer case and the two in the Gauss case and that even as they talked, Lieutenant Colonel Raymond Orr was already putting the final touches to the special gallows that he was constructing for the occasion.

Two days later, on July 8, their secret was no longer a secret. Colonel Eley, flanked by both chaplains, entered the corridor in death row and informed first Walter Beyer and then Berthold Seidel, Hans Demme, Willi Scholz, and Hans Schomer that the execution of their sentences would be carried out at midnight the following evening. Then Colonel Eley left the two chaplains to salvage whatever peace of mind they could for the prisoners in the awful gloom of that block of cells.

The following night no one was able to sleep in death row. The lights burned there until the last of the five were led out at somewhere around four o'clock in the morning. The other nine prisoners watched with quiet despair and a vitriolic sense of injustice, but there was nothing they could say, even to each other, and they finally went to sleep after the sun had risen in the very early hours of the morning of July 10, 1945.

When Colonel Eley and the chaplains arrived again two days later, there was no wonder as to the reason for their visit. Erich Gauss and Rudolf Straub listened and silently accepted the information that they would be hanged the next evening. And so, on the morning of July 14, all that remained of the fifteen German prisoners of war condemned to death were Helmut Fischer and his six companions.

Their case was still unresolved. No word had come from Washington, and they were left with only the conflicting moods of hope because of Menschner's reprieve and despair because of the execution of the seven defendants in the Beyer and Gauss cases. As the days passed, they slowly sank back into the normal routine. Chaplain Towle continued to visit them each day; they talked candidly and at length about their own lives and what they would do if they ever got out of their predicament. And they waited sullenly for the news of their fate, which appeared, as time went on, would never be forthcoming. Stengel often said laughingly to the chaplain: "You don't think they've forgotten about us, do you?"

But they were far from being forgotten.

The evening of August 23 was a typical stifling hot Kansas night. Some of the prisoners were dressed only in their shorts and T-shirts and all of them were barefoot. Fischer and Fritz Franke were talking between the bars that separated their two cells; Guenther Kuelsen was writing a letter; Ludwig and Reyak were playing checkers; Otto Stengel was working on a drawing of the face of Christ that he had started several days earlier; and Rolf Wizuy was simply lying on his bunk staring up at the ceiling. It was 9:25 P.M., thirty-five minutes before the lights were scheduled to go out.

All seven of the prisoners heard the clatter of heavy, fast-stepping footsteps before anyone appeared at the barred door to the corridor, and they all paused in what they were doing to look toward the door. Even Wizuy pushed himself up on one elbow to see who was coming at that hour of the night. A guard swung the door open and in marched Colonel Eley, followed by two other officers and the two chaplains. The guard who had opened the door called the prisoners to attention, and the seven men moved quickly to that position, each standing by his bunk. Colonel Eley moved just beyond Helmut Fischer's cell, almost directly in front of Fritz Franke, and the other officers formed a compact little group behind him. Colonel Eley had several papers in his hand, but he looked up and down the line of cells at the men standing rigidly in each. Then he looked down at the top sheet of paper and began to read.

"General Court Martial Orders Number 406: Charge: violation of the 92nd Article of War. Specification: In that Prisoner of War Helmut Fischer, Prisoner of War Fritz Franke, Prisoner of War Guenther Kuelsen, Prisoner of War Heinrich Ludwig, Prisoner of War Bernhard Reyak, Prisoner of War Otto Stengel, and Prisoner of War Rolf Wizuy, all of Prisoner of War Processing Station, Angel Island, California, acting jointly and in pursuance of common intent, did, at Prisoner of War Camp, Papago Park, Phoenix, Arizona, on or about March 12, 1944, with malice aforethought, willfully, deliberately, feloniously, unlawfully, and with premeditation kill one Prisoner of War Werner Drechsler, a human being, by strangulation.

"Pleas to the specification and charge by each accused: Not guilty.

"Findings of the specification and charge as to each accused: Guilty.

"Sentence as to each accused: To be hanged by the neck until dead."

Colonel Eley paused and shuffled the papers in his hand, placing the one he had just finished under the others, and then continued.

"The sentence having been approved by the reviewing authority, the record of trial forwarded for the action of the President, and the record of trial having been examined by the Board of Review in the Judge Advocate General's office; and the Board of Review having submitted its opinion in writing to the Judge Advocate General, and the record of trial, the opinion of the Board of Review, and the recommendations of the Judge Advocate General having been transmitted directly to the Secretary of War for the action of the President, and having been laid before the President, the following are his orders thereon:

"In the foregoing case of German Prisoner of War Helmut Fischer, Fritz Franke, Guenther Kuelsen, Heinrich Ludwig, Bernhard Reyak, Otto Stengel, and Rolf Wizuy, the sentence of each accused is confirmed and will be carried into execution under the direction of, and at a time and place to be designated by the Commandant, United States Disciplinary Barracks, Fort Leavenworth, Kansas."

Colonel Eley looked up from the paper, his eyes again wandering down the line of cells, and then he added:

"The orders signed by the President of the United States and issued by the Secretary of War will be carried out here August 25, 1945, commencing at zero zero zero one hours of that date."

Colonel Eley did an abrupt about-face and walked swiftly back down the corridor and out of the cell block. His entourage, with the exception of the two chaplains, followed close at his heels, and as the barred door closed behind them the guard shouted, "At ease." But the prisoners had already sunk into that position.

Chaplain Towle had the guard unlock the cell doors so that the men could gather in the corridor with him and Chaplain Sagar. The men walked slowly out into the corridor; some of them did not even bother to bring their chairs along. Kuelsen sat back on his bunk and picked up the letter he had been writing, then crumpled it into a ball and threw it on the floor of his cell.

Otto Stengel was the first to speak: "The bastards, the rotten goddamned bastards," he said, addressing the whole group. "Why the fuck are they doing this? They don't understand, not at all. I thought after all this time, they'd understand." But then his voice began to crack and he stopped.

Rolf Wizuy, who was standing next to Stengel near the table looked over at him and with a surprising degree of calmness said: "It doesn't matter any more, Otto. It's all over."

"They're still bastards," Ludwig intoned. "Whether it's all

over or not, they're still bastards." And then he slumped down into the chair he had brought out from his cell.

Guenther Kuelsen joined the others in the corridor and asked Chaplain Towle: "That's tomorrow night, isn't it?"

"Yes, at midnight."

Helmut Fischer was sitting at the table when Kuelsen came out, his head in his hands, staring down at the coarse grains of wood. He looked up when Kuelsen spoke and sat back in his chair, but said nothing.

"I'll be here all day tomorrow," the chaplain continued. "I've made arrangements so that the cells will be open all day." There was an awkward silence and the chaplain seemed to be searching for something to say. "You'll all want to write letters home tomorrow, I'm sure. Is there anything you need?"

"No," Fischer answered for the group, and the others nodded in agreement.

"They don't give you much time once they make up their minds, do they?" Fritz Franke asked bitterly.

"You wouldn't want a lot of time, I'd think. Would you, once you finally knew?" Chaplain Towle asked.

"I suppose not. I don't really give a shit any more."

Stengel walked around the table, shuffling slowly but constantly moving. "What good is it going to do for them to kill us? The war's over. Don't they know that?" he asked rhetorically. "I have a wife and children in Germany, maybe starving to death right now, I don't know. Who's going to help them?"

"Take it easy, Otto," Fischer said.

But Stengel barely paused. "It's not for killing a traitor. It's because they're still fighting the war. We did our duty and they're going to hang us for it. It's stupid, it's goddamned stupid. And there's nothing we can do about it, just sit here and let it happen." And then looking directly at

Chaplain Towle, Stengel said, "Why are they doing this to us?" Before the chaplain could answer, however, Fischer spoke up. "It doesn't matter why now. It's going to happen, that's it."

"You think I don't know that?" Stengel said.

"We all knew it right along," Fischer began again. "We all knew this might happen, and now it has. All we can do now is die like good German sailors. We all agreed to that. We have nothing to be ashamed of."

"I'm not ashamed of anything. I'm proud I did my duty. I'm saying they're wrong, that's all. And I'm trying to find out why the hell they're doing it. I think I at least have the right to know. Can somebody tell me that?"

"Shut up, Otto. You're just making it worse," Fischer said, staring coldly up at Stengel.

Stengel did not answer, but he stopped pacing.

Fischer then turned to the chaplain. "We will die as good Germans, just as we lived." He looked then at the others in the corridor and in their impassive, sullen faces he could see that they were all in agreement. Even Otto Stengel nodded his head slowly in concurrence.

"You know you will be allowed to wear your uniforms," the chaplain said. "You'll want to, I imagine."

Fischer spoke for the group. "Yes, what's left of them. We don't have full uniforms, you know. Only what we had on the submarine."

"I'll see that they're gotten out of storage and cleaned up for you tomorrow."

At a few minutes before ten o'clock, the guard reappeared at the door to the corridor and told them that the lights would be turned out in two minutes.

Chaplain Towle stood up uneasily. "Is there anything else I can do tonight?"

Fischer shook his head. "No, not tonight." Fischer looked

directly at the chaplain. "It's wrong, you know. What they're doing to us is wrong." He paused and looked around the corridor. "You will be here tomorrow?"

"Tomorrow, of course."

"Early?"

"If you'd like, yes, early."

Chaplain Towle, looking at the others, said, "Good night now," and then turned and left the corridor. The seven men went back into their cells and shortly after the guard had locked them in, the lights went out.

The prisoners were roused at 5:30 the next morning, but most of them were already awake in their cots. They were served a breakfast of French toast, bacon, cereal, an orange, and coffee. Surprisingly they were all very hungry. Chaplain Towle arrived shortly after eight o'clock, and though the cell doors were opened, not all the prisoners left their cells. Some were writing letters, trying to communicate to their families some form of hope despite the fact that all of theirs was now gone. Guenther Kuelsen wrote with this in mind.

In prison
August 24, 1945

Dear Parents, Grandparents, Lilo, Erich, Friends,

With these lines, I would like to take leave of you all, and would like to, at the same time, thank you for all the good things you have done for me. Fate, unfortunately, does not want that I should see whole what I have left whole. With the expiration of this day, I will depart from this world, and enter the great army. Just you stay strong, endure, and be united. Germany will live, even if we have to die. I was prepared for my sentence, and took it easily, as you all know me. It just isn't a "soldier's death," but one has to yield. I will also overcome that in the belief in my Fatherland. God help me.

Now with what I personally have, there is not much to settle; the money that may still be in my account, you will be able to use. You will probably also receive all other belongings. Stay healthy and lively—heads up. This wishes you as I take leave your son, grandchild, brother, friend,

Guenther

When he finished the letter, Kuelsen joined some of the others in the corridor. Fischer and Stengel were still in their cells writing letters. Chaplain Towle talked to the men in the corridor for awhile and then walked into Fischer's cell. "Can I help you with the letter at all?"

Fischer looked up. "No, I'm almost through," he said, and then ignored the chaplain.

Chaplain Towle could sense almost immediately that through the night, much of the bittterness that Fischer had felt over the last months had come back. It may have been from the expression on his face or the curtness of his words and movements, but whatever it was, it was there. The chaplain sat on Fischer's bunk while he was finishing the letter. Fischer finally folded up the self-mailing piece of POW stationery and tossed it onto the bunk next to the chaplain.

"There's really not much you can say, is there?" he asked, nodding toward the letter.

"I don't know; I think there's probably a lot you could say if you wanted to."

"I don't want to tell my family everything I feel. It's hard enough on them. I don't want to make it worse. But I feel now Otto was right last night."

Fischer and the chaplain talked for quite some time, and in the course of their conversation the question of religion finally came up. Fischer repeated his feeling that he had been deserted by God and religion. Some of the others gathered at the door to Fischer's cell and joined the conversation to express feelings very similar to Fischer's.

At 11:30 the men had lunch. Chaplain Towle stayed with them and asked to have some food brought down so that he could eat with them. In the afternoon the men went back to writing letters and just talking. In a way, it seemed almost like an ordinary day in the basement of the castle.

Finally, the chaplain went back to Fischer to try again. They talked for a little while, but as it dragged on, the chaplain became irritated.

"Are you going to take all that bitterness with you into eternity?" he asked.

"I guess so. Why not?"

"At midnight you're going to face God. Don't you know that? And whether you think it's just or unjust, your life here is going to be over. Whatever's happened here isn't going to matter anymore. It's just going to be between you and Him. You've got to make your own choice about your eternal life and you've got to make it here, today."

The chaplain sat back and breathed heavily. He had not intended to get so carried away, but he had said what he wanted to say.

Fischer remained silent, staring at the chaplain. The other prisoners were listening, but none of them said anything, either.

Finally, Chaplain Towle broke the silence. "I don't mean to give you a sermon, but I meant every word I said. I think it's terribly important. And I think you should, too." The chaplain started to get up, but Fischer put out his hand, motioning him to stay.

"I think maybe you're right," Fischer said.

The chaplain spent the rest of the afternoon talking to each of the other prisoners, helping some of them with their letters home. The others, following Fischer's lead, were much more amenable now to the chaplain's talk about religion, and all talked freely about it. Fritz Franke was still the most silent of all and Otto Stengel the most verbal, but they all in their own way emitted the same feelings of deep frustration and resignation. The men were told that dinner would be beef pot pie, but that they could have

something else if they wished—the Army obviously not want-
ing to break with the tradition of the occasion by not offer-
ing one of the last amenities afforded to condemned men.
Bernhard Reyak and Rolf Wizuy said they didn't care, but
the others opted for Southern fried chicken, a dish they had
never had before becoming prisoners of war but had learned
to like over the last two years.

In the evening, the seven men were allowed to put their German uniforms on, and then many of them went back to writing letters. At ten o'clock, Chaplain Towle told them that he
would have to leave because he had been ordered to report to
Colonel Eley's office.

When Chaplain Towle arrived in the commandant's office,
a number of other officers were already there along with the
newspaper and radio reporters who had been invited by the
Fort Leavenworth Public Information Office to witness the executions. It was dreadfully quiet in the room, the chaplain
thought. Colonel Eley briefed all of them on the procedure that
would be followed, where they would stand, and so forth. The
reporters surprisingly had very few questions. Each had been
given a folder that contained personal data on each of the condemned, a copy of the orders that had been confirmed by the
President, the news release on the operation and construction of
the gallows, and a menu of the food served in the disciplinary
barracks that day.

Back in the basement of the castle as it neared midnight,
Guenther Kuelsen was the only prisoner still writing a letter. It was his third of the day and it was very short.

In prison
August 24, 1945

Dear Parents and Family:

With this card I once more address myself to you. My last hour
draws closer and closer and at the same time I feel very close to

you. I see you in my thoughts, and I know you are remaining strong. Don't take it so hard. One can't tie any bonds with the powers of fate. It has to be like this. Once again, best, best wishes. As always,

Your Guenther

After the briefing, the chaplain returned to the basement of the castle to wait with the men. A few minutes before midnight, the hollow echo of footsteps could be heard approaching the corridor, and Chaplain Towle felt a terrible lump growing in his throat. The men were silent, they were all standing, peering out from their cells at the door. Chaplain Towle was standing in the corridor next to Fischer's cell.

The door was opened, and a lieutenant led the way into the corridor. Behind him were a sergeant, six guards with rifles, and two guards with keys. The lieutenant said crisply, "Helmut Fischer," and one of the guards with keys moved quickly over to unlock the cell door. Fischer was allowed to walk down the row of cells and say good-bye to his comrades. It was a similar scene to the one enacted three weeks earlier when Edgar Menschner departed, only this time there was no gaiety. Fischer shook hands with each man and when he reached Stengel's cell, Stengel reached out and clutched him by the arm and said simply, "Comrade." Fischer nodded his head, a faint smile on his lips and repeated the word.

Fischer stopped at Wizuy's cell and said, "We die as soldiers, Rolf."

As Fischer turned to walk back down the corridor he looked over his shoulder and said. "Don't forget, friend." Wizuy did not answer but stared after Fischer, who took his place between the guards, three on each side, one man with keys in front, and the other at the rear. The lieutenant and the sergeant marched the troop out of the corridor, and the door was shut and locked behind them. The chaplain walked next to Fischer in silence up the stairs through another barred door and out into the rotunda of the castle. The footsteps clattered loudly, and Fischer looked over at the chaplain and saw that he was shaking. "You're nervous. I'm the one who should be nervous." he said with a faint smile.

"I am, I know."

The door to the main entrance was opened and the marching men continued out of the rotunda and then out of the building. Outside Fischer looked around him and then up at the sky; it was the first time he had been outdoors since his arrival at Fort Leavenworth about eight months earlier.

It was an extremely hot night. The moon, bright in the sky, illuminated much of the prison yard.

The men marched along the brick walkway and then turned toward the salvage warehouse. The distance from the castle to the building that housed the gallows was about 150 yards. Light poured out of the large entranceway and down the wooden ramp that led to it; the entrance was normally used by trucks. They marched up the ramp and into the warehouse; it was very bright inside.

Colonel Eley was awaiting them, standing at attention directly in front of the gallows. Fischer with an emotionless expression on his face could see the platform and the noose hanging quite still above it as he approached the colonel. Off to the side was a sergeant standing next to a large brakelike lever that rose out of the floor, and Fischer knew that he was the actual executioner. The group stopped a few feet before Colonel Eley. Along one wall of the building there stood a number of army officers who had been appointed witnesses to the executions. Against the opposite wall were the news reporters, silently watching every movement in the scene unfolding before them. Near Colonel Eley were also a number of enlisted men, who had various assignments to carry out in the operation.

Colonel Eley had everyone called to attention and then read

the death sentence. Helmut Fischer had heard the words before, and he stared straight ahead as the sharp, clear voice of Colonel Eley sliced through the silence. When he finished he looked at Fischer and asked, "Do you have a last statement you wish to make?"

"No. I would only like to thank the chaplain." He looked over at Chaplain Towle for a fleeting moment and then turned back to Colonel Eley.

Colonel Eley said, "May God have mercy on your soul," and he and the two other officers stepped to the side. Fischer was led onto the platform several feet above ground level and shown the black circle on which he was to stand. He turned to face the audience but stared straight ahead toward the large doorway he had come in a few minutes earlier. Three enlisted men moved onto the platform quickly. One knelt down and began tying a rope around Fischer's ankles, another gently pulled his arms behind his back and began to tie them. The third man, a sergeant, stood by holding a black hood. When Fischer's hands and feet were securely bound, the sergeant stepped forward. Fischer's eyes, which had seen a scant twenty-two years of life, darted quickly around the room before the black hood shut everything from view. The sergeant reached up and pulled the noose down and, after placing it around Fischer's neck, tightened the large knot. Fischer stood rigidly at attention, not a movement, not even a quiver in his military bearing.

The sergeant stepped from the platform and approached Colonel Eley. The room was absolutely silent; all eyes were on the hooded, bound figure who stood alone now on the black circle. The sergeant stood before Colonel Eley and gave a stiff salute, which the colonel returned. Then, without a word, the colonel turned to the sergeant standing by the large lever, raised his arm straight out to the side, only his index finger extended, and then let it fall smartly to his side. The sergeant plunged the lever forward and the sharp grating noise as the trap door bolt sprang open tore through everyone in the room like an electric shock. Fischer's rigid body hurtled downward. Almost immediately the rope suddenly became taut and seemed actually to jump back upwards. For a moment there wasn't another sound in the room. Chaplain Towle stared at the taut rope, now swaying gently from side to side. The awful silence was broken by the shuffling of feet and the clearing of throats, but no words were spoken.

Chaplain Towle suddenly turned toward the entrance and began walking quickly toward it. As he neared it, he began to run—down the ramp and around the building and down the slight incline at the back. He entered the only door to the elevator shaft and went inside. Three doctors and another officer were standing there, looking up emotionlessly at the body twitching and jumping in convulsion above them. Chaplain Towle looked at the body and then quickly at the officers. One of the doctors, with a reassuring but stupid smile, said, "Don't worry, father; he's unconscious."

The chaplain did not say anything but quickly grabbed the step ladder in front of the body and climbed up it. He took a pocket knife out and cut a long slit across the front of the black hood and then fumbled in his pocket for the oils to anoint Fischer. When he finished, one of the doctors mounted the ladder with his stethoscope in hand, but the chaplain did not wait for the final pronouncement and went back out the way he came in. He knew Helmut Fischer was dead. When he arrived back at the front of the building, the guard was already formed to march back to the castle and get Fritz Franke. He joined them, and they began the long trek across the yard.

Fritz Franke was ready when he heard the footsteps approaching. He threw his narrow shoulders back in what appeared to be an uncomfortable position and stood staring straight at the door through which the guard detail would enter. He said a concise good-bye to each of his comrades and shook hands with all of them. Franke marched stiffly and when he was outside in the yard barely even looked around him.

When he stood before Colonel Eley and listened to the execution orders being read, he stared directly into the colonel's eyes. The corner of his mouth was slightly curled in an almost impish expression; and for all his twenty-one years he looked more like a school boy being reprimanded than a soldier about to be executed for murder. The colonel asked him if he had a last statement, and Franke replied curtly, "No." Then he turned slightly toward the chaplain, and there was a momentary trace of a smile before he walked up and took his place on the gallows. After he had been bound and the hood and noose had been placed on him, Colonel Eley conducted the same ritual, and Chaplain Towle hurried out and around the building to anoint the second of the seven men.

When he entered the elevator shaft, the first thing to catch his eye was not the hanging body of Fritz Franke but the bare feet of Helmut Fischer sticking out of an Army blanket in the corner of the room. Then he tended to the body of Fritz Franke.

The reporters were allowed to make the trip back to get Guenther Kuelsen, and they walked with the chaplain behind the guard detail. In death row they stood at a discreet distance as Kuelsen made his way down the row of cells saying good-bye and watched as Rolf Wizuy's arm came out between the bars of the last cell to pat his friend on the back as he was leaving.

Kuelsen followed the same path as Fischer and Franke across the prison yard, occasionally reaching up to brush the strawlike blond hair from his eyes. The reporters followed in a disorganized troop, looking like a band of curious onlookers hurrying after a funeral procession.

The only statement Guenther Kuelsen had to make was

to thank the chaplain for his help over the past few months. "I did appreciate it," he added just before turning to march to the gallows. He stood straight and militarily correct, and like the others before him, he did not falter once. Just before the hood was placed on his head he tried one last time to shake the hair from his eyes with a snap of his head, but it fell right back down. Shortly after one o'clock in the morning he plummeted into the basement of the salvage warehouse.

The reporters did not go back for Heinrich Ludwig. They stayed in the warehouse talking to each other and to some of the army officers. The initial shock had worn off somewhat, but the gruesome drama that was still far from over was enough to stilt their conversation considerably.

The four remaining men in death row talked very little while they were waiting; even Otto Stengel was at a loss for words. They all felt the men who had gone before them were actually the lucky ones because for them it was all over. They did not have to wait, to think about what was happening while they were waiting. Ludwig seemed almost pleased when the guards finally arrived to take him. As he walked with the chaplain, he talked quite a bit, so much so that Chaplain Towle was somewhat taken back because Ludwig had been one of the most detached of the seven throughout their acquaintance at Fort Leavenworth. When Ludwig faced Colonel Eley, he had only a dull, mute expression on his face and his shoulders sagged slightly. His last statement was brief, "My only thanks are for the presence of the chaplains." He would not see his twenty-sixth birthday, and as he stood on the black circle with the two enlisted men tying his hands and feet, he still looked much younger than twenty-five. At 1:30 A.M. the trapdoor sprang open, and the sudden jolt at the end of the seven-foot fall broke Heinrich Ludwig's neck in one clean fracture.

Chaplain Towle noticed the three pairs of feet now sticking

out of the blankets as he arrived to anoint Ludwig. He had to wait for a minute or two because the body was jerking so violently that he couldn't get up on the ladder. "Can't you cover up their feet?" he asked one of the medical officers. But he was told that the blankets were not big enough and that the army, with military preciseness, had provided them with only seven blankets.

There seemed to be a deep fear behind the eyes of Bernhard Reyak when the guard arrived for him. Chaplain Towle noticed that Reyak's chunky hands were trembling —but his full face was strong and emotionless. At twenty-one, his short stocky body was in excellent physical condition despite his long ordeal as a prisoner of war, and he walked resolutely to his death, talking occasionally to the chaplain as they went, but appeared deeply absorbed in his own thoughts.

When the colonel asked him for his last words, Reyak did not answer. The colonel repeated the question and Reyak, his mind apparently returning to the reality of the moment, abruptly answered, "No." The black hood scarcely fit over his head and some of his features could faintly be discerned underneath it. He stood at attention until the trap door sprung out from under him. At two o'clock in the morning he was pronounced dead.

Otto Stengel and Rolf Wizuy were the only ones left when the guard detail returned to death row. Stengel was standing at the door of his cell when the group arrived. He shook hands with Wizuy and then suddenly turned to the lieutenant, "I want to take the picture of my wife and children with me. I want it buried with me." The lieutenant hesitated for a moment, and Chaplain Towle said, "I'll get it for you," went into the cell after it and placed it in Stengel's shirt pocket. Outside, Stengel was almost his normal self. He looked at the mall and remarked to the chaplain, "Nice flowers, aren't they? It's been a long time since I've seen flowers." He talked almost incessantly as they walked and even told the chaplain he liked the last meal but that the portion of fried chicken had been too skimpy. As they entered the brightly lit warehouse, however, he became deathly silent and stood before Colonel Eley at rigid attention. To the traditional question, he said that he did want to make a statement. "I am fortunate that I have known the chaplain. And I think the colonel was very correct in handling us and we received excellent treatment while here."

Chaplain Towle was startled by the statement and tried in his mind to make it jell with the bitter feelings of Stengel only the night before. He could not understand Stengel's sudden compassion, but then he remembered that he had had difficulty understanding the moods and thoughts of Stengel all along. Stengel turned and walked almost jauntily to the gallows, but when he looked out at all of the people staring up at him, he snapped to attention.

His days of news-gathering were over. At the age of twenty-six, the oldest of the seven men went to his death with his family's picture in his pocket. He hung in the basement for only five minutes before he was pronounced dead; his was the quickest death of all seven.

Rolf Wizuy was sitting on his bunk staring idly at the floor when they came for him. He looked up but did not rise. Chaplain Towle noticed immediately that Wizuy was trembling; the boy's whole body seemed to be shaking. The chaplain stepped into the cell as if to help him get up, but Wizuy quickly got up under his own power. "I'm all right," he said as he started out of the cell. Then he returned to the Chaplain and said, "There's nobody left to say good-bye to," and shook his head.

Chaplain Towle trailed behind slightly, and as he reached the door from the corridor, he turned back and looked at the empty cells. The seven doors were still open; there were no inhabitants left in the death row. He thought briefly of the men sitting around the table in the corridor talking with him, and then as he hurried to catch up with Rolf Wizuy, the whole hollow, sickening feeling that it was over forever descended on him, completely and dreadfully, and he deeply hoped he would never see that corridor again.

Wizuy walked between the guards with the same coltish unsteadiness that he had shown when he stormed down the aisle of his barracks to meet Helmut Fischer just after he had learned of Werner Drechsler's arrival at the camp in Papago Park. His eyes nervously flitted about the prison yard, and he was mumbling a prayer under his breath. When he reached the ramp, he stumbled momentarily, but he caught himself, and then, very erectly, he marched in to face Colonel Eley. His last statement was also only to thank Chaplain Towle. He was still mumbling the prayer under the black hood when the noise of the trap door cut off his words. At the age of twenty-three, he was the last member of the group to die in the last mass execution in the United States.

Chaplain Towle went down to anoint him, and then stayed until Wizuy was officially pronounced dead. It took eighteen minutes for this finally to come about. The chaplain watched the grim procedure as the doctors went up and down the step ladder checking to see if death had taken place. When the three doctors all agreed that he was dead, Wizuy was lowered and the noose taken from his neck. The black hood was stripped off and the bonds on his feet and hands were cut, and his shoes were removed. An enlisted man then wrapped the body in a blanket and placed it next to the other six. Chaplain Towle looked again at the fourteen feet now sticking out, shook his head, and then quickly left the building. It was 2:48 in the morning; the entire operation had taken only three hours.

Chaplain Towle declined a ride back to his quarters, electing to walk by himself. He was exhausted and drained, but he knew he would never go to sleep that night. When he did get home, he sat in a chair and stared out the window until the sun finally came up.

That afternoon, August 25, 1945, the seven men were buried in a wooded graveyard set on the side of a hill just west of the disciplinary barracks. Chaplain Towle officiated at the funeral services and the burial, and Colonel Eley and a number of other officers attended.

A week after the executions, an army newspaper, the *Fort Leavenworth News,* carried the skeletal story of the hangings of the seven German prisoners of war.

Seven German prisoners of war were hanged early last Saturday morning at the United States Disciplinary Barracks in the greatest mass hanging yet held at the Ft. Leavenworth institution.

The seven men were condemned to death for the murder of a fellow prisoner, Werner Drechsler, at a prisoner of war camp in Papago Park, Phoenix, Ariz. They received their sentence after a court martial held at Florence, Ariz., on Aug. 16, 1944. . . .

The prisoners were notified last Thursday night [Aug. 23, 1945], 24 hours before their executions, that the time had been set. The men were received at the USDB last Jan. 29.

The trap was sprung on the first man at 12:10 and the last man went to his death at 2:48 A.M. A new system for mass hangings has been devised at the institution which saved more than an hour in the procedure.

The **Naval Institute Press** is the book-publishing arm of the U.S. Naval Institute, a private, nonprofit, membership society for sea service professionals and others who share an interest in naval and maritime affairs. Established in 1873 at the U.S. Naval Academy in Annapolis, Maryland, where its offices remain today, the Naval Institute has members worldwide.

Members of the Naval Institute support the education programs of the society and receive the influential monthly magazine *Proceedings* and discounts on fine nautical prints and on ship and aircraft photos. They also have access to the transcripts of the Institute's Oral History Program and get discounted admission to any of the Institute-sponsored seminars offered around the country.

The Naval Institute also publishes *Naval History* magazine. This colorful bimonthly is filled with entertaining and thought-provoking articles, first-person reminiscences, and dramatic art and photography. Members receive a discount on *Naval History* subscriptions.

The Naval Institute's book-publishing program, begun in 1898 with basic guides to naval practices, has broadened its scope in recent years to include books of more general interest. Now the Naval Institute Press publishes about 100 titles each year, ranging from how-to books on boating and navigation to battle histories, biographies, ship and aircraft guides, and novels. Institute members receive discounts of 20 to 50 percent on the Press's nearly 600 books in print.

Full-time students are eligible for special half-price membership rates. Life memberships are also available.

For a free catalog describing Naval Institute Press books currently available, and for further information about subscribing to *Naval History* magazine or about joining the U.S. Naval Institute, please write to:

Membership Department
U.S. Naval Institute
118 Maryland Avenue
Annapolis, MD 21402-5035
Telephone: (800) 233-8764
Fax: (410) 269-7940
Web address: www.usni.org